Also by Jane Doerfer

The Pantry Gourmet

The Legal Sea Foods Cookbook
(with George Berkowitz)

GOING
SOLO
IN
THE
KITCHEN

GOING SOLO IN THE KITCHEN

Jane Doerfer

ALFRED A. KNOPF
NEW YORK
2014

To my wonderful children,
Joanna and Andrew Doerfer

Many thanks to my skillful editors, Kathy Zuckerman and Judith Jones, and to all the other creative people at Knopf who made this book possible.

This Is a Borzoi Book
Published by Alfred A. Knopf, Inc.

Copyright © 1995 by Jane Doerfer
All rights reserved under International
and Pan-American Copyright Conventions.
Published in the United States by
Alfred A. Knopf, Inc., New York, and
simultaneously in Canada by Random
House of Canada Limited, Toronto.
Distributed by Random House, Inc., New York.

Library of Congress Cataloging-in-Publication Data
Doerfer, Jane.
Going solo in the kitchen / by Jane Doerfer. — 1st ed.
p.   cm.
Includes index.
ISBN 0-679-42486-5
1. Cookery for one.   I. Title.
TX652.D59   1995
641.5'61—dc20   94-38776   CIP

Manufactured in the United States of America
Published May 21, 1995
First Paperback Edition Published September 10, 1998
Reprinted Eleven Times
Thirteenth Printing, December 2014

CONTENTS

INTRODUCTION

I cook for myself because I like to eat well. I also want to prepare economical meals that are good for me and are centered around seasonal food. It's as simple as that.

Your reasons for solo cooking might be quite different. Maybe you're bored with eating take-out every night, or perhaps you're recently divorced or widowed—or on a budget. We may begin solo cooking for different reasons, but we end up with the same reality: Nothing tastes quite as good as a meal you've thought about and taken the time to prepare and enjoy. By cooking at home, you feed both your psyche and palate.

Actually, cooking for yourself isn't difficult—like anything else, it just sounds difficult if you haven't mastered the basics. Solo cooking is really much easier than cooking for others: It takes far less time, is less costly, and is less emotionally charged. (If your food doesn't come out well, you're the only one who knows it.) It's probably one of the few arenas in your life where you are totally in control. You can eat when and what you like every night. (When asparagus is in season, and if you're an asparagus freak, you can savor it until your skin turns green.) If you're in the mood for smoked salmon, or a T-bone steak—prohibitively expensive if purchased in quantity—when you're buying for one they're the same price as a container of Chinese take-out or a big deli sandwich.

And, if you're particular about your health, cooking is just good sense because you know exactly what you're putting in your body. It's a shame to spend hours keeping in shape, and then blow it all in five minutes at the fast-food counter. Most prepared foods get their flavor from fats and sugar—and are loaded with preservatives. Even if you're buying healthful convenience foods, they always taste the same.

The first step in cooking solo is to make a commitment to mastering the mechanics: deciding your menus, doing the shopping, learning to store food without wasting half of it, and preparing the meals. Even if you're an experienced cook, you may need to reframe the way you operate—and you may need to buy a new set of smaller cooking utensils. However, now that you've purchased this book, the hardest part is over: You no longer have to convert a recipe designed for several persons down to proportions suitable for one.

I've been cooking for myself for several years. I also teach other people how to cook at my Going Solo in the Kitchen cooking school. In the process, I've learned exactly which shortcuts and techniques make life easier when you're cooking alone. In the following chapters I'll describe the best ways to make shopping and storage work for you, explain tips for freezing food, and give you more than 350 recipes for all kinds of flavorful foods—including ethnic and vegetarian specialties—as well as some of those old-fashioned favorites, such as roast chicken or pot roast, that you may crave but hesitate to cook for one.

Like many of you, I have a busy schedule. I may enjoy cooking, but that doesn't mean that I want to spend hours in the kitchen. As I believe that the best everyday food is simple food, the majority of the recipes in this book can be prepared in fewer than 30 minutes—many in under 20 minutes. I've included several meals-in-one and numerous master recipes that can be made on the weekend and recycled into new-tasting meals during the week. I've also given you recipes for a few breads (such as biscuits), nonalcoholic fruit drinks (great in the afternoon, after work), and desserts that are delicious and use up small amounts of fruits that otherwise might spoil. I suggest ingredients that are readily available in most supermarkets, no matter where you live. I've also given you some discretion in the portions, so that you can select recipes and adjust amounts depending upon your appetite.

My style of cooking is based on the best of what's seasonally available—lots of vegetables and herbs—and little fat. For many years I was *Horticulture* magazine's food columnist. Instead of writing for cooks, I was developing recipes for gardeners—whose main concern was using up the bounty they had produced. This experience convinced me that the very best-tasting flavors originate with fresh vegetables and herbs. It may take a few more minutes to chop raw ingredients, but you always feel good when your food gets its flavor from the earth, not the lard bucket.

I enjoy cooking for myself. I find it a joyous, satisfying experience. I hope that you will too.

GOING
SOLO
IN
THE
KITCHEN

GETTING STARTED

SELECTING KITCHEN EQUIPMENT

You don't need a lot of utensils or gadgets to cook well for yourself. But your pots and pans should be the right scale for small-portion cooking—and they should be durable. If you're equipping a kitchen for the first time, it's tempting to buy a prepackaged set of pots and call it a day. Sometimes these sets are just what you need (because they're frequently the smaller sizes)—other times, they're too large in scale to be practical for a solo cook. Taking the time to find exactly what you want will make the mechanics of cooking much easier in the long run.

Pots and Pans

I have found that cooking in correct-sized pots is far more critical when you are cooking small portions than when you are cooking in quantity. If you're braising a small amount of chicken and vegetables, for example, the flavor of the sauce will be more concentrated when you cook it in a smaller casserole than when you make do with a larger one. This doesn't mean you should rush out and buy the smallest pans on the market. The very smallest sizes, such as 6-inch frying pans or 1-quart pots, are almost too small to be truly useful.

Three sizes of pots that are particularly handy for solo cooks are:
- A 2-quart stove-top and ovenproof casserole with a lid
- An 8–12-inch skillet
- A 9 1/2-inch oval au gratin baking dish

Heavy, durable equipment is always important when you're cooking, but it's particularly significant when you're trying to cook with less fat. In a lightweight pan, foods will tend to burn and scorch as the pan will have a greater number of hot spots than a heavier pan. For panfrying, some cooks swear by stainless-steel utensils with a core of aluminum on the bottom; others opt for copper lined with tin—or their treasured old cast-iron skillets. (Some of the inexpensive cast-iron skillets imported from the Far East have small surface pitting and cannot be seasoned correctly so that food won't stick.) Aluminum is the least versatile choice because it reacts with acids. With the exception of the baked goods, all of the recipes in this book were cooked in nonreactive pans (stainless steel or enamel).

I've cooked for years in casseroles made of enameled cast iron, which is a good material for low-fat cooking. This cookware is fabricated by several firms, such as Le Creuset in France or Chantal in Germany. Although these pots are initially quite expensive, they will pay for themselves over time. Enamel doesn't react with acids as does aluminum, so you can easily cook with acidic ingredients like tomatoes, wine, and citrus juices. Le Creuset makes a handy 2-quart casserole designed with options of both steamer and double-boiler inserts, as well as a 2-quart pan with a cover that does double duty as an 8-inch skillet (particularly useful if your storage space is limited). Chantal's line, which is lighter in weight, includes a wok for two with a tempered glass lid that's a good size for cooking soups and braised dishes. These are but two of the many companies that make enameled cookware, but if you go this route, buy cautiously because a lot of the stylish-looking enamelware on the market chips easily.

(By the way, flea markets and thrift stores are prime sources for used enameled pans. I've bought several for less than $5 apiece. If their interior surfaces are stained from use, just soak them in a bleach and water solution overnight to lighten or remove the stains. Do not buy them if the surfaces are chipped or crazed.)

If you're trying to cook with less fat, the coated nonstick cookware is appealing, but you might not realize that many of these coated surfaces are not meant for high-heat cooking. Some coated nonstick cookware, particularly inexpensive brands, will pit or flake when you're using it for stir-fries and other intense-heat applications.

You'll also need a large stockpot for cooking pasta or rice—or simmering soup. A 6- to 8-quart pot should be sufficient for virtually anything you would cook. If you cannot find a good quality source for equipment near you, Bridge Kitchenware (at 214 East 52nd Street, New York, New York 10022) sells a vast range of cooking equipment by mail, including stainless-steel cookware from France. It is also a good source for durable baking equipment. Bridge's catalog department frequently runs specials that are not available at the store. There is a small fee for the catalog.

Potato Peelers and Knives

The simple $2 swivel-blade potato peeler found at your local hardware store is one of the most valuable kitchen tools you can own. With it you can peel not only potatoes, but also tomatoes, peppers, cucumbers, zucchini, carrots, or any other thin-skinned vegetables. (You can even make cheese curls.) But it must be sharp. These peelers are so durable that we tend to use them year after year, long after they should be discarded. Check yours; if it won't peel a tomato or pepper easily, it's time to replace it.

You'll need only a few knives: a chef's knife for chopping, a paring knife, and a bread knife. Many professional cooks prefer carbon steel for blades because it holds an edge well, but carbon steel rusts (and reacts with some vegetables), and is hard to find. Most knives on the market today are made with a stainless-steel alloy. When you're buying a knife, be sure to pick it up and see how it balances in your hand. A comfortable pairing of hand and knife size is far more important than most people realize. Also, of greater import than the brand of knife you buy is whether or not you keep it sharp. It will take you twice as long to chop food with a dull knife than with a sharp one. You're also much more likely to cut yourself. You should wash knives by hand, not in the dishwasher, because the heat of the dishwasher can crack the handles. If you store them carefully, your knives will last for years. (To protect the points of your knives from snapping off, stick them in used wine corks.) Professional chefs often use sharpening stones to keep their knives in prime condition. These work beautifully, but for the average cook there's an easier (and less expensive) alternative. You can buy a hand-held sharpening tool designed for fishing and hunting knives that works equally well on kitchen knives. It has the advantage of having fixed blades so you don't have to figure out the correct sharpening angle. A mail-order source for one such tool, the Super Sharpener, is Byer's Creative Sales and Manufacturing Company, P.O. Box 550, Whitefish, Montana 59937.

Food Processors, Blenders, and Mixers

A food processor is handy, but not essential. Here's one time when the solo cook has an advantage: The new inexpensive mini-sized food processors are just the right size for one. However, with a sharp knife—and a steady hand—you'll be able to chop just about anything.

Blenders are practical for puréeing soups, making breadcrumbs, or blending fruit drinks. When you're selecting a blender, remember that plastic containers scratch and can melt in a dishwasher: Glass containers are more expensive, but are well worth the few extra dollars. Make sure you buy a blender that comes apart for cleaning. (Blenders are another yard-sale or thrift-store standby. Just plug them in to make sure they work before buying.)

Unless you do a lot of baking, an inexpensive hand-held electric mixer is all you need.

Other Kitchen Equipment

If you are just starting out and do not own any measuring spoons, cups, or mixing bowls—all the backup paraphernalia necessary to cook—several companies sell starter kits containing a range of items for less than you could buy them individually. These kits are available at most discount and department stores. At a minimum, you'll need a large mixing bowl (about 2 quarts), a set of measuring spoons, a 1-quart glass liquid measuring cup, a set of dry measuring cups, an 8-inch square pan, a cookie sheet, a wooden spoon, a professional-quality whip for smoothing sauces and gravies, a spatula, and an oven mitt (or two). A cutting board small enough to put under the faucet (or in the dishwasher) is also handy. I find a pepper mill essential in cooking. PepperMate, available from East Hampton Industries in East Hampton, New York, is a good-quality brand.

Practical Considerations

When you're on a budget, equipping a kitchen—even as a solo cook—can be expensive. You don't have to purchase everything at once, but instead of buying an interim set of cheap pots that will tend to burn everything in sight, you might spend a few minutes checking out the housewares department at your local thrift store. Goodwill Industries and the Salvation Army, for example, have regional stores throughout the country. Their housewares departments are treasure troves for used kitchen utensils, such as frying and cake pans. They are also good spots to pick up cast-off dinner and serving plates. (It's fun to coordinate your dinner plates with your food—earthenware for peasant casseroles, fancier china for fish dishes, or different-colored plates to set off vegetables, such as glazed black dishes for broccoli and tomatoes. Plain white is the most practical choice. And, since you're buying for one, nothing has to match.) In addition, you can equip your kitchen for a few dollars and know that the money you're spending is supporting a charitable cause. Then, when you can afford it, you can trade up and give your pots back to the thrift store so that someone else can get a start.

SHOPPING FOR FOOD

For many of us who are single, supermarket shopping is a chore—yet another task to be sandwiched in at the end of the day. Even though we constitute a sizeable proportion of the population, singles at the supermarket might as well be invisible. It takes us longer to shop because we need to hunt for what we want amidst the meat and staples packed in family-sized portions. Only at the produce department do we gain a respite, because often fruits and vegetables are displayed and sold by the piece. Is it any wonder that so many of us head right for the frozen food section (where the convenience foods are packaged for one), load up on a week's worth of microwave dinners or diet meals, and leave?

There's a certain amount of basic planning that's necessary to avoid this scenario. You can get away with buying whatever looks appealing and deciding what to do with it at a later date when you have a family (or roommates) to feed. But if you're living alone, you need to be more restrained—otherwise you can end up with a tremendous amount of spoilage.

Successful shopping really begins before you walk out of the house. When you take the time to survey what is in the refrigerator and to decide what you're in the mood to eat (and to check the newspaper for supermarket money-saving specials), you're less likely to run out of steam and settle for convenience foods. During the week, add items you need to a shopping list attached to the refrigerator. If you load up on nonperishable staples, such as flour or sugar, once a month, your weekly sprint will be much easier.

Selecting a Market

No matter where you live, there's usually one market more responsive to your requests as a solo shopper than the competition. The problem is finding it. If you live in a cosmopolitan area with a sizeable population of singles, locating such a market is usually just a matter of legwork. Virtually every city has dozens of butcher or fish shops—or fruit markets—where you can establish yourself as a regular customer and buy exactly what you want. Although these shops may be more expensive on an item-by-item basis than the supermarkets, ultimately they may be less costly because you buy only what you need. In a small-town or suburban setting, however, your only option may be a large chain supermarket that caters to a clientele of families. If you can establish a friendly relationship with the key staff (see *A Personal Strategy for Shopping,* page 11) it makes your shopping much easier—particularly when you're buying meat or produce.

Dealing with the Butcher

A friendly butcher can be your best resource at the market. If you treat him—or her—with consideration, he'll be more than willing to cut smaller portions for you—or to halve and repackage large roasts. When

> *"I love food shopping. I enjoy being surrounded by all those beautiful things. It's like window shopping at the very high end. I shop in the European way at little gourmet stores and markets where everyone knows me. I never go to the supermarket except to pick up paper towels. Of course, I live in a city neighborhood where I can shop like this. These personal connections make everyday living much more pleasant."*
>
> Laurie Werner, travel writer

I'm buying a lamb roast or a turkey breast, I'll ask the meat man to halve it and pack both portions separately. I may request that the meat be boned and that the scraps and bones be included in my order (to simmer for stock). I'll use one portion immediately and freeze the other. When items are on sale, I explain that I am perfectly willing to pay a fee for repackaging, but I've never been charged. Because I think ground meat and poultry lose quality once frozen, I always ask for freshly ground meat in half-pound portions.

Having a friendly butcher is particularly helpful when preparing an item in several different ways. For example, when pork butt is on sale, I'll buy about four pounds. (Pork butt is the standard cut for Chinese stir-fries.) I'll ask the butcher to grind one pound—which I'll include in Chinese meatballs or in meat loaf mixtures—and to divide the remaining meat into two portions, one to be thinly sliced for stir-fries, the other left whole for roasting or braising. Even subtracting for waste, from a four-pound pork butt I end up with at least six meals: two with the ground meat, one with the stir-fried pork, and three with the roast and leftovers.

(I realize that often by the time you get to the market the line of people waiting for individual service is long or the meat market staff is off-duty, in which case and with a little patience you can repackage your meat and poultry at home. For example, I've suggested how to cut up a chicken on page 126.)

Shopping for Fruits and Vegetables

The most common complaint I hear from single cooks is that they buy far too much produce at the market, run out of ideas on ways to use it up, and let it spoil. Or they're asked out to dinner or work late several nights in a row and the food rots.

It's tempting to load up on produce. (I do it more often than I'd like to admit.) A little self-knowledge is the key. If you anticipate a busy week at work, and you know from past experience that probably you won't be home until 8 or 9 p.m., don't buy perishables such as greens or corn that should be used up immediately. Instead you can purchase vegetables, such as carrots, turnips, yams, cabbages, or spaghetti squashes, that will stay in good condition until you have time to cook again. (Or maybe you should decide that it's an ideal week to eat out. Having the flexibility to choose when—and what—you're going to eat is a major perk of the single state.)

Many of us stockpile produce because we're trying to eat in a more healthy manner. But frequently we're unrealistic about the amount of fruits and vegetables one person can reasonably consume before they spoil. We like the looks of the peaches, so we pick out three or four; then the pears are tempting, so we toss a few in the basket. We haven't had a ripe cantaloupe in a while—and they're on sale—so we add one to the pile. Of course, apples are loaded with fiber, and bananas with potassium . . . pretty soon we've filled a shopping basket with two weeks' worth of perishables. Then we repeat the pattern at the vegetable aisle.

If you consistently purchase too much, as I once did, you'll need to retrain your eye to select only what you need. Before you head for the market, it's important to inventory the contents of your refrigerator. Rather than just opening the door and giving a cursory look, I've found it helpful to remove all the perishables and put them on the counter. Some of the over-the-hill vegetables will have enough flavor to simmer for a vegetable stock, others should be jettisoned. The pepper with a rotten spot near the stem doesn't need to be discarded; you can trim it and use in a stuffing or in casseroles. You can dunk a bag of questionable spinach in a sink full of lukewarm water and separate the rotten leaves from those with promise. Then you can stem the remaining spinach, dry it and wrap it loosely in paper towels, and refrigerate it for a forthcoming dinner. Even wilted celery and scallions make a flavorful bed for a roast chicken. If you cut up ripe peaches, bananas, and grapes, and toss them with fresh orange or lime juice, you'll end up with a delicious light fruit salad lunch. By the time you've finished your inventory, you may find that you have the ingredients for three or four meals without moving an inch.

Also, it helps to analyze if there's a consistent pattern to your shopping. Do you usually buy twice as much lettuce as you consume? Do you stock up on fresh herbs and never open the packages? Or is splurging on take-out at the deli counter your downfall? You might try adding up the cost of the food you're throwing away. One week's waste may be such a sobering total that you'll be inspired to change your pattern of shopping.

A PERSONAL STRATEGY FOR SHOPPING

Since I became single a few years ago, I've lived in a major city as well as rural communities in both the North and the South. Shopping in the city was hectic but satisfying, for I could always find what I wanted. Life changed dramatically once I moved to the rural world, where my local shopping options were limited to supermarkets with heavily advertised convenience foods, mounds of family-sized packs of meats, and staples in amounts more suitable for feeding a football team than a lone cook.

After checking out the quality of the meat and produce at the available stores, I picked the one where I planned to do most of my business.

My shopping strategy was simple: I wanted to establish a friendly relationship with the market's key personnel. I began by introducing myself to the store manager, explaining that I liked the store and wanted to shop there, but that as a single cook I needed to buy meat and produce in smaller amounts than his market offered. I asked what he could do to accommodate me. (I've done this in every community I've lived in since I became single, and the response has always been positive.) Once I'd received a commitment, I requested an introduction to the meat and produce department heads. I explained the situation again, chatted for a while, and memorized their names for future reference.

This step established both a personal tone and a framework for my future requests. When any problem arose with their staff, I could always point out (courteously) that I was merely asking for a service that their supervisors agreed to provide. It also made shopping more pleasant because I knew people by name and they, in turn, recognized me. Of equal importance for me as a small-town shopper was that once I established a friendly relationship with the managers, they were willing to order specialized foods, such as balsamic vinegar or basmati rice. (I've found that even the most obscure items are listed in the specialty food ordering catalogs that most managers have. It helps, of course, if you can rustle up enough fellow cooks to insure that the items continue to be stocked.)

All this may sound quite basic, but most single people don't take the time to establish these supermarket friendships, which can save them a lot of aggravation later on.

STORAGE

Years ago, while I was writing a cookbook about pantry foods, I experimented with numerous ways of storing food. I discovered that most foods stay in good condition much longer than you might realize: the key is taking the time to store them carefully. And, of course, having a refrigerator in good condition with a reliable temperature mechanism is essential.

If the meat or poultry you've bought is tightly sealed in plastic wrap, loosen the wrap before putting it away in the refrigerator. Meat loosely wrapped stays fresh longer than meat that is tightly wrapped. Most ground meat has a shelf life of no longer than a day or two; poultry, two days—and chops or roasts, three to four days. If you've ended up with more perishable meat than you anticipated, it's best to freeze it at this stage rather than waiting until it's on the verge of spoiling. Previously frozen fish (discernible at the market by the puddle of water in which it sits) should be lightly covered with plastic wrap and stored for no more than a day. Recently caught fish will stay in decent condition for three days if stored, lightly covered with plastic wrap or foil, in the coldest part of the refrigerator, usually the bottom shelf in the back.

With the exception of potatoes, onions, and winter squash (which should be kept in a cool, dry place), most vegetables should be refrigerated as soon as possible. In general, I find it's best to leave vegetables such as peppers, carrots, summer squash, scallions, beets, and tomatoes unwashed until you use them unless you're super-careful about drying them off. Any extra moisture leads to rot. Either put them in the vegetable compartment or place them loosely in heavy unsealed plastic bags. Keep fresh ears of corn in their husks and try to cook them as soon as possible. The longer corn sits around, the faster the sugars in the corn turn to starches—and the older the corn tastes. If you're already past the optimum flavor stage (usually the case by the time the corn has reached a commercial market) you can refrigerate ears of corn for two days in their husks.

You can refrigerate greens such as spinach or kale, unwashed, in an unsealed plastic bag, but taking a few minutes to prepare the lettuce leaves before storing them makes life a lot easier when you're fixing dinner. After you put away the rest of the produce, just fill a sink with *luke-*

warm, not cold water, which makes the soil wash off more easily. Twist the stems off the lettuces so that the leaves are separated, and dunk them in and out of water to remove any soil adhering to the leaves. Check each leaf and remove any rotten or bruised spots. Drain the lettuce leaves in a colander and dry them either by hand or in a salad spinner. (I think a salad spinner is well worth the few dollars it costs, but if space is tight—forget it.) If you have a soft-textured lettuce, such as oak leaf, salad bowl, or ruby, don't be too vigorous, or you'll bruise the leaves and they will spoil faster. Then, either layer the leaves in paper toweling or in clean dishtowels, roll them up, and place them in a large, unsealed plastic bag on the center shelf of the refrigerator. Leaving the bags unsealed allows the moisture to evaporate. Using this method, the lettuce will stay crisp for about four to five days.

You can hold most fruits at room temperature unless your kitchen temperature is more than 70°F, in which case you should refrigerate them. Fruits such as pears continue to ripen at room temperature and will stop ripening once they are refrigerated. (You can ripen them in a paper bag on the counter. Most commercially available pears, such as Bartlett or Anjou, will ripen within three to four days. Bananas ripen virtually overnight. I find that when I mound fruit in a bowl on the kitchen counter (where I see it every time I walk in the room), I'm less likely to waste it than when it's hidden away in the refrigerator.

When I was experimenting with storage techniques I learned that prepared foods keep longer if you refrigerate them in glass rather than plastic. (Pickled foods, in particular, sometimes last three to four days longer.) Ingredients such as cottage cheese, sour cream, and yogurt will keep better if you store them upside down so that the contents are pressed against the lid, preventing air from getting in.

Most foods kept in short-term storage have a much fresher flavor when salt is omitted, particularly when onions, garlic, peppers, or cucumbers are included in the recipe. Hummus made with salt, for example, often develops a strong—almost unpleasant—flavor in storage, but when you prepare it without salt, the hummus tastes fresh for days. (You can always add salt before serving.) That's the reason I often suggest that you leave out the salt until serving. The salt tends to draw out any bitter juices.

Maximizing the Freezer

The way I use a freezer has changed since I became a solo cook. At one time, when I was cooking for a family of four, I stockpiled large amounts of food. I filled a large free-standing freezer to the brim with meat specials, vegetables from the garden, and casseroles of family favorites. My goal was long-term storage.

Now that I'm single, I don't need a big freezer: The standard freezer compartment in my refrigerator is more than adequate. Rather than thinking of my freezer as a long-term storage unit, I regard it more as a cold storage pantry for ingredients that make my meals more interesting. I freeze hard-to-find or exotic ingredients, unusual flours, herbs and spices, servings of leftovers, small amounts of vegetables, and portions of foods, such as bacon or salt pork, that I use so infrequently that they would spoil in the refrigerator. If I go out of town unexpectedly, I'll freeze any perishable vegetables and fruits whole and use them in casseroles or fruit drinks. I store bags of commercially frozen vegetables, such as okra, lima beans, and corn, and add them to soups for lunch or supper. By using the freezer to hold many different kinds of ingredients, I make my cooking much more versatile and keep any spoilage to a minimum.

Freezing Ingredients

Even a small freezer is an excellent holding station for short-term storage up to a month. If you use a freezer for long-term storage of fruits and vegetables, you may wish to consult a freezing cookbook or a bulletin from the U.S. Department of Agriculture. It's handy to keep a roll of freezer paper, tape, scissors, and a marking pen near the refrigerator so you won't be tempted to freeze foods without rewrapping them. You should not freeze food only in aluminum foil because it tends to tear if it shifts in storage. A supply of heavyweight plastic bags is handy for short-term storage of vegetables and fruits. A set of heavy plastic containers that can go from the freezer to the microwave is particularly useful for storing leftover casseroles or braised main dishes. I save plastic yogurt or sour cream containers because they're just the right size for freezing soups.

Here are some useful freezer standbys:

Bacon, ham, and salt pork. These pork-based items store reasonably enough in the freezer—particularly a country ham, which has a less pulpy texture than hams that have been pumped with water (between the water and the chemicals they're scarcely worth buying). I package bacon into 2-strip portions and wrap them individually; ham, cut into small chunks and stored in a heavy plastic bag; and salt pork, into 1/4-cup sizes, just right for baked beans.

Bread. If bread is stored in freezer bags it retains its quality in the freezer. (The plastic wrap in which most store-bought bread is packaged is not meant for freezer storage, and the bread tends to dry out.) When I bake bread, I cut it into slices once it's cooled and immediately store it in the freezer in 3–4 slice portions. Any leftover French or Italian bread freezes well. Cut it into serving portions before freezing individually.

Breadcrumbs. Purée stale bread in a blender, or put it in a paper bag and crush with a rolling pin or wine bottle. Store breadcrumbs in a jar in the freezer and use as needed.

Cheese. Cheese freezes well when it's grated, poorly when it's frozen whole, because its texture changes, becoming more crumbly when frozen. (An exception is creamy, high-fat cheeses such as Brie, which do all right when they're already ripened correctly.) This isn't a problem if you're using cheese as an ingredient in cooking. You can grate dribs of cheese and store them either in individual plastic containers or mix them together in a large container such as a recycled yogurt or sour cream carton for use in cooking. Cream cheese freezes well with only a slight loss in texture. I cut it into 1-ounce portions, wrap them in plastic wrap, and store them in a plastic bag.

Coffee. Coffee should be stored either in the refrigerator or freezer. You can grind whole beans while they're still frozen.

Cream and sour cream. Ultra-pasteurized cream has a long shelf life, but you can freeze it and use for whipped cream. Partially thaw the cream and whip it while it is still slightly frozen. If you let it thaw completely, it will separate. Sour cream separates when defrosted, but it will still work adequately in baked goods.

Fish. As fish has little connective tissue it loses texture rapidly in the freezer unless it is held at a lower temperature than meat and poultry. It's best to freeze fish purely as a temporary measure and use it up within one month. Be sure to wrap it tightly in freezer paper or plastic wrap. Many commercial freezing operations freeze fish in water. It's up to you.

Fruits. Soft fruits and berries, such as raspberries, freeze well enough to be used as ingredients in baking but they do lose texture. (If you cook blueberries while they're still frozen, there's little loss of quality.) The flesh of stone fruits, such as peaches, darkens in the freezer, but you can freeze ripe fruit whole, run it under the hot water faucet to loosen the peel, and use the frozen flesh puréed in recipes or citrus-based drinks (see pages 285–86). I freeze bananas whole. Their skins blacken in the freezer but I run them under the hot water faucet, softening their skins, then peel them immediately and purée while they're still frozen for citrus drinks and cakes. If you wait to use the frozen banana until it defrosts, you'll be faced with a soggy mess.

Gingerroot. In the past I covered peeled fresh gingerroot with sherry and put it in the refrigerator. The ginger perfumed the sherry (which could then be used for cooking), and the sherry kept the ginger from spoiling. That's still a good method, but now I prefer to freeze whole ginger, skin and all, in a plastic bag. To use in recipes, all you need to do is scrape off the peel while it's still frozen, and grate whatever you need on a hand grater. It's as easy to grate frozen as it is fresh ginger, and your eyes won't water. Then place the frozen gingerroot back in the freezer.

Herbs. The oils in herbs make them taste best fresh, but frozen herbs are preferable to dried. Many supermarkets sell the plastic containers of fresh herbs airshipped from California. As a single cook, you'll be hard-pressed to use up even a small container before they rot. You can chop the herbs in the quantity you prefer, put them in ice-cube trays, cover with water, and freeze them, or, if you'd like a larger quantity, freeze them in coated paper cups. Once they're frozen you can transfer them into plastic bags for storage and defrost as needed. If you're in a hurry, you can freeze whole herbs in their plastic containers (or on a cookie sheet) and mince them while they're still frozen. A few herbs, such as tarragon or basil, darken in the freezer, but their flavor is still acceptable.

Lemon zest. When you're grating the zest from a fresh lemon, freeze any extra zest in plastic wrap and add it to cakes or casseroles for extra flavor.

Meat and poultry. Meat and poultry have enough connective tissue so that they withstand freezing well. However, you should rewrap them before storing because supermarket plastic wrap was never designed as freezer wrap. It's too thin and you'll often end up with freezer burn. Just put the meat in heavy plastic bags or wrap in freezer paper or plastic wrap. Aluminum foil tends to tear as contents are moved around in the freezer. Use it up within three months.

Nuts. Nuts freeze well, although they soften slightly when defrosted. It's handy to chop them first, then store each kind of nut in individual heavy plastic bags.

Peppers. Hot peppers give a zing to food (and are a good salt substitute), but most people wouldn't use them every day. Fortunately, hot peppers freeze well if you peel them first (the skin toughens in the freezer). The most readily available—and easiest to peel—are jalapeño peppers. Peel jalapeños with a vegetable peeler, seed them, and mince the flesh. Then you need only spread the minced pieces out on a cookie sheet in the freezer. Once the individual pepper pieces are frozen (a matter of a few minutes), you can scrape them up with a spatula and store them in a re-sealable plastic bag, where you can measure them easily when you need a small quantity. The frozen minced pieces defrost almost immediately at room temperature and can be used virtually interchangeably with fresh peppers. Bell peppers must be peeled before freezing because their flesh toughens. I follow the same procedure as for hot peppers, but I also slice some in strips so that I have the luxury of using more than one color of pepper in a dish. (Yellow and red peppers are frequently in the reduced produce section. When I see them I buy whatever is available and freeze them in this manner.)

Pesto. Freezing pesto in ice-cube trays works well. Two or three cubes will give you enough pesto for one serving of pasta.

Stocks. Stocks freeze beautifully. If you pour the liquid into an ice-cube tray, freeze it, then remove and store the frozen cubes in a plastic bag, you'll have a handy supply of stocks for a quick meal. One ice cube equals about 2 tablespoons.

Tahini. This Middle Eastern sesame seed paste is usually sold in a 16-ounce bottle, making it an impractical choice for a solo cook because the sesame seeds can turn rancid unless you use the paste on a regular basis. I freeze the commercial tahini in 1/4-cup portions and defrost it in the re-frigerator. Be sure to stir the tahini before you divide it up.

Vegetables (uncooked). Commercially frozen artichoke hearts, peas, corn, and lima beans are useful ingredients to have on hand for dinners or soups. Most other vegetables are better fresh. When you're going out of town and the fresh vegetables in your refrigerator would spoil otherwise, place them on a cookie sheet, freeze them, and use them in soups. This, of course, is not the optimum way to freeze vegetables (green vegetables, for example, traditionally are blanched first) but it works well when you're in a rush. I freeze tomatoes whole, run them under the hot water faucet (the skin peels right off), then cook them while still frozen. Vegetables with a high water content, such as celery, end up with ice crystals, which affects the texture, but they're still OK for flavoring soups or casseroles.

Vegetables (cooked). If you don't feel like eating up cooked vegetable leftovers, freeze them in plastic containers and use for soups or meals later on. Cooked winter squash, for example, freezes beautifully. Freeze any leftover cooked vegetables except for potatoes and cauliflower, which become watery.

SALADS

After a busy day, it's great to come home to a meal that needs only a minute or two of preparation before you dive in. A main course salad fits the bill perfectly because you can assemble most ingredients in advance. Of course, if you're choosing salads that are chock-full of vegetables and herbs (and virtually no oil), you're also eating smart. And, if you're a frugal cook, you'll be conjuring up some of your salads with leftovers that you've saved for precisely this reason. Any leftovers that are enhanced by a marinade or dressing can be recycled into a salad. For example, you need only some cooked rice or pasta—and some steamed broccoli or blanched green beans—to put together a simple vegetarian cold salad; just toss with oil, vinegar, and herbs, and dinner is ready. And if you want a heartier repast, you can add paper-thin slices of meat or poultry—or some diced cheese.

Although it's sometimes easier as a single cook to concentrate on main-course meal-in-one salads, don't ignore their usefulness as an accompaniment to other foods. A simple green salad, with a touch of olive oil, vinegar, and fresh herbs, whets the appetite—and is the ideal foil to a grilled piece of fish or meat—while a ripe tomato and sweet onion salad, sprinkled with basil, always makes poultry taste better.

While you can sometimes fudge with less than perfect ingredients in preparing casseroles or soups, you'll need top-quality ingredients for salads. Nothing is less appetizing than lettuce that is turning brown, vegetables that are limp, or meats or cheese that have dried out in the refrigerator. The lettuces should be washed and dried, while vegetables ought to be crisp and full of vegetable juices (if you can bend a carrot or zucchini—put it in the stockpot or roasting pan, not the salad). Any leftover meat, poultry, fish, or cheese that you're adding to a composed salad should be fresh-tasting. To perk up the flavor of poultry, meat, or fish, marinate in lemon or lime juice for a few minutes before adding to the salad.

Salads are really just cooked or raw ingredients served cold in some sort of marinade (such as oil and vinegar) or dressing (such as mayonnaise). The biggest mistake that novice cooks make in assembling salads is to use too much dressing. The purpose of a dressing is to accentuate and balance the flavors of the ingredients and, in the process, to moisten them. That's it.

If you don't have the inclination—or time—to make salad dressing from scratch, keep bottles of olive oil and red wine vinegar handy and use them to moisten your tossed salad greens. Drizzle a little olive oil over the greens till the leaves glisten, toss salad to coat the leaves, then add a few drops of vinegar. Good-quality oils and vinegars bring out the flavors of the greens and herbs; bottled dressings overwhelm them—and make the salads always taste similar.

I mention this because single cooks tell me that as a rule they rarely bother to make salad dressings. Preparing a simple oil and vinegar dressing takes only about a minute longer than shaking a bottle of store-bought dressing. Even when you're buying high-quality olive oils and specialty vinegars, homemade dressing is less expensive than the bottled brands—and it sure tastes better. By varying the vinegars and oils you

> *"It's only recently that I've started cooking for myself. Before I found the whole procedure rather mystifying. But because I've become more health oriented, I feel more comfortable when I know what I'm putting into my body, rather than something that may taste wonderful but has too much fat. As a result, I've changed a lot of my habits: In the past I would buy a jar of tomato sauce; now I'm more likely to make my own. I especially like to prepare salads because I love to cut up vegetables. It's so methodical and precise, I find it relaxing. I also enjoy arranging the ingredients so that they look beautiful. I would still prefer to cook for other people and hear their appreciation, but I'm amazed at how much I like cooking for myself and how good the food tastes."*
>
> Judy Blatman, public relations director

MAYONNAISE

At one time, before eating raw eggs became such a risk because of the possibility of salmonella bacteria in the yolks, I prepared mayonnaise from scratch using either a blender or food processor. Now I buy a commercial mayonnaise, such as Hellmann's, which is available in a reduced-fat version. I find that adding 1/4–1/2 teaspoon fresh lemon juice for each 1/4 cup mayonnaise freshens the flavor.

use—and by adding different herbs—your salads can taste different night after night.

I keep on hand five kinds of vinegars: cider, red wine, rice wine, sherry, and balsamic. While that might sound like overkill, few condiments give you as much variety, particularly if you eat green salads daily. Depending upon the salad, I interchange the cider, red wine, and rice wine vinegars (and store them in the refrigerator so they don't continue to ferment and become overly acidic). I use sherry and balsamic vinegars in moderation—usually just for flavoring—a dash of either deepens the flavor of ingredients. (They're also wonderful additions to sauces and, if you're on a low-salt diet, help compensate for the lack of salt.)

Good-quality olive oil is a must for a green salad, but you don't need to stock up on $20 bottles of Italian extra-virgin oil. For everyday living, a less expensive virgin oil from the Lucca region of Italy—or one of the flavorful oils from Spain—will suffice. However, buying olive oil in gallon containers is a poor idea because a single cook can't possibly use the oil up before it starts to go slightly rancid. It's wiser to spend a little more for smaller containers (which also gives you the opportunity to keep shopping around until you find an oil you like). You should store olive oil in a cool, dry place, such as the cupboard—not the refrigerator. If you like a less assertively flavored oil, canola is a healthful alternative.

This chapter includes several basic salads, such as green, spinach, and tomato and onion—as well as main-course suggestions. Remember that these are only a starting point for your own salad fixings. When you get in the habit of assessing your leftovers with salads in mind, you'll come up with some wonderful original creations and have the satisfaction of not wasting food.

By the way, if you miscalculate the amount of green salad you're going to eat, just add it to the stockpot, vinegar and all.

BASIC SALAD DRESSING

Good-quality salad greens should be the main attraction of a salad, and the dressing should complement, not overpower, them. Different vinegars add variety without disguising the taste of the greens. The standard vinegar is apple cider vinegar, but you must keep it refrigerated, otherwise it will continue to ferment and become overly acidic. Other good choices include wine vinegar, rice wine vinegar, and sherry vinegar. A drop of balsamic vinegar goes a long way.

The choice of oil is a matter of personal taste. Many people prefer to use only olive oil; others find the flavor too strong and like to cut it with a little vegetable oil. To accent olive oil's fruity taste (and to intensify the flavor of less expensive oils), soak a few black olives that have been preserved in oil in the olive oil for a week before using.

This is my mother's dressing, which uses less oil than traditional dressings. Add additional oil if you wish. Leftover dressing stays in good condition for several days if refrigerated in a covered glass jar.

(Makes about 1/2 cup dressing)

1 clove garlic	Salt
Dry mustard	3 tablespoons cider vinegar
Freshly ground black pepper	1/3 cup oil

Halve the garlic, remove the green germ in the middle, and place in a glass jar with a cover along with a generous pinch of dry mustard, a grinding of black pepper, and salt to taste. Add the vinegar, cover the jar, and shake to incorporate the ingredients. Uncover the jar and let the mixture sit for at least 1/2 hour and up to 4 hours. Strain out the garlic and add the oil. Cover the jar and shake once again. Use sparingly on the greens.

BLUE CHEESE DRESSING

If you have a small amount of a Roquefort-style blue cheese, use it up in this creamy salad dressing. Omit the garlic if you plan to store the dressing.

(Makes about 1/3 cup)

1 tablespoon softened crumbled
   blue cheese
2 teaspoons lemon juice or 1
   teaspoon vinegar
1/4–1/3 cup low-fat sour cream
   or nonfat yogurt

1/2 teaspoon minced garlic
   (optional)
Salt and freshly ground black
   pepper
1 teaspoon water (optional)

Mix together the cheese, lemon juice, sour cream, and garlic, if using. (If you want a homogenous dressing, beat it in a mixer.) Taste and season with salt and freshly ground black pepper. Add 1 teaspoon water if you prefer a more liquid dressing. Let sit for about 1/2 hour before serving to let the flavors meld.

VARIATION

Grilled Chicken and Blue Cheese Composed Salad. Thinly slice a *chicken breast* grilled without the skin. Arrange it in a mound on a bed of crisp *romaine lettuce*. Surround with 1 quartered *hard-boiled egg* and half a peeled, sliced *avocado* that's been moistened with lemon juice and generously sprinkled with freshly ground black pepper. Crumble a piece of cooked *bacon* on the top. Serve with the dressing on the side.

LEFTOVERS

Store any leftover dressing in a covered jar in the refrigerator, where it will stay in good condition for at least 1 week.

SWEET-SOUR POPPY SEED DRESSING

This is less sweet than many poppy seed dressings. Taste it and add additional sugar if you wish. It's quite good with *Fruit Salad* (page 40) or tossed with sliced raw cabbage or fennel and some grated carrot. If stored in a covered jar in the refrigerator, the dressing will stay in good condition for about 1 week.

Note: The fried fish variation is tasty. If you don't mind poppy seeds with your fish, you can also recycle any leftover dressing. *(Makes about 1/2 cup)*

2 tablespoons white or cider
   vinegar
1 tablespoon orange juice
   (optional)
2 tablespoons sugar

Dry mustard
Salt
1–2 tablespoons oil
2 tablespoons nonfat yogurt
2 teaspoons poppy seeds

Place the vinegar, orange juice, if using, sugar, a pinch of dry mustard, salt, oil, and yogurt in a large bowl and whip together until combined, or purée in a blender. Stir in the poppy seeds.

VARIATION

Use the dressing (minus the poppy seeds) as a marinade for *Southern-Style Fried Grouper or Catfish* (page 109).

GREENS SALAD

I call this a "greens" salad because ideally you would use more than one salad green. If you have your own garden or access to fresh lettuce at a farmers' market or specialty vegetable shop, you know how delicious tender, new lettuce leaves taste, and how nice it is to vary the flavor by adding more than one variety of greens. You can also change the flavor with slightly bitter-tasting leaves (arugula) or bland leaves (corn salad/mâche). When I'm buying lettuce at the supermarket, I look for salad bowl, ruby red, Boston or Bibb lettuce. I realize you may not have a choice of lettuces in your area, but the produce manager of the market may be more amenable to stocking them than you may think. You have nothing to lose by asking (try commandeering your friends into making similar requests).

(Serves 1)

1 1/2–2 cups lettuce leaves, cleaned, washed, and dried
2–3 tablespoons salad dressing (see previous pages)

Freshly ground black pepper (optional)

Toss the lettuce with the dressing. Serve immediately. Generously sprinkle with black pepper if you wish.

VARIATIONS

With cherry or plum tomatoes. Add 1/2 cup sliced *tomatoes* along with the dressing.

With cucumbers and/or peppers. Add 1/4–1/3 cup sliced *cucumber* and/or chopped *bell pepper*. Remember that these vegetables are often waxed, so you may wish to peel them.

With cooked asparagus, carrot, and scallion. Peel and thinly slice a stalk of cooked *asparagus* and a small *carrot*. Add them along to the salad with a chopped *scallion*.

With fresh herbs. Add 1–2 tablespoons finely chopped herbs such as *basil, parsley, sweet marjoram, chervil,* or *lovage*.

FRESH SPINACH SALAD

Freshly harvested spinach has a delicate texture that's a far cry from the washed spinach you find at the supermarket.

(Serves 1)

2 cups fresh spinach
1 clove garlic
2 teaspoons lemon juice or rice wine vinegar
Salt

Dry mustard
1–2 tablespoons olive oil
Freshly ground black pepper (optional)

Wash the spinach, removing any tough stems. Dry thoroughly and tear into large pieces (leave whole if baby spinach). Roll up in a kitchen towel and refrigerate until using.

Fresh Spinach Salad (continued)

Smash the garlic clove with the flat side of a knife and place in a glass container with the lemon juice or vinegar. Add a pinch of salt and dry mustard and let sit for at least 1/2 hour. Stir in the oil. Toss with the spinach, taste, and season with black pepper if you wish. Serve immediately.

VARIATION

Main Course Spinach Salad. For a main-course salad add 1 finely chopped *hard-boiled egg* and 1/3 cup sliced *mushrooms*. It's also good with a slice or two of crumbled cooked *bacon*. You could also add 1 tablespoon freshly grated *Parmesan cheese* and a dash of *nutmeg*.

SLICED TOMATO AND SWEET ONION SALAD

When perfectly ripe tomatoes are in season, this salad is virtually a meal-in-one, with a slice of country bread and a hunk of cheese. The secret touch is to soak the onions for 30 minutes in ice water to crisp them before combining with the tomatoes. Vine-ripe tomatoes are a must—as is fresh basil.

(Serves 1)

1/3 cup peeled and thinly sliced sweet onion

2 medium ripe tomatoes, sliced about 1/2 inch thick

2 teaspoons mild vinegar, such as white wine

2–3 teaspoons olive oil

Sugar

Salt and freshly ground black pepper

1 tablespoon minced basil

Place the onion slices in a bowl of ice water loaded with ice cubes. Let sit for 30 minutes. Drain, pat dry, and layer on a plate with the tomatoes. In a glass container, mix together the vinegar, olive oil, a pinch of sugar, and salt and pepper to taste. Pour over the tomatoes and onions. Sprinkle with the basil.

VARIATION

With lemon zest. Substitute *lemon juice* for the vinegar and sprinkle 1 teaspoon *lemon zest* over the salad before serving.

LEFTOVERS

Drain the tomatoes and onions and purée them with *V-8 or tomato juice.* Served over ice, it's a refreshing summer beverage. Or, drain the tomatoes and onions, pat them dry, and chop them. Use as a topping for a *small pizza* or, if you have just a tablespoon or two, an English muffin. Add grated *mozzarella and/or Parmesan cheese* and melt in the oven.

WALDORF SALAD

Even when the refrigerator is virtually bare, with a crisp apple, celery, mayonnaise, walnuts, and lemon juice on hand, you can put together this famous salad, served for much of this century at New York City's Waldorf-Astoria Hotel. I like a mixture of fresh fennel and celery—and prefer to cut the mayonnaise with yogurt.

(Serves 1)

1 large crisp apple, such as Granny Smith, peeled and diced into 1/2-inch pieces (about 11/4 cups)
1/3 cup diced celery or a mixture of celery and fennel
2 teaspoons fresh lemon juice

1/4 cup reduced-fat mayonnaise—or a mixture of 2 tablespoons mayonnaise and 2 tablespoons nonfat yogurt
1/4 cup chopped walnuts
Boston lettuce (optional)

Mix together the apple, celery, and lemon juice. Combine with the mayonnaise and walnuts. Taste and add more lemon juice if needed. Mound on lettuce leaves, if you like.

VARIATIONS

With lemon zest. Add 1 teaspoon minced *lemon zest.*

With pineapple. Add 1/4 cup finely sliced drained *canned pineapple.* Substitute *pecans* for the walnuts.

COLESLAW

This easy-to-make coleslaw can be dressed up as much as you wish. Add grated carrots and peppers, celery, onions, horseradish, sugar, and vinegar—all are traditional ingredients used in this favorite American salad. For a crisper salad, soak the shredded cabbage in ice water for 1 hour before draining it and tossing with the dressing. This is particularly attractive made with shredded red cabbage and carrots.

(Serves 1)

2 tablespoons yogurt
1/4 cup mayonnaise
1/4 teaspoon cider vinegar

1/8 teaspoon dry mustard
2 cups finely shredded cabbage

Mix together the yogurt, mayonnaise, cider vinegar, and dry mustard. Toss with the cabbage. Serve immediately, or let sit for an hour to wilt slightly.

VARIATIONS

With carrots and peppers. Add 1/3 cup grated *carrot* and 3 tablespoons chopped *bell pepper*.

With carrots and raisins. Add 1/2 cup grated *carrot* and 3 tablespoons *raisins*.

With celery and onions. Add 1/4 cup diced *celery* and 2 tablespoons chopped *onion* or *scallion*.

With mustard. Add 2 teaspoons *Dijon mustard*.

Sweet-and-Sour Coleslaw. Add 1 teaspoon *sugar* and increase vinegar to 2–3 teaspoons.

With horseradish. Stir in 1–2 teaspoons *prepared horseradish*.

With sour cream. Substitute *sour cream* for the yogurt.

With anise or celery seeds. Add 1 teaspoon *anise or celery seeds* and 1/4 cup chopped *fennel* (optional).

LEFTOVERS

Drain and use as a filling in *sandwiches* such as turkey, coleslaw, corned beef, and Russian dressing on rye bread; coleslaw and Swiss cheese on rye; or grilled rye bread stuffed with mustard, Swiss cheese, coleslaw, and roast beef or pastrami.

GREEK SALAD

This is a satisfying meal-in-one to eat after a hard day at work. A mixture of soft-texture lettuces and baby spinach leaves is especially good, but use iceberg lettuce if you prefer. Arugula is frequently added in Greece. Vary the proportions of vegetables and olive oil and lemon juice to suit your taste.

(Serves 1)

1/2 cucumber
1 large ripe tomato
1/2 green pepper, halved top to bottom
2/3–1 cup mixed salad greens
1/4 red Bermuda onion or 2 scallions

Kalamata (Greek) olives (optional)
2 tablespoons feta cheese
Lemon juice
Olive oil

If the cucumber is garden fresh, leave the skin on. Otherwise, peel and seed the cucumber and cut into 1/2-inch slices. Core the tomato and cut it into wedges. Thinly slice the bell pepper into rings, discarding the seeds and stem end.

Place the salad greens in a shallow bowl. Arrange the tomato, cucumber, and green pepper in a circle around the edge. Slice the onion into strips and scatter over the vegetables. If you like, add a few Kalamata olives to the plate. Crumble the feta cheese in the center. Drizzle with lemon juice and olive oil to taste. Then, after you've admired your handiwork, toss the salad.

VARIATION

Tossed Greek Salad. Toss all the solid ingredients together, then moisten with olive oil to taste, then with lemon juice. (About 1 tablespoon olive oil to 1/2 tablespoon lemon juice works well.)

CAESAR SALAD

This salad, invented in Tijuana, Mexico, by a restaurateur who had an unexpected batch of customers arrive after the kitchen was closed, is one that you *always* should eat at home, not in a restaurant. Many restaurant chefs still use the classic method of making a Caesar salad, which is to bind the dressing together with a coddled egg (an egg boiled for 1 minute). The egg white cooks slightly and thickens, helping the dressing adhere to the lettuce leaves. Personnel at the Egg Board say that an egg must be boiled for 3 to 5 minutes to kill any salmonella bacteria should they be in the yolk.

However, the egg is but one of the flavors in a Caesar salad—and a minor one at that. You can easily omit it—or you can boil the egg for five minutes and use only the yolk, discarding the solidified white. This recipe uses the yolk because it gives more of the classic Caesar salad flavor, but I also add a drop or two of balsamic vinegar. Anyway, after you've munched your way through the croutons, Parmesan cheese, and the anchovies, you'll barely notice the omission.

(Serves 1)

1 egg
2 teaspoons olive oil
1–2 teaspoons lemon juice or
   cider vinegar
Balsamic vinegar
6 medium romaine lettuce
   leaves, broken crosswise into
   2-inch-wide pieces

Freshly ground black pepper
2–4 anchovies, coarsely
   chopped (optional)
Croutons (page 256)
2 tablespoons grated Parmesan
   cheese

Bring a small pot of water to a boil, add the egg, and gently boil for 5 minutes. Run it under cold water, crack open the shell, and place the yolk in a glass bowl. Beat it with a fork or a whip. Add the olive oil, lemon juice, and a dash of balsamic vinegar. Place the lettuce in a salad bowl and toss with the dressing. Sprinkle with a generous amount of black pepper. Top with the anchovies, if using, and croutons to taste. Sprinkle on the Parmesan cheese, and toss again.

VARIATIONS

With sliced beef. Add 1/2 cup thinly sliced rare *roast beef or* sliced *leftover steak* (grilled is particularly nice). Use *red wine vinegar.*

With garlic. Add 1 teaspoon finely minced *garlic* to the dressing.

SALAD NIÇOISE

When baby potatoes, tomatoes, and green beans are in season, there's no better salad to whet your appetite. At other times of the year, increase the amount of basil, chives, and capers to pick up the flavor. The waxy, yellow-fleshed fingerling potatoes, available at many gourmet fruit and vegetable stores or farmers' markets, are particularly good with this combination. I like the taste of the beans and tomatoes without a dressing, but the French would toss them in oil and vinegar. Taste, and add additional oil and vinegar if you prefer.

(Serves 1)

6–8 baby potatoes, about 1–1 1/2 inches in diameter— or 2 boiling potatoes, halved

2 tablespoons chopped scallion or sweet onion

1/2 teaspoon minced chives

1 tablespoon olive oil

2 teaspoons white wine or rice wine vinegar

1 teaspoon chopped basil (optional)

1/4 teaspoon Dijon or Creole mustard (optional)

Salt and freshly ground black pepper

A 3 1/4-ounce can tuna fish packed in water, drained

1 large ripe tomato, quartered

2 ounces cooked trimmed green beans (3/4–1 cup)

1 hard-boiled egg, peeled and quartered (see below)

6–8 brine-cured black olives (such as the small imported olives from Provence)

3–4 anchovies (optional)

1/2 teaspoon capers (optional)

Bring a large pot of water to a boil, add the potatoes, lower the heat to a gentle boil, and cook until done, about 10–12 minutes. (Baby potatoes

Salad Niçoise (continued)

will cook through slightly faster. Potatoes 1 inch in diameter, for example, will be done in 8–10 minutes.) Slice the potatoes 1/2 inch thick. Gently combine with the scallion, chives, olive oil, vinegar, and optional basil and mustard. Season with salt and pepper. Place the potato salad in the middle of a platter. Surround the potatoes with the tuna fish, tomato, green beans, and egg quarters. Garnish with olives, and, if you like, anchovies and capers.

HARD-BOILING AN EGG

An easy way to hard-boil an egg is to place it in a pot of water, bring to a boil, gently boil for about 15 seconds, and then let sit in the water for 30 minutes before peeling. A medium egg will be cooked through without being rubbery.

ITALIAN TOMATO AND BREAD SALAD

This salad, once a peasant dish, is now a chic addition to many restaurant menus in northern Italy. And no wonder, for assembled with densely textured fresh croutons, ripe tomatoes, and virgin—or extra-virgin—olive oil, it's the essence of what a summer meal ought to offer. The lime juice isn't traditional—but it adds flavor.

(Serves 1)

1 cup peeled, seeded, and chopped ripe tomatoes (preferably both red and yellow varieties)

1/4 cup chopped scallions, both white and light green parts of stem

2 tablespoons chopped parsley leaves

1–2 tablespoons olive oil

1 tablespoon lime or lemon juice

Salt

1 cup freshly made *Croutons* (page 256)

Mix together the tomatoes, scallions, parsley, olive oil, and juice. Taste and season with salt. Press down lightly with the palm of your hand to release the tomato juices. Toss with the croutons. Let sit for at least 15 minutes before serving. This is a good light main course or a nice accompaniment to roast pork served at room temperature and fresh corn on the cob.

VARIATION

With cucumbers and mint. Add 1/2 cup peeled, seeded, and diced *cucumbers* and 1 teaspoon chopped *mint* to the other ingredients.

RED ONION, BEEF, AND CAPER SALAD

This salad, which should be served at room temperature, can be made either with leftover roast beef, roast beef from the deli—or with pan-seared raw beef, as below. (Cut the beef on the serving plate so that the beef juices mingle with the dressing.) Ask the butcher to slice about 1/4 pound paper-thin pieces from a roast—preferably a sirloin tip. Crisping the onion in the water adds texture.

(Serves 1)

Red Bermuda onion
Olive oil (for pan)
3–4 ounces raw beef, sliced
    paper thin
Freshly ground black pepper
2–3 teaspoons olive oil

2 teaspoons red wine or cider
    vinegar
Balsamic vinegar (optional)
1 teaspoon minced capers
1 tomato, sliced and halved

Cut slices from a Bermuda onion and separate into rings. The number of slices you cut depends upon your taste. I like about 1/3 of a medium-sized red onion. Put the slices into a bowl filled with ice and water. Set aside.

Film the bottom of a large, heavy frying pan with oil (about 2 teaspoons should do). Heat the pan until hot and add the beef slices. Sear them on one side until they almost cook through, approximately 1–2 minutes. Generously sprinkle the slices with black pepper and turn them for just a moment. Lift them from the pan and place on a plate. Cool the slices slightly, then cut them into 1-inch-wide pieces.

Red Onion, Beef, and Caper Salad (continued)

Mix together the olive oil, red wine vinegar, a dash of balsamic vinegar, if using, and the capers. Drain the onion rings and pat dry. Toss the beef with the caper dressing. Mound it in the center of a plate and top with the sliced onions. Surround with the tomato slices.

VARIATIONS

With leftover cooked roast beef, deli beef, or corned beef. Slice the beef and marinate it in the caper sauce for at least 1 hour. Add a dash of *hot pepper sauce and/or* 1/4 teaspoon *Dijon or Creole mustard.* Mound on the plate and proceed as above.

With potato salad. Substitute *Potato Salad* (page 43) for the tomato. Reverse the arrangement. Place the salad in the center of a plate and surround with the beef. Sprinkle with 1 teaspoon minced *parsley.*

COOKED VEGETABLE SALADS

Borrowing from a time-honored tradition among European cooks, I often recycle cooked vegetables from the evening before into the following day's salads. Even a small amount of vegetables will reappear in another guise: sometimes in a vinaigrette as an antipasto offering or even dressed with mayonnaise as a composed salad. I frequently cook extra vegetables that complement each other two nights in a row so that I can put together a salad for dinner the following night. When you're planning to make cooked vegetable salads, be sure to leave the vegetables as crisp as possible, and dry them off and store them in glass, not plastic, containers in the refrigerator. I put a doubled-up piece of paper toweling under the vegetables to absorb any excess moisture.

Here are some ways to use up cooked vegetables in salads:

• Slice a baked beet into 1/4-inch strips. Toss with oil, vinegar, and chopped scallions. Serve on a bed of raw spinach, arugula, or corn salad (mâche) greens.

• Briefly marinate cooked cauliflower and broccoli florets in lime juice. Toss with a little olive oil and fresh basil.

• Chill cooked asparagus. Arrange in a fan shape and drizzle with a vinaigrette sauce. Garnish with chopped hard-boiled eggs.

- Chill roasted red peppers. Mix them with slivers of red onion and sliced anchovies in an oil and vinegar dressing.
- Dice cooked carrots and mix with cooked peas. Gently mix with mayonnaise flavored with lemon juice. Serve on a bed of lettuce. Garnish with capers if you wish.
- Make a yogurt-tahini dressing and drizzle over cooked broccoli, cauliflower, or beans. (Or serve it as a dip for barely cooked vegetables.) Mix together 1 tablespoon yogurt, 1 teaspoon tahini (sesame seed paste), 1 teaspoon lime juice, and 1/4 teaspoon honey.
- Mash the yolk of a hard-boiled egg and mix with oil and vinegar. Toss with cooked asparagus, beans, and peas. Chop the egg white and mix together with chopped parsley. Sprinkle over the top.

AVOCADO, PAPAYA, AND SHRIMP SALAD

This salad, which takes less than five minutes to assemble, satisfies the appetite on a hot summer night. If you don't want to turn on the stove, buy cooked shrimp. You can use a standard oil and vinegar dressing, but the citrus juices enhance the delicate flavors. Be sure to coat the avocado slices with the dressing so they don't darken from being exposed to the air.

(Serves 1)

1 tablespoon lemon, lime, or orange juice (or a combination)

1 1/2 tablespoons lightly flavored vegetable oil

1/2–1 teaspoon minced chives or parsley (optional)

2–3 ounces peeled cooked shrimp

1/2 ripe avocado

1/4 super-ripe papaya

Chicory leaves

Mix together the citrus juice(s), oil, and the herb, if using. Toss the shrimp in the dressing and let sit while you peel and slice the avocado and papaya. Place the chicory leaves on a plate, lift the shrimp out of the dressing, and place them in the center of the chicory. Arrange the avo-

Avocado, Papaya, and Shrimp Salad (continued)
cado and papaya alternately in a pinwheel fashion around the shrimp.
Spoon over the dressing. Serve with French bread.

VARIATION

Colorful Shellfish Salad. This basic salad is a splashy centerpiece for a
Sunday brunch or supper. Just increase the amounts to suit the number
of guests you have, and add a small amount of cooked shelled *mussels*
and *lobster.* Serve with fresh fruit shortcakes or sugar cookies and fresh
fruit for dessert.

FISH SALAD

The lemon juice freshens the flavor of this salad, which utilizes leftover
cooked fish. If you marinate the fish in the citrus juice and pepper for
several hours, it will absorb more of the citrus taste than if you wait until
assembling the salad.

(Serves 1)

1 grapefruit
1 cup leftover cooked white-
    fleshed fish—such as cod,
    grouper, monkfish, or hake—
    skinned, boned, and cut into
    strips
2 tablespoons freshly squeezed
    lemon, lime, or grapefruit
    juice
Freshly ground black pepper

1 tablespoon peeled, seeded,
    and chopped tomato
2 tablespoons chopped fennel
    or celery
1 tablespoon olive or canola oil
2 teaspoons minced parsley or
    sweet marjoram
Salt
Lettuce leaves (about 4 from a
    Bibb or Boston lettuce)

Peel the grapefruit, pull apart to divide into halves, and set one half
aside for another use. Holding the halved grapefruit over a small bowl
to catch the juices, peel away the membrane of each section and slice it
into smaller pieces. You should end up with only flesh—no membrane.
Set the grapefruit aside. (You can use the grapefruit juice—rather than
lemon juice—to moisten the fish. However, the lemon juice gives a
sharper flavor.)

Mix together the fish, juice, and a generous amount of black pepper;

let sit for at least 20 minutes to let the fish absorb some of the juice (or refrigerate for no more than 12 hours). Add the tomato, fennel, oil, and parsley. Taste and season with salt.

Arrange the lettuce leaves on a dinner plate, mound the fish salad in the center, and surround with grapefruit sections.

VARIATION

Lemon Shrimp Salad. Substitute 1 cup cooked *shrimp,* or equal amounts of cooked *shrimp and mussels,* for the fish. Omit the tomato and grapefruit.

RUSSIAN SALAD

Leftover cooked vegetables form the base of this salad, popular throughout Europe, where it's often used as part of a cold appetizer platter or as a stuffing for vegetables (such as tomatoes). It's usually served coated with lots of additional mayonnaise, a step to omit if you are avoiding extra fat.

(Serves 1)

1 small boiled potato, peeled and cut into 1/2-inch dice (about 3/4 cup)
1/3 cup cooked green beans cut into 1-inch lengths
1/4 cup cooked carrot cut into 1/2-inch dice
1/4 cup cooked peas
1 tablespoon lemon juice

1/3–1/2 cup reduced-fat mayonnaise—or a combination of half mayonnaise, half yogurt
Salt and freshly ground black pepper
Cayenne pepper or hot pepper sauce (optional)
Lettuce or chicory leaves

Mix together the potato, green beans, carrot, peas, and lemon juice. Let sit for 10–20 minutes. Mix with the mayonnaise. Taste and season with salt, pepper, and a dash of cayenne pepper or hot pepper sauce, if using. Serve on a bed of lettuce or chicory leaves.

VARIATIONS

With artichoke hearts and/or cooked mussels. Surround with commercially *pickled artichokes* and/or 6–8 cooked, shelled *mussels.*

Russian Salad (continued)

With cooked shrimp. Omit the carrots and beans. Add 1/2 cup diced cooked *shrimp* and 1/4 cup chopped *celery or fennel* to the mayonnaise.

With cauliflower or broccoli. Omit the peas and carrots. Substitute equal amounts of cooked *cauliflower or broccoli florets.*

With pickle, Hungarian-style. Add 1–2 teaspoons diced *dill pickle.*

LEFTOVERS

Use to stuff a raw tomato (or half a tomato). Halve an unpeeled *tomato,* and, using a sharp knife, hollow out both halves. (The peel helps it retain its shape.) Sprinkle with salt and pepper. Add minced *lemon zest* to the salad to perk up the flavor (1/2 cup of salad would require 1/4 teaspoon zest). Stuff the tomato and sprinkle with minced *celery leaves or parsley.* Surround with a quartered *hard-boiled egg.*

COUSCOUS AND SWEET POTATO SALAD

The new instant couscous is an excellent standby for days when you're harried, for you can cook it in 5 minutes. Use as the foundation for any number of vegetable salads, such as this version with leftover sweet potato, which takes less than 10 minutes to assemble. The rich flavor of the sweet potato compensates for the lack of oil.

(Serves 1)

1/2 cup salted water
1/2 to 1 teaspoon olive oil
1/3 cup dried instant couscous
3 tablespoons peeled, seeded, and cooked *Roasted Red Pepper* (page 63) or chopped fresh peppers
1/4 cup sliced scallions
1 tablespoon sliced celery (optional)

1/2–2/3 cup cooked sweet potato, cut into 1/2-inch-thick pieces
1–2 tablespoons orange juice
Cumin
Cinnamon
Salt
Lettuce (optional)
Orange or lime slices, for garnish

Bring the water to a boil and stir in the olive oil and couscous. Remove the pan from the heat, cover, and let sit for 5 minutes. You will end up with about 1 cup cooked couscous. In the same pot, toss the couscous with the red pepper, scallions, celery, sweet potato, and orange juice. Season with a pinch each of cumin and cinnamon and salt to taste. If you wish, mound the couscous on lettuce leaves and garnish with a slice of orange or lime. You can either eat the salad right away, or wait about 30 minutes to allow the flavors to meld.

VARIATIONS

With tomato. Omit the sweet potato, cumin, and cinnamon and substitute 1/2 cup peeled, seeded, and chopped *tomato* and 2 teaspoons chopped *coriander or parsley.*

With broccoli and/or cauliflower. Omit the sweet potato and substitute 3/4 cup cooked *broccoli or cauliflower florets.*

Note: Any leftover *Oven-Fried Sweet Potato* (page 66) is particularly flavorful in this salad.

TABBOULEH

Tabbouleh, a popular Middle Eastern salad, makes a wonderful summer meal. If you're going to hold the tabbouleh for more than one day, add the tomatoes and cucumbers just before serving.

(Makes about 1 1/4 cups)

1/2 cup bulgur wheat	1 tablespoon freshly squeezed
1/3 cup chopped onion	lemon juice
2 tablespoons chopped mint	2–3 teaspoons olive oil
2 tablespoons finely chopped	Salt and freshly ground black
parsley	pepper
1 cup chopped tomato	
1/2 cup coarsely chopped	
cucumber	

Cover the bulgur with water, and let stand for at least 1 hour until softened. Taste the bulgur. If the grains are soft yet chewy, drain, place in a clean towel, and squeeze the bulgur dry. Put it in a bowl. Toss with the onion, mint, parsley, tomato, and cucumber. Then stir in the lemon juice, oil, and salt and pepper to taste.

FRUIT SALAD

Sometimes, a fresh fruit salad is all you want for dinner—particularly on a muggy evening. It's a handy way to use up small portions of fruit, but the fruit you use should be of high quality. Save those less-than-perfect fruits for *Baked Mixed Fruit Crisp* (see page 274). You can vary the fruit depending upon the season, but try to include a diced tart apple for crunch and contrast.

(Serves 1)

1/4 cup mixed orange and lemon juice or 1/4 cup orange juice
1 teaspoon sugar (optional)
1/2 teaspoon minced orange zest
1/2 cup sliced strawberries (about 1/5 pint) or whole blackberries or raspberries
1/3 cup sliced banana (about 1/2 banana)

1/2 cup peeled, seeded, and sliced peaches, pears, cantaloupe, or oranges (flesh only)
1/2 cup peeled and sliced apple
6–8 halved red or Thompson grapes

Place the juice in a large glass bowl. Add the optional sugar, zest, strawberries, banana, peaches, apple, and grapes. Be sure that the apple and banana are coated with juice so that they don't turn brown. Either eat immediately, or refrigerate, covered, for up to 2 hours.

VARIATIONS

With blueberries. Add 1/3 cup whole *blueberries.*
With Sweet-Sour Poppy Seed Dressing. Drain the fruit, reserving the juices for a puréed fruit drink (see page 286). Place on a plate and spoon 2 tablespoons of *Sweet-Sour Poppy Seed Dressing* (page 24) in a band across the top.

SCANDINAVIAN-STYLE CUCUMBER SALAD

Throughout Sweden and Denmark, food is often accompanied by a sweet-sour marinated cucumber salad. The Danes use it to garnish their open-faced sandwiches, while the Swedes serve it with their smorgasbord offerings. It's particularly good with little meatballs, beef dishes, and simply prepared baked fish. Taste and adjust the amount of sugar and vinegar to your palate.

(Makes 1 cup)

1 medium cucumber   2 tablespoons cider vinegar
2 tablespoons sugar

Peel the cucumber and score the skin with the tines of a fork. (Scoring means to run the fork tines down the cucumber. It makes a decorative scallop and also starts the cucumber juices flowing.) Thinly slice the cucumber. Place the slices in a bowl and sprinkle with the sugar. Press down firmly on the slices to release the cucumber juices. Add the vinegar. Toss the cucumber slices and refrigerate for about an hour or until chilled.

VARIATION

With dill. Add 2 teaspoons chopped *dill* just before serving.

LEFTOVERS

Any leftover cucumbers will keep for about 1 week if stored in a covered glass dish. Use them in sandwiches such as tuna fish or meatloaf, add to salads such as potato, or snack on them as a pick-me-up. Save any leftover juices for salad dressings.

With soy sauce and sesame oil. Drain any leftover cucumbers and season to taste with dashes of *soy sauce* and *Oriental sesame oil*. Serve with Chinese stir-fries.

GERMAN POTATO SALAD

In Germany you're more likely to be served sliced waxy yellow potatoes in a vinaigrette and parsley sauce than this Americanized version. But on a frosty winter's night, this tastes wonderful with grilled bratwurst and beer. If you can locate German fingerling potatoes (yellow waxy finger-shaped potatoes) at a farmers' market, buy them for this recipe.

(Makes 1 generous serving)

2 slices lean bacon
1/3 cup chopped onion
1 tablespoon flour
1/2 cup warm water or beef
    broth
1 teaspoon sugar
1–2 tablespoons cider vinegar

1 teaspoon celery seeds
    (optional)
11/3 cups sliced cooked waxy-
    textured potatoes
Salt and freshly ground black
    pepper

In a heavy nonreactive frying pan, cook the bacon until crisp. Remove from the pan, crumble, and set aside. Remove all but 1 tablespoon of the fat from the pan. Cook the onion in the fat for 2 minutes, stirring occasionally. Do not let brown. Off the heat stir in the flour. Place the pan back on the stove, and cook for 2 minutes, stirring constantly. Stir in the warm water. Cook, stirring occasionally, until the mixture has thickened. Add the sugar, cider vinegar, celery seeds, if using, and reserved bacon, adjusting the amount of sugar and vinegar to suit your taste. If the sauce is too thick, stir in additional water a tablespoon at a time. Place the potatoes in the pan, and toss until the slices are covered with the sauce. Taste and season with salt and pepper.

VARIATIONS

With mustard. Add 1–2 teaspoons *Dijon mustard.*

With cornichons. Add 1 tablespoon chopped *cornichons* (small pickled cucumbers).

With country ham. Replace the bacon fat with *butter* and substitute 1 tablespoon minced *country ham* for the bacon.

With herbs. Omit the bacon. Use 1 tablespoon *butter.* Stir in 2 tablespoons chopped herbs, such as a combination of *tarragon and parsley; chervil, winter or summer savory*—or *lovage.*

POTATO SALAD

This is my mother's potato salad—simple, hearty, and delicious. Potato salad is too much trouble to make for just one meal, but if you wait to add the salt until just before serving, the salad will stay digestible for at least 3 days.

(Makes about 2¹/₂ cups)

3 medium potatoes
¹/₄ teaspoon dry mustard
2 teaspoons cider vinegar
¹/₃ cup diced onion, preferably
    sweet
1 hard-boiled egg, coarsely
    chopped (optional)
¹/₂–³/₄ cup diced celery

1–2 tablespoons chopped
    parsley or lovage
¹/₃–¹/₂ cup mayonnaise
1–2 tablespoons yogurt
    (optional)
Salt and freshly ground black
    pepper (optional)

Boil the potatoes until cooked through, drain, and peel them. Cut into ¹/₂-inch cubes. While still warm, sprinkle with dry mustard and toss with the cider vinegar. Stir in the onion, optional hard-boiled egg, celery, and parsley. Mix in the mayonnaise and yogurt, if using. Let sit for at least 1 hour so that the flavors meld. Wait to season until serving. Store any leftover salad in a glass bowl in the refrigerator. This is delicious with grilled pork or chicken—or with an all-vegetable platter of sliced tomatoes and *Scandinavian-Style Cucumber Salad* (page 41).

VARIATIONS

With diced pickles. Mix in 2 tablespoons snipped *dill* or diced *sweet pickles* before adding the mayonnaise.

With pickle relish, Southern-style. Add 1 tablespoon *spicy brown mustard* and 1–2 tablespoons *pickle relish.*

FENNEL AND RAW MUSHROOM SALAD

This salad is satisfying by itself—or as an accompaniment to roast pork or chicken. Black pepper accentuates fennel's clean taste.

(Serves 1)

3/4 cup very thinly sliced raw
   mushrooms
1 1/2–2 cups thinly sliced raw
   fennel
1–2 teaspoons olive oil

1–2 teaspoons fresh lemon juice
1/2 teaspoon minced lemon zest
Freshly ground black pepper
Salt (optional)

Arrange the mushrooms down the center of a plate and flank with the fennel. Mix together the olive oil, lemon juice, and lemon zest and drizzle over the fennel and mushrooms. Sprinkle with black pepper and season with salt if you wish.

VARIATION

Fennel and Mushroom Soup. Omit the oil or reduce to 1/2 teaspoon. Wait to add the lemon juice until you taste the soup. Simmer the fennel and mushrooms in 1–1 1/2 cups of *chicken, beef, or vegetable stock* for 10 minutes. Coarsely purée the mixture in a blender along with the lemon zest. Taste and season with black pepper and salt.

HURRY-UP GUACAMOLE

You can make guacamole as simple or complex as you wish. In Mexico, it's often just avocado mashed with lime juice and salt. This version with jalapeño peppers and onions takes about 4 minutes to prepare. Guacamole is delicious with *Burritos with Leftover Beef* (page 174) or as a snack with nonfat tortilla chips. It's a great way to use up half an avocado. (Or, if you're starting from scratch, rub the surface of the remaining avocado with oil and citrus juice or vinegar and wrap it in plastic wrap before refrigerating it.)

(Makes 1/4–1/3 cup)

1/2–1 teaspoon fresh or frozen
    peeled, seeded, and minced
    jalapeño pepper (optional)
1 tablespoon chopped onion
1/2 teaspoon olive oil

1/4–1/3 cup mashed avocado
1 teaspoon lime juice
Salt and freshly ground black
    pepper
Cumin (optional)

Put the jalapeño pepper, if using, and onion in a small microwaveable glass dish, stir in the olive oil, and microwave until the vegetables are cooked through but retain some texture (about 1 1/2 minutes). Or sauté slowly for 5 minutes in a small frying pan. Stir into the mashed avocado. Add lime juice. Taste and season with salt, pepper, and, if you like, a pinch of cumin. You can eat the guacamole immediately—or leave it for 1/2 hour so that the flavors meld.

VARIATION

With hot pepper sauce. Omit the jalapeño pepper. Substitute a dash of *hot pepper sauce.*

BROWN RICE SALAD WITH PEANUTS

This simple salad takes about 2 minutes to assemble. Serve it with grilled mackerel or pork chops. The sherry vinegar is essential.

(Serves 1)

1 cup cooked brown rice
2 teaspoons sherry vinegar
2 teaspoons canola or vegetable
    oil
Salt and freshly ground black
    pepper (optional)

1/4 cup chopped dry-roasted
    peanuts
1 tablespoon chopped chives or
    scallion greens

Mix together the rice, vinegar, and oil. Season with salt and pepper if you wish. Sprinkle with the peanuts and chives.

VARIATION

With tangerine segments. Substitute 1/3 cup chopped *walnuts* for the peanuts and omit the chives. Use 1 teaspoon sherry vinegar and *tangerine*

Brown Rice Salad with Peanuts (continued)
juice to taste. Mound the salad on a few leaves of loose *leaf lettuce,* such as salad bowl. Sprinkle with the walnuts. Surround with peeled *tangerine segments.*

TUNA RICE SALAD

The lime juice and black pepper set off the flavor of the beans. Omit the anchovies if you wish. This is a good way to use up leftover cooked green beans and rice.

(Serves 1)

1/4 pound trimmed green beans (or 11/2 cups cooked green beans)
11/4 cups cooked rice
2 tablespoons chopped celery with leaves
2 tablespoons scallion greens
A 31/4-ounce can tuna fish in water, drained
1 tablespoon peeled, seeded, and chopped fresh tomato
1 tablespoon chopped coriander or parsley (or a combination of both)

1 teaspoon chopped anchovies (optional)
11/2 tablespoons peeled, seeded, and minced jalapeño pepper
2 teaspoons olive oil
1 teaspoon rice wine vinegar or lime juice
Salt (optional)
Lime juice
Freshly ground black pepper
1 ripe tomato

Bring a pot of water to the boil, add the beans, and boil for 2 minutes. Pour the beans into a colander and run it under cold water. Drain the beans and place them on a clean dishtowel to absorb any moisture. They should be cooked through but retain some texture.

Mix together the rice, celery, scallions, tuna fish, tomato, coriander, anchovies, and pepper. Toss first with the olive oil and then with the rice vinegar. Let sit for 15 minutes to meld the flavors. Taste and correct seasonings, adding salt if you wish.

Mound the rice salad in the middle of a plate. Divide the green beans into two equal portions and fan them out on the sides of the rice.

Squeeze lime juice over the beans and sprinkle with black pepper. Cut the tomato into eighths and arrange it on the top and bottom of the plate. Serve at room temperature.

VARIATION

With cooked fava beans and red pepper. Substitute 1$1/2$ cups cooked *fava beans* for the green beans. Toss with 2 tablespoons charred, peeled, and chopped *Roasted Red Pepper* (page 63). Proceed as above.

BABA GHANOUSH

Also known as eggplant caviar, this Middle Eastern specialty is a great pick-me-up on a summer night as part of an appetizer platter (along with hummus, stuffed grape leaves, and pita bread). If you omit the salt, this version tastes fresh for several days.

(Makes about 1$1/2$ cups)

A 1-pound eggplant
1 clove garlic
2–3 tablespoons lemon juice
$1/4$–$1/3$ cup tahini (sesame seed paste)
Cayenne pepper (optional)

Salt (optional)
Olive oil
Chopped red onion
Chopped fresh mint
Boston lettuce or pita bread

Place the eggplant in a shallow baking pan. Insert a stainless-steel fork in the eggplant up to the point where the tines end. The fork conducts the heat into the center of the eggplant so that it cooks faster. Bake the eggplant in a preheated 425°F oven until cooked through and soft, about 35–40 minutes. It's all right if the eggplant chars, for in some versions of this dish, the eggplant is cooked over coals, which gives it a smoky flavor.

While the eggplant is still warm, remove the skin. Cool slightly and drain off the juices, which tend to be bitter. Chop and mash the garlic with a knife and place it in a mixing bowl. Add the eggplant pulp, lemon juice, and tahini to taste. Vary the proportions depending upon whether you want the lemon or the sesame flavor to dominate. Beat with a mixer until incorporated. (Or you can pulse in a food processor.) Taste and, if you wish, season with cayenne pepper and salt.

Baba Ghanoush (continued)

To serve, place a portion on a plate, make a depression in the center, and fill with olive oil (about 1 teaspoon). Garnish with chopped onion and mint. Serve with lettuce or pita bread to use as a scoop. This baba ghanoush will keep, refrigerated, for almost 2 weeks.

VARIATIONS

Russian-style Eggplant Caviar. Omit the tahini and add 3 tablespoons each cooked chopped *bell peppers* and *tomatoes* and 1 teaspoon chopped fresh *coriander.*

With chickpeas. Omit the tahini and add 1/3 cup cooked chopped *onions* and 1/4 cup cooked chopped *tomatoes.* Just before serving, stir in 3/4 cup cooked whole *chickpeas.*

FARMERS' MARKETS AND FARM STANDS

An exciting aspect of our renewed interest in gardening and healthful eating is the emerging network of farmers' markets—even in the cities—where you can buy fruits and vegetables at their peak points of flavor. No matter where you live, there's likely to be a market—or a farm stand—nearby that sells fresh produce in season. I urge you to search one out and to take the time to shop there at least occasionally. Savoring fresh fruits and vegetables in season is one of the cook's great pleasures. And even the most self-sufficient among us can relish the sociability and new friendships found at a farmers' market.

These markets remind us that food shopping is an enjoyable experience, not a chore. They also allow us to simplify and reframe our style of cooking. Farm-fresh vegetables and fruits require little from you as a cook but respect. Baby carrots don't even need peeling; steamed or simmered in water and served plain or with a dusting of herbs they're a far cry from the coarsely textured supermarket staples. A handful of sugar-sweet cherry tomatoes is an addictive snack. Have you ever tasted a sautéed fresh rutabaga? Or steamed kohlrabi? How about a strawberry that's so juicy you practically need a bib to protect your clothes?

Wherever I travel, I hunt out the local farmers' markets and spend some time browsing and tasting the regional specialties. Even now, 20 years later, I can recall a molasses shoofly pie I ate at a rural Pennsylvania market. Or, the hundreds of crocks filled with pickled peppers at Budapest's Central Market. When you leave a farmers' market, you take home memories as well as produce.

ITALIAN GREENS AND BEAN SALAD

You can make this salad with canned white beans. Imported ones usually have more texture. Broccoli rabe (rapini) can be found at many supermarkets throughout the winter and early spring. Young broccoli rabe has small leaves and a bright green bud much like an underdeveloped broccoli head. If it's overaged, the green is exceptionally bitter. The tip-off is huge buds that have flowered. Don't buy these greens—they're on the verge of being inedible. The stems of winter greens should be trimmed with a vegetable peeler.

(Serves 1)

1/3 pound broccoli rabe
Half of a 1-pound can of white
    kidney beans
2 tablespoons chopped
    coriander
1 tablespoon lemon juice

1/4 cup chopped scallions
1–2 tablespoons olive oil
Cayenne pepper (optional)
Salt (optional)
2–3 pieces anchovies (optional)

Trim the broccoli rabe and blanch it in a pot of boiling water for 3–4 minutes, depending upon the thickness of the stems. Plunge into cold water to stop the cooking process and drain. Coarsely chop.

Drain the beans, gently rinse them with lukewarm water, drain again, and toss with the broccoli rabe, coriander, lemon juice, scallions, and the oil. Taste and correct seasonings, adding a pinch of cayenne pepper and salt if you wish. Top with the anchovies, if using.

VARIATIONS

With tangerines. Omit the anchovies and add 2 tablespoons chopped

Italian Greens and Bean Salad (continued)

sweet marjoram. Replace the lemon juice with *tangerine juice* and garnish with *tangerine slices.*

With leftover broccoli. Substitute 1 cup cooked sliced *broccoli* for the broccoli rabe.

BROWN RICE, CARROT, AND ZUCCHINI SALAD

Cook up extra brown rice for this hearty salad that's good either for a light supper or a lunch-box special. Remember that warm rice absorbs the dressing better than refrigerated rice—so if you have time, toss the rice with the tahini, vinegar, and oil right after it cooks. The tahini is available at health-food stores as well as the Middle Eastern food or gourmet sections of most supermarkets.

(Serves 1)

1 cup cooked brown rice
1–2 tablespoons tahini (sesame seed paste)
1 tablespoon olive or canola oil
$1^1/2$ tablespoons cider or sherry vinegar or fresh lemon juice
$1/4$ cup diced scallions, including the green tops

$1/4$ cup grated carrot
2–3 tablespoons diced celery
$1/2$ cup diced raw zucchini or summer squash (optional)
Salt and freshly ground black pepper
Cabbage

Toss the rice with the tahini, oil, and vinegar. Stir in the scallions, carrot, celery, and zucchini, if using. Taste and season with salt and pepper. Serve on a bed of shredded raw cabbage—or use the tender inner leaves of the cabbage as an edible scoop.

RED PEPPER AND POTATO COMPOSED SALAD

The sweet taste of the roasted pepper and scallions sets off the meaty taste of the beans. Vary the amount of beans to suit your taste. The salad looks best made with potatoes no more than 2 inches in diameter. Red bliss or yellow fingerlings work well. This is an excellent way to use up leftover blanched beans or cooked potatoes.

(Makes 1 generous serving)

1 bunch scallions (about 10)
1 large red pepper
1/3–1/2 pound green beans,
    trimmed

1/2 pound sliced cooked waxy
    potatoes

Dressing

1 clove garlic, smashed
2 tablespoons mild rice wine
    vinegar
1/4 teaspoon dry mustard
Salt and freshly ground black
    pepper

2 tablespoons olive oil
1/4–1/2 teaspoon Dijon mustard
2 teaspoons minced sweet
    marjoram

To roast the scallions and the pepper, halve and seed the pepper and place in the rear of a broiling pan; arrange the scallions in front. Broil the scallions for about 1 minute, turning once. Watch carefully; they burn fast. Remove them from the oven and continue roasting the pepper another 4–8 minutes, or until the skin is blackened. Or, if you have a gas stove, put the peppers at the side of the burners, so the skins are blistered by the flame. (You can also roast the scallions this way.) Run the halves under cold running water so that the blackened skins can be pulled off easily. Dry them and cut into strips. Set aside. Chop the scallions into large pieces, and set aside.

Blanch the green beans in a large pot of boiling water for about 2 minutes. They should be barely cooked and crunchy. Plunge them into cold water to stop the cooking process, drain, and set aside.

To make the dressing: Place the garlic in a glass bottle with a lid, add the vinegar, dry mustard, a pinch of salt, and black pepper to taste. Let marinate for at least 30 minutes. Add the oil, Dijon mustard, and the sweet marjoram. Taste and correct seasonings if necessary.

Arrange the salad: Mix together the beans, two thirds of the pepper strips, and the scallions. Put the potatoes in the center of a serving dish and surround with the beans. Pour the dressing over the salad, and garnish the potatoes with the remaining pepper strips. Let sit for at least 30 minutes before serving.

Red Pepper and Potato Composed Salad (continued)

VARIATION

With tuna and hard-boiled egg. Flake a drained 3¹/₄-ounce can of *tuna fish packed in water* in the center of the platter, and surround with the vegetables. Garnish with a quartered *hard-boiled egg.*

LEFTOVERS

This salad keeps well for a day or two in the refrigerator. The beans lose some color, but the flavor is fine. It's a good take-to-work lunch.

TOMATO AND FETA CHEESE SALAD

The saltiness of the cheese plays against the acidity of the tomato.

(Serves 1)

1 ripe tomato	1 tablespoon chopped corian-
Salt	der, mint, or sweet marjoram
¹/₄ teaspoon freshly ground	1 ounce feta cheese
black pepper	2 tablespoons sliced scallions
1 cup washed, trimmed, and	2 teaspoons olive oil
dried spinach leaves	2 teaspoons lime juice

Cut the tomato into wedges and sprinkle with salt and pepper. Let sit while you assemble the salad. Mix the spinach with the herbs and place on a plate. Crumble the feta cheese in the center of the plate. Arrange the tomato wedges in a circle around it. Sprinkle with the scallions. Mix together the olive oil and lime juice and drizzle over the tomatoes.

QUICK-TO-MAKE SALADS

• Make a raw zucchini, yellow summer squash, and cucumber salad. Halve the unpeeled vegetables, remove the seeds, and cut them into 1-inch pieces. Toss with chopped Bermuda onion and an oil-and-vinegar dressing. Garnish with cherry tomatoes.

- Thinly slice raw fennel and carrots. Marinate in an oil-and-vinegar dressing and serve on a bed of peeled and thinly sliced oranges. Sprinkle with chives, if you wish.
- Slice raw mushrooms over cooked green beans. Sprinkle with chopped chives or scallions and a generous amount of freshly ground black pepper. Drizzle with olive oil and lemon juice.
- Alternate slices of peeled grapefruit with sliced avocado. Drizzle with grapefruit juice and sprinkle with black pepper and/or chopped chives.
- Grate carrots and toss with freshly ground black pepper or lemon juice and oil. Or
- Grate carrots and toss in mayonnaise flavored with a trace amount of horseradish sauce.
- Make a pepper and tomato salad. Thinly slice green peppers into rings. Cut a ripe tomato into wedges and sprinkle with pinches of sugar and salt. Mound the tomatoes in the center of a plate and surround with the green pepper rings. Drizzle with an oil-and-vinegar vinaigrette. Garnish with chopped scallions or chives.
- Grate radishes and moisten with yogurt or sour cream.
- Mix together bean sprouts and slivered scallions. Toss with a pinch of sugar and soy sauce and a drop of Oriental sesame oil.
- Thinly slice raw zucchini and toss with lime juice and olive oil.
- Quarter leftover brussels sprouts. Toss with a mustard vinaigrette and sprinkle with chives or crumbled cooked bacon before serving.
- Buy small or pullet eggs. Hard-boil them, then cut them into quarters and arrange on a platter alternately with scallion fans (scallions trimmed to within 2 inches of their bases, then thinly sliced down to the white base, and soaked in ice water until the greens fan out).
- Combine leftover rice with equal parts of freshly chopped tomatoes, chopped cucumbers, and cooked peas (frozen is fine). Season with salt and pepper and a small amount of oil and vinegar.
- Toss together both yellow wax and green beans, arrange on a serving plate, and sprinkle with chopped scallions. Drizzle with a mustard vinaigrette.
- Alternate slices of tomato and mozzarella cheese. Drizzle with olive oil and garnish with basil leaves. Flank with fresh fennel, if you wish.
- Arrange peeled and sliced oranges on a plate and top with shredded

radishes that have been tossed in a lemon juice and oil dressing. Sprinkle with chives.

- Slice Chinese cabbage into slivers. Toss with chunks of cooked chicken mixed with mayonnaise into which you have added a good-quality curry powder and lemon juice to taste, along with sliced fennel or celery if you wish.

- Prepare a sweet-and-sour sauerkraut relish salad. Rinse sauerkraut and combine with diced celery, onions, and green peppers. Marinate in a dressing made with sugar (or honey) and vinegar.

- Try a main-dish corned beef and potato salad. Mix together diced potatoes, celery or fennel, pickles, onions, cubes of corned beef, and mayonnaise. Add Dijon mustard to taste.

VEGETABLES

Too often, single cooks pass up the healthful benefits of cooking with fresh vegetables for the convenience afforded by their frozen counterparts. Frozen vegetables are fine in the occasional soup or stew (or in a pinch), but they lack the fresh vegetable juices that add so much flavor to even the most basic preparations. As many fresh vegetables cook in minutes, in less than 10 minutes, for example, you can sauté a generous helping of baby spinach or steam some tender sliced carrots and sprinkle them with minced herbs. Also, unlike when you're chopping vegetables to feed a family, when you're cooking for one, the preparation time is minimal—especially when you keep your chopping knife honed.

And, should you get a little carried away with the chef's knife, you can freeze the leftovers and use them in soups and stews (see *Storage*, page 12). Though most supermarkets now stock frozen packets of peppers,

> "I'm the stir-fry king. The kind of food I like is simple—such as the Chinese style of cooking where it's cooked for just a short period of time. The food tastes fresh and alive, and I think it's better for you. I eat a lot of vegetables, rice, and pasta—not much meat. Once in a blue moon I'll do the pseudo-Mexican thing with a tortilla, corn, beans, and rice. I also eat a lot of fruit; sometimes fruit is almost a meal in itself. I love eating alone. I can cook what I want, I can eat at whatever hour I want (and sometimes that's a very late hour), and some of the things I eat, I don't think anyone else would like. I don't like to waste food—so I'll put just about anything between two pieces of bread."
>
> *George Benoit, carpenter*

onions, and tomatoes, when you keep a plastic bag in the freezer for any chopped surplus, you're ahead of the game.

If you tend to opt for frozen rather than fresh vegetables because waste is a problem, try shopping with a week's menu on hand so that you don't purchase more than you need. It's also useful to design your menus to use up the most perishable vegetables a day or two after you go shopping and save the "keepers" for later on.

Certain vegetables are useful always to have on hand. Although I shop for perishables weekly, I usually keep at least one sweet or red onion, carrots, and celery in the refrigerator and bags of corn, peas, lima beans, and okra in the freezer. Many supermarkets mark down peppers when they get small bruised spots. It's handy (and frugal) to buy a supply and peel, chop, and freeze them for cooked preparations. I keep canned chickpeas and beets (much better baked, but canned will do for a quick marinated beet salad) on the pantry shelf along with potatoes (both Irish and sweet). In the winter, I always have a butternut squash on hand. Even once it's cut, the raw squash will keep for several days in the refrigerator.

Why not try a few weeks of selecting your vegetables, and designing your menus around them. If you're trying to fit more vegetables into your life, it's an easy way to start.

In this chapter I've given you quick recipes for vegetable side dishes as well as a number of vegetable main courses, such as two of my favorites, *Vegetable Stew* and *Chickpeas with Potatoes*. Fresh vegetables taste great, they're good for you, and they don't break the bank. What more could you want?

BOILED ARTICHOKE

An artichoke, once a delicacy only for the wealthy, is now commonly available almost year round. It's a vegetable to savor—particularly alone. But count on at least 40 minutes to cook a good-sized artichoke—and another 20 minutes to eat it leaf by leaf.

(Serves 1)

A 5–8-ounce artichoke	1–2 lemons
2 quarts water	Mayonnaise or melted butter
Salt	

Trim the artichoke stem and remove about 1–1¹/₂ inches from the top of the artichoke. Bring the water to a boil in a stainless-steel pot, add salt to taste, and the juice of 1 lemon. Once the water comes to a boil, add the artichoke. Gently boil for 30–40 minutes, or until a leaf comes out easily when you pull on it. Immediately run the artichoke under cold water to stop the cooking process, then drain it.

Before serving, pull out the center leaves and scrape out the inedible "choke" with a spoon. Serve with mayonnaise or melted butter into which you have squeezed lemon juice to taste.

CAREFREE ASPARAGUS

There's a certain sensual pleasure to be found in slowly eating asparagus with your fingers, piece by piece, while you're alone. Thanks to my friend Nancy Curtis for sharing this easy technique for cooking asparagus. It is particularly useful if you'd like to have extra asparagus on hand for salads.

(Makes 1 serving)

6–8 stalks asparagus   Boiling water

A savvy produce manager knows that bunches of asparagus should be displayed with their stems standing in water, which keeps the flesh hydrated and tender. Fortunately, if you crave asparagus and can only find it wrapped in plastic at the supermarket vegetable counter, there's still a way to improve its texture. Break off each stalk at its base (if you're truly frugal you can chop the stalks and simmer them for a soup base). Using a sharp paring knife, selectively remove any tough skin from the stems. You can usually spot it—the skin is dry-looking.

Place the asparagus in a large glass or stainless-steel bowl and cover with enough boiling water so that the asparagus floats. Let it sit in the water until it is lukewarm. The asparagus will be slightly cooked and will retain texture. You can eat it immediately, plain or dipped in a butter-lime sauce (2 parts butter to one part lime juice). Or you can drain the stalks, wrap them in a kitchen towel, and store in the refrigerator until cold, then serve with a mayonnaise thinned with lemon juice and garnished with minced chives. (If you have a garden, the chive blossoms are

Carefree Asparagus (continued)

beautiful used as a garnish.) You can even recook them by sautéing garlic and the asparagus in olive oil for a minute. To serve, drizzle with a touch of balsamic vinegar and soy sauce, the olive-garlic oil, and lots of freshly ground black pepper.

LEFTOVERS

Asparagus, Mushroom, and Scallion Pizza. See page 261.

Asparagus and Ham Appetizer. Squeeze *lemon juice* to taste over 3–4 stalks of asparagus and drizzle with *olive oil* (about 1/2 teaspoon). Sprinkle generously with *black pepper*. Wrap in 1 slice of boiled *ham*. Arrange on a plate and flank with a quartered *hard-boiled egg*. Or you could omit the lemon juice and olive oil and spread one side of the ham with *mayonnaise* or a *mustard*-mayonnaise mixture and wrap the asparagus stalks in it.

ROASTED ASPARAGUS

This is great finger food. Don't bother to trim the asparagus ends, just nibble down the stems to the tough cores and discard them. The amount of asparagus depends upon your appetite.

(Serves 1)

6–8 pieces asparagus   Freshly ground black pepper
1/2–1 teaspoon olive oil   Salt

Wash and dry the asparagus. Place the olive oil on a baking sheet and roll the asparagus in it. Sprinkle with black pepper. Bake in a preheated 450°F oven for 10–15 minutes, or until the asparagus is lightly browned. Sprinkle with salt before serving.

BROCCOLI WITH LEMON

A bit of fresh lemon or lime juice complements the flavor of broccoli far better than butter. If you're using broccoli stems, peel them first.

(Makes about 3/4 cup broccoli)

1 cup broccoli florets or a combi-
    nation of florets and stems,
    cut into 1-inch diagonal pieces

Freshly ground black pepper
1/2 lemon or lime

Bring a pot of water to a boil. Add the broccoli and boil, uncovered, for just about 2 minutes, or until the broccoli is barely cooked through. Remove from the heat, drain, sprinkle with black pepper, and squeeze over lemon or lime juice to taste.

STEAMED CARROTS

Garden-fresh carrots taste great as is—or with a dusting of minced fresh herbs, such as parsley or dill. Stored carrots often are improved with a citrus glaze (see Variations). If you don't have a steamer, you can use a metal colander placed in a large pot, but the water level should be below the carrots.

(Serves 1)

2 medium carrots

Water

If the carrots are recently harvested, you don't need to peel them, just wash off the soil. Otherwise, peel the carrots, cut them into 1/4-inch-thick slices, and place in a steamer basket. (You should have about 1 cup sliced carrots, but the amount depends upon how many carrots you prefer.) Place 3/4 cup water in the bottom of the steamer pot. Bring it to a boil, add the steamer basket, and cover the pot. Steam the carrots for 4–5 minutes, or until cooked through. (Check the texture after 3 minutes by spearing a carrot with a fork.)

VARIATIONS

With herbs. Toss the cooked carrots with 1 teaspoon minced *parsley or sweet marjoram* or 1/2 teaspoon minced *chives, tarragon, or dill.*

With lime juice and honey. Heat 1 tablespoon of the liquid left from steaming the carrots either in the steamer (if it's small and nonreactive), or in a small nonreactive frying pan. Bring the liquid to a boil, stir in 1

Steamed Carrots (continued)

teaspoon *honey,* and cook for about 30 seconds over high heat, stirring constantly, until the liquid cooks down almost to a glaze. Add 1 teaspoon *lime juice* (about 1/4 lime), stir until the juice is incorporated, and add the carrots. Toss until the carrots are coated with the sauce. If you wish, add a pinch of *cumin.*

With butter and sugar. In a small frying pan melt 1/2 teaspoon *butter.* Stir in 1/4 teaspoon *sugar,* and continue stirring until the sugar foams. Add 1 teaspoon either water or *lemon juice* and toss with the carrots.

Note: You can freeze any leftover carrot liquid to use in soups or stews.

BLANCHED CAULIFLOWER

Cauliflower is often passed over by solo cooks because it's usually sold by the head and it doesn't keep—or freeze—well. If you shop at a supermarket that has a salad bar, however, see if cauliflower florets are a salad bar ingredient—and buy enough for one meal. (The florets have been trimmed, so you need only give them a quick once-over before cooking them.) If you blanch cauliflower for just a few minutes, it gains a delicate flavor and texture.

(Serves 1)

Water	11/2 cups cauliflower florets
Salt	1/4 lemon

Bring a pot of water to a boil, add salt to taste and the cauliflower florets. Gently boil, uncovered, for about 3–4 minutes. Drain and serve with lemon.

VARIATIONS

With herbs. Just before serving sprinkle with 1 teaspoon minced *chives, coriander, or parsley.*

With breadcrumbs. While the cauliflower is cooking, melt 1/2–1 teaspoon *butter* in a frying pan. Stir in 11/2 tablespoons *breadcrumbs* and cook over medium heat, stirring frequently, until the crumbs are browned, about 3 minutes. Drain the cauliflower and sprinkle with the breadcrumbs.

With anchovies and breadcrumbs. Stir 1–2 mashed *anchovies* into the butter before you brown the *breadcrumbs.*

SAUTÉED CUCUMBERS WITH LEMONGRASS

Cooked cucumbers have a subtle flavor and tender texture that marries well with delicately flavored fish such as sole or monkfish. Lemongrass, used so often in Thai food, is a virtually indestructible herb that grows in warm climates. Many supermarkets now stock it in the fresh herbs section—but if you can't find it substitute dill or parsley. Be sure to check if the cucumber you've bought is waxed, in which case peel it first—otherwise, if the skin is tender, leave it on for color.

(Serves 1)

1 medium-sized cucumber	2 teaspoons chopped lemon-
1 teaspoon butter	grass, dill, or parsley
Sugar	1 juicy lime (optional)

Remove the tip of the stem end of the cucumber, and halve it lengthwise (any bitterness will be concentrated near the stem). Peel if necessary. Remove the seeds and cut each half into 1/2-inch wide crescent-shaped pieces. Bring a pot of water to the boil, add the cucumber pieces, and boil them, gently, for about 3 minutes. Drain and dry them.

Heat the butter in a heavy frying pan, add the cucumber pieces and a pinch of sugar, and cook, stirring occasionally, for 5 minutes. Stir in the herbs and cook 1 minute longer. Taste and season with lime juice if you wish. Serve immediately.

FRESH GARDEN PEAS

You owe it to yourself to find a source for fresh peas in season, for they're so good with just a smidgen of butter and herbs. I count on 1/2 pound of fresh peas per portion.

(Serves 1)

1/2 cup shelled peas (about 1/2 pound)
1/4–1/2 teaspoon butter

1/2 teaspoon chopped herbs, such as mint or sweet marjoram

Bring a pot of water to a boil, add the peas, lower the heat to a gentle boil, and boil for no more than 2 minutes.

Taste a pea to see if it's cooked through. Drain the peas, put back in the pan, and stir in the butter and herbs. Serve immediately.

VARIATIONS

With fresh mushrooms. Before cooking the peas, heat 1/2–1 teaspoon butter in a pan. Add 1/4–1/3 cup sliced *white mushrooms,* stir to make sure they are coated with butter, and cook for 1 minute, stirring. Add 1 tablespoon water and *salt* and *pepper* to taste. Cover the pan and cook over medium heat for 2 minutes. Meanwhile boil the peas. Drain the peas, add them to the mushrooms, and serve immediately.

With scallion. Add 1 tablespoon minced *scallion* before serving.

With pasta. Toss cooked peas with 2 ounces cooked *spaghetti,* 1/2 teaspoon minced *lemon zest,* and 1 tablespoon grated *Parmesan cheese.* Season to taste. You could also add *mushrooms* for a mushroom-pea pasta sauce.

SAUTÉED SNOW PEAS

This technique is also good with sugar snap peas.

(Serves 1)

3–4 ounces snow or sugar snap peas
2 teaspoons butter
Salt and freshly ground black pepper

1/2 teaspoon minced sweet marjoram or mint

String the snow peas by pulling the tips down their sides to remove the strings. Wash, dry, and set them aside. Heat the butter in a heavy frying pan, stir in the peas, and stir and toss continuously until they are a bright green, about 2 minutes. Season to taste with salt, pepper, and sweet marjoram.

ROASTED RED PEPPER

Home-roasted red peppers are tremendously versatile. They're a great dieting aid: Even a slice or two, chopped up and added to vegetable dishes, gives a sweet, mellow flavor, particularly to beans, broccoli, and summer squash. Several strips of roasted peppers eaten plain, or arranged on a toasted piece of French bread brushed with olive oil, are a wonderful snack at the end of a busy day. You can broil as many peppers as you wish, but cover them with olive oil before you store them. Roasted peppers keep at least a week in the refrigerator.

(Makes 1/3 cup roasted pepper)

1 large thick-fleshed red pepper   Olive oil
Garlic

Halve the pepper and remove the seeds. Place it cut side down on a broiling pan lined with aluminum foil and broil in a preheated oven for 5–8 minutes, or until the skin is blackened. Remove the pan from the oven, enclose the pepper in the foil, and let it sit for 10–15 minutes. Peel the pepper with a paring knife or your fingers. The skin will lift right off. Pat the halves dry and slice them into 1/2-inch-wide pieces. Put them into a clean glass jar with a lid, add a smashed clove of garlic, and top with olive oil (about 2 tablespoons). Store in the refrigerator.

Note: Use what's left of the garlic-and-pepper-flavored oil to give flavor to sautéed chicken or vegetables.

SAUTÉED NEW POTATOES WITH CHIVES

At farmers' markets when the potatoes are coming into season, you can buy tiny new potatoes about 1 inch in diameter, or if you have a garden, you can steal them from your plants. I steam them in their skins—or cook them in this combined sauté/pan-steam manner, which gives the flavor of fat without all the calories. You'll need a heavy frying pan (or stove-top casserole) with a cover. This recipe works fine with larger potatoes: just cut them into equal-sized pieces.

(Serves 1)

1 tablespoon olive oil	Salt and freshly ground black
1 tablespoon butter	pepper
7–8 whole new potatoes with	2 teaspoons chopped chives
skins (or cut into 1-inch	
pieces)	

Heat together the olive oil and butter. Rinse and dry the potatoes and toss them in the fat for about 2 minutes, moving them around constantly. Discard all but a thin film of fat, cover the pan, and cook slowly for 10–15 minutes, or until cooked through. Stir occasionally. Remove from the heat and sprinkle with salt and pepper to taste and chopped chives.

VARIATION

With garlic. Add 1 teaspoon chopped *garlic* along with the potatoes.

ACCORDION BAKED POTATO

Slicing potatoes in this way is popular in Denmark, where making everyday objects attractive is a philosophy of life. These potatoes are usually coated with butter and topped with a light coating of breadcrumbs. Equally good is the version below, which has only a featherlike coating of olive oil. As the potato cooks, the slices fan out like an accordion and brown slightly. (Vary the width of the slices depending upon how crisp you'd like them to be.) The slightly crunchy exterior contrasts nicely with the smooth interior of the potato. (And since you're alone, you can relish the potato slice by slice by eating with your fingers.)

(Serves 1)

1 mealy-textured potato, such as russet (Idaho)	Salt and freshly ground black pepper (optional)
1/2–1 teaspoon olive oil	

Peel the potato and pat it dry. Put the potato on the counter and with a sharp paring knife slice it crosswise about two-thirds through in 1/4-inch parallel cuts. Coat the entire surface of the potato with olive oil. (The most efficient way to do this is to put the olive oil in the palm of one hand and roll the potato in it with the other hand.) Place the potato in a preheated 425°F oven for 35–55 minutes. The cooking time depends upon the size and variety of potato. Remove the potato from the oven, let sit for 5 minutes, and season with salt and pepper, if you wish.

VARIATIONS

With breadcrumbs and butter. Coat the potato with 1 teaspoon melted *butter*. Bake for 20 minutes and sprinkle with 2 teaspoons fresh, dry *breadcrumbs*. Proceed as above.

With the skin. If you are using a fresh, thin-skinned potato, don't bother to peel it. Proceed as above.

Accordian Baked Onion. Place an *onion* stem side down on the counter. Trim the base and cut it halfway through into eighths. Turn the onion over in the palm of your hand, put it on the counter, and press down slightly. Repeat the olive oil treatment and bake as above, checking after 30 minutes. Remember that the fresher the onion, the quicker it will cook.

OVEN-FRIED POTATOES

A little vegetable oil goes a long way in this takeoff on fried potatoes. Rinsing the potatoes until the water is clear makes them crisper. You can vary the amount of potatoes to suit your appetite.

(Serves 1)

1 large mealy-fleshed potato, such as russet (Idaho)	1/2–1 teaspoon canola or olive oil Salt

Peel the potato and cut it into 3/4-inch-thick slices. Either place the slices in a colander and run cold water over them until the water runs clear, or soak them in a bowl of cold water. Drain the potato slices and thoroughly dry them. Put the oil on a baking sheet and one by one, roll the slices in the oil (as you get to the end, it may look as if you're running out of oil, but you want to give them only a light coating).

Bake the potato slices in a preheated 450°F oven for 15 minutes, turn them, and lower the heat to 425 and cook 5–10 minutes longer. Test after 5 minutes to see if they are cooked through. Sprinkle with salt before serving.

VARIATION

Oven-Fried Sweet Potato. **Roasting** *sweet potatoes* this way accentuates their rich flavor. Any extra potato would be particularly good in *Couscous and Sweet Potato Salad* (page 38).

MASHED POTATOES

Mashed potatoes are one of those comfort foods best made in larger amounts, but the leftovers are so useful that even solo cooks can enjoy them. Texture is all-important in preparing excellent mashed potatoes. The key is to start with mealy-textured potatoes rather than waxy ones, and to treat them gently. (At the market, pick out baking potatoes.) You must *never* whip them with a mixer, which gives them a gluey texture.

Use a masher—or, better still, a ricer, an implement that pushes the cooked potatoes through small holes (you see it often at yard sales).

(Makes 1 generous serving)

1¹/2 cups peeled and cubed raw potatoes	1–2 teaspoons butter
Water	1 tablespoon sour cream (optional)
Salt	Freshly ground black pepper
About 1 tablespoon milk	

Cover the potatoes with water salted to taste, bring to a boil, and lower the heat to a gentle boil. Boil the potatoes until they are cooked through, about 15 minutes for 1-inch pieces. Drain off the water (saving it for potato bread or stews), either mash or rice the potatoes, add milk (the amount will depend on the moisture in the potatoes), butter, and sour cream, if using. Increase the amount of milk if you are omitting the sour cream. Taste and season with salt and pepper.

VARIATIONS

With scallions. Stir in 2 tablespoons chopped fresh *scallions* before serving.

With horseradish. Stir in 1–2 teaspoons prepared horseradish before serving.

LEFTOVERS

Mashed Potato Pancakes

This is an excellent way to use up a small amount of leftover potatoes.

(Makes 2 thick 3-inch pancakes)

2 teaspoons butter	¹/3 cup leftover mashed potato
2 tablespoons chopped onion	
2 teaspoons chopped pepper (a combination of sweet and hot is good)	3–4 tablespoons cornmeal (preferably stone-ground)
1 medium egg	Salt and freshly ground black pepper

Heat 1 teaspoon of the butter in a nonreactive frying pan. Add the

Mashed Potato Pancakes (continued)

onion and pepper and cook over medium heat, stirring constantly, for 1 minute. Pour in just enough water to cover (about 2 tablespoons) and continue cooking, stirring frequently, until the onion is translucent and the water has evaporated. This will take about 5 minutes. Set aside.

Beat the egg in a bowl. Stir in the potato, cornmeal, reserved vegetables, and salt and pepper to taste. You want just enough cornmeal so that the mixture holds together.

Halve the potato mixture, forming 2 patties. Heat the remaining 1 teaspoon butter in a heavy small frying pan and cook the potato cakes over medium heat, turning once, until they are cooked through and lightly browned. This will take 5–10 minutes. Serve immediately. Either chicken breasts or shrimp sautéed in butter and tossed with lime juice and a dash of cayenne pepper or hot pepper sauce just before serving would make a good accompaniment.

Variations

With corn. Add 1/2–3/4 cup cooked *corn*.

With leftover greens. Using your hands, squeeze the cooked greens until dry. Chop them. You can add anywhere from 1/4–3/4 cup chopped *greens* along with the potatoes. Add a pinch of *nutmeg*.

Baked Leftover Mashed Potatoes

The French often recycle mashed potatoes by binding them with egg and cheese or cream and piping them through a pastry bag. If, like most of us, you do not own a pastry bag, smooth the mashed potatoes out in a small baking dish, swirling the surface to give it a slight pattern as it browns.

(Serves 1)

1 medium egg	1 tablespoon butter, softened
3/4–1 cup leftover mashed potatoes, at room temperature	1/8–1/4 teaspoon grated nutmeg
	1 tablespoon chopped parsley (optional)
1 teaspoon flour	Salt

Beat the egg. Stir in the potatoes, flour, butter, nutmeg, and parsley, if using. Season with salt to taste. Spread in a buttered baking dish and bake in a preheated 400°F oven for 15–20 minutes, or until cooked through and lightly browned.

Variations

With garlic. Heat the butter in a frying pan and sauté 2 teaspoons minced *garlic* over medium heat, stirring frequently, for 3 minutes. Do not let the garlic brown. Add to the potato mixture and proceed as above.

With Parmesan cheese. Add 1 tablespoon grated *Parmesan* cheese to the potato mixture and proceed as above.

Mashed Potato and Escarole Casserole (page 87)

Whole Wheat Potato Bread (page 255)

SAUTÉED SUMMER SQUASH OR ZUCCHINI

You can grate the squash and onion in just a minute on an old-fashioned standing grater—or use the food processor. A combination of both yellow squash and zucchini is attractive.

(Serves 1)

1/2–3/4 cup grated yellow
    summer squash or zucchini
1/2–1 teaspoon olive oil
1 tablespoon grated onion

2 tablespoons chopped parsley
    or a combination of parsley
    and coriander

Gently squeeze the summer squash to remove some of the vegetable juices. Set it aside. Heat the olive oil in a heavy frying pan. Add the onion and summer squash. Cook, stirring constantly, for about 3 minutes, or until cooked through. Stir in the parsley and serve immediately.

SPICY PURÉED SWEET POTATOES

If you've never eaten fresh sweet potatoes, you're in for a treat. Sweetened canned potatoes bear little resemblance to the rich-tasting, densely textured roots so popular in the South. Just like corn, there are many cultivars of sweet potato, but unlike corn, they're not called by name. As I never know whether I'm getting a dry- or moist-textured potato, I prefer to steam or gently boil sweet potatoes to keep them moist. I usually prepare a little extra to add to breads or biscuits or to make *Sweet Potato Pudding Dessert* (see Variation). I think honey brings out the flavor of the potatoes far better than sugar. This goes well with robust-flavored poultry, meats, or fish that can hold their own, such as roasted duck or lamb, or baked mackerel or bluefish.

(Makes about 2 cups)

3 cups peeled and cubed raw	Cinnamon
sweet potatoes	Nutmeg
1 tablespoon butter, softened	Salt
1 tablespoon honey	

Place the sweet potatoes in a steamer or cover with water and gently boil them until a knife inserted into the flesh goes in easily and the potatoes are cooked through. The sweet potatoes will be done in 20–25 minutes, depending upon the method used.

Drain and purée the sweet potatoes in a food processor, pulsing on and off just until their texture is smooth, or put through a food mill. Remove to a bowl and beat in the butter and honey. Taste and season with a dash of cinnamon and nutmeg, and salt. Serve hot.

VARIATION

Sweet Potato Pudding Dessert. (Serves 1–2.) Use 1 1/2 cups leftover sweet potatoes. Beat together with 1 additional tablespoon butter and 1 additional tablespoon honey. Add 1/4 teaspoon each cinnamon and nutmeg, and a dash of *cloves.* Beat in 1 medium *egg.* Put in a shallow 7-inch ovenproof dish and bake in a preheated 350°F oven for about 30 minutes, or until cooked through. Serve either hot or at room temperature with cream or *Quick Butterscotch Sauce* (page 277).

LEFTOVERS

The pudding is rich, so occasionally I'll eat only half and create another dessert by smoothing it back in the dish, covering with an egg-white meringue, and browning it in the oven. To make the meringue, beat 1 *egg white* until it forms soft peaks, and then add 4 teaspoons *sugar*, a teaspoon at a time. Continue beating until the egg whites stand in stiff peaks. Swirl on top of the sweet potatoes and bake in a preheated 400°F oven for 15 minutes.

If you have only a few spoonfuls left, add to beef, lamb, and pork stews. The sweet potato will thicken the stews while adding a depth of flavor.

SAUTÉED CHERRY TOMATOES WITH HERBS

The acids in the tomatoes make this an excellent counterpoint to rich, oily fish such as bluefish or mackerel, or a lamb chop.

(Serves 1)

1–2 teaspoons butter or olive oil
1 teaspoon minced fresh garlic
6–10 thick-fleshed cherry
   tomatoes, about 1 inch in
   diameter

1–2 teaspoons minced fresh
   chives or dill (optional)
Salt (optional)

Heat the butter in a heavy frying pan over moderate heat. Add the garlic and cook, stirring constantly, for 1 minute. Stir in the tomatoes, and continue to cook for 3 minutes, or until they are barely cooked. Sprinkle with chives, if using, and cook, stirring, 30 seconds longer. Taste and season with salt if you wish. Serve immediately.

FRIED GREEN TOMATOES

Long before Fannie Flagg's book (and the ensuing movie) made the idea of eating green tomatoes popular, country folk enjoyed this dish. In the Midwest, cooks encase tomatoes in an egg-flour batter; in the South they tend to use cornmeal. Some people even sprinkle the tomatoes with brown sugar before adding the coating. But whatever the preliminaries, the frying fat comes from cured pork—either ham or bacon. As a result, most fried tomatoes are far too greasy. This version uses a touch of cured fat for flavor and omits the egg coating (which serves as a sponge to absorb the fat). A fried tomato is a tasty accompaniment to baked fish, such as flounder or hake. If you're a gardener or can locate them at a farmers' market, try making this recipe with low-acid yellow tomatoes. Regardless of the variety of tomato, they should be mature, and on the verge of turning ripe.

(Serves 1)

1 large green tomato
Salt and freshly ground black
   pepper
Finely ground cornmeal
   (preferably white)

1–2 tablespoons bacon or ham
   fat or a combination of cured
   fat and butter

Cut the tomato into thick slices, and salt and pepper them. Dip the slices into cornmeal. Heat the fat in a heavy frying pan, brown the slices on one side, then turn and brown on the other. Serve immediately. The tomatoes get soggy as they sit.

Note: If you store ham fat or bacon slices in the freezer, it takes only a minute or two to render (melt) the fat in the microwave (or just a little longer in a frying pan).

SALSA

Why buy salsa, when this takes only a few minutes to put together and tastes so fresh? Omit the salt until serving unless you plan to polish off the salsa in one evening.

(Makes about 1³/₄ cups)

1¹/₂ cups peeled, seeded, and chopped ripe tomatoes
¹/₃ cup chopped Bermuda onion
2 teaspoons minced jalapeño pepper

1 tablespoon freshly squeezed orange juice
1 tablespoon freshly squeezed lime juice
1 tablespoon chopped coriander
Salt (optional)

In a large bowl, mix the tomatoes, onion, pepper, orange juice, lime juice, coriander, and salt to taste. Cover the bowl with plastic wrap and let sit for at least an hour before serving so that the flavors will meld.

BRUSCHETTA

Olive oil takes center stage in bruschetta, the Italian grilled appetizer based on leftover peasant bread. It's hard to believe that a few simple ingredients could taste so sublime—but why not, when you're using virgin olive oil, ripe tomatoes, and a firm-textured loaf of French or Italian bread. Try this some summer evening for a quick, light supper.

(Serves 1)

2 tablespoons olive oil
1 teaspoon fresh garlic
1 cup peeled, seeded, and coarsely chopped ripe tomato

Salt and freshly ground black pepper
3 pieces leftover French bread, cut ¹/₂ inch thick on the diagonal

Heat 1¹/₂ tablespoons of the olive oil in a heavy enameled or stainless-

Bruschetta (continued)

steel pan. Add the garlic, lower the heat, and cook for 1 minute, stirring constantly. Stir in the tomato, and cook, stirring frequently, until it thickens to almost a marmalade consistency. This will take about 8–10 minutes. Remove from the heat, taste, and season with salt and freshly ground black pepper. Heat a frying pan, add the bread, and quickly pan-toast it until the surfaces are barely browned. Drizzle with the remaining olive oil, and sprinkle with black pepper. Top with the cooked tomatoes.

Note: If your tomatoes taste bland, add a dash of red wine vinegar just before the tomatoes are reduced.

VARIATION

With tomatoes and cucumbers. Grill the bread as above and drizzle with olive oil. Sprinkle with freshly ground black pepper. Toss together 3/4 cup peeled, seeded, and chopped tomatoes with 2 tablespoons peeled, seeded, and chopped *cucumbers,* and 1 tablespoon chopped *scallion.* Barely moisten with olive oil and serve over the grilled bread.

BAKED BEANS

In England, people eat baked beans on toast for breakfast and the fast-food joints sell baked bean sandwiches. The English know that these beans are a filling snack food. I like baked beans occasionally, but I prefer them less sweet than standard versions. If you have a sweet tooth, increase the amount of brown sugar. You can make baked beans with virtually any white, dried shell bean: In Maine, where baked beans are standard Saturday night fare, and virtually every grange dinner features them, cooks use Jacob's Cattle, a speckled bean that's been cultivated for centuries. In other parts of the country, you're more likely to find them made with navy, great northern, or pinto beans. Whichever bean you decide upon, be sure to bake the beans for three to four hours—they just won't taste right unless you do.

(Makes 4 cups)

2 cups dried beans
1 teaspoon chopped garlic
    (optional)
2 ounces salt pork or fatback
2 tablespoons catsup or cocktail
    sauce

2 teaspoons dry mustard
1/4 cup dark brown sugar
1/4 cup molasses
Freshly ground black pepper
Lemon juice (optional)

Wash the beans and pick out any stones that may be among them (a common occurrence in generic packaged beans). Cover them with water, add the garlic, if using, bring to a boil, and boil slowly for 30 minutes, adding additional water if necessary. Cover the pan and let the beans soak for 2 hours. (The traditional way to rehydrate beans is to let them soak overnight, but often they start to ferment, which can give you indigestion.) Drain the beans, saving the soaking liquid.

Cut off a thin slice of the salt pork and place it in the bottom of a 6-cup covered ovenproof casserole or bean pot. Combine the beans with 1 cup of the soaking liquid, the catsup, mustard, brown sugar, and molasses, and add to the pot. Slice almost through the rest of the salt pork several times and place it on top of the beans. Cover the pan and bake in a preheated 300°F oven for about 4 hours, stirring occasionally. Watch toward the end of the cooking time and add additional liquid if necessary so that the beans stay moist. Taste and season with freshly ground black pepper and a touch of lemon juice if the beans are too sweet.

VARIATION

With onions. Add 1 cup chopped *onions* halfway through the cooking time.

LEFTOVERS

Summer Squash, Baked Bean, and Tomato Soup

Believe it or not, baked beans make a decent base for a vegetable soup. Fresh tomatoes work best with this recipe because of their high acid content which counteracts the sweetness of the beans, but canned tomatoes are also OK. Serve with *Cornbread* (page 269) or a coarse country-style whole wheat or rye bread.

Summer Squash, Baked Bean and Tomato Soup (continued)

2 cups leftover baked beans	1 cup chopped celery
1^1/3 cups beef stock, water, or tomato juice—or a combination of all three	1/2 cup chopped onion
	1 cup coarsely chopped yellow summer squash or zucchini
2 cups peeled, seeded, and chopped tomatoes	2 slices bacon, cooked and crumbled (optional)

Put the baked beans, stock, tomatoes, celery, and onion in a large pot. Bring the mixture to a boil, reduce the heat, and simmer slowly for about 30 minutes. Add the summer squash and cook 5–10 minutes longer, depending upon the texture you want the squash to have. Serve with crumbled bacon on top, if you like.

Variation

Puréed Bean Soup. **Omit the squash and cook the soup about 45 minutes. Purée the soup in a food processor. Taste and add a touch of *sherry vinegar or lemon juice* if necessary. Garnish with the bacon bits.**

RED BEANS AND RICE

This is a perfectly balanced meal-in-one, with the advantage of reheating well either on top of the stove or in a microwave. I make 2 cups of beans to have enough left over for soup. I find that preparing the beans as below cuts down on flatulence. There's usually no need for salt because the ham is salty.

(Makes 1 serving)

1 cup dried red kidney beans	1 teaspoon chopped garlic
1/2 a ham hock (about 4 ounces), or ham scraps	Cooked rice (see page 220) to taste
3/4 cup chopped onion (about 1 medium)	

Place the beans in a heavy stove-top pan and cover with 5 cups water. Bring the water to a boil, and boil the beans for 5 minutes. Let the beans sit in the water for 30 minutes, then drain them. Cover once again with fresh water, add the ham hock, onion, and garlic, and bring the liquid to a boil. Lower the heat, cover the pan, and simmer slowly for at least 2 hours, stirring occasionally and adding water as needed. When the beans are ready, they should be cooked through yet still retain some liquid to pour over the rice. Remove the ham hock, and shred any meat, which is then added to the beans. Serve over cooked rice with *Cornbread* (page 29).

VARIATIONS

With hot peppers. Add 2–3 tablespoons chopped *hot peppers* about 30 minutes before the beans are done. Proceed as above.

With tomatoes. Stir in 1/2 cup peeled, seeded, and chopped *tomatoes* just before removing from the heat.

LEFTOVERS

Red Bean Soup—Plain and Fancy

Both versions of this soup are tasty; it depends upon your mood. In the soup below the rich taste of the beans contrasts with the crisp texture of the bok choy slices. When the greens are less fresh, try the first variation, simmering them longer and adding the corn and tomatoes just before serving.

(Serves 1)

2/3–1 cup leftover red beans
11/3 cups broth or water
1/3 cup chopped sweet onion
1 teaspoon chopped garlic
11/2 cups coarsely chopped bok choy (Chinese cabbage) or Swiss chard leaves
Salt and freshly ground black pepper
Hot sauce (optional)

Put the red beans in a large stove-top pot. Add the broth, onion, and garlic. Bring the mixture to a boil, cover the pan, and simmer over moderate heat for about 20 minutes. Stir in the bok choy, uncover the pan, and boil for 1 minute, stirring constantly. Season with salt, pepper, and/or hot sauce to taste.

Red Bean Soup (continued)

Variations

With corn, coriander, and tomatoes. Proceed as above. Add the bok choy along with 1/2 cup fresh or frozen *corn* kernels. Simmer for 5 minutes, stirring frequently so that the beans don't burn. Remove from the heat and stir in 2 tablespoons peeled, seeded, and chopped fresh *tomato* and 2 tablespoons chopped *fresh coriander.* Let sit for 5 minutes before serving. Taste and season with salt and pepper if you wish.

With lima beans and summer squash. Proceed as above. Add the bok choy along with 1/2 cup fresh or frozen *lima beans* and 1 cup chopped *summer squash or zucchini.* Simmer for 5 minutes, stirring frequently. Just before serving, stir in 2 tablespoons *scallion greens.* Taste and season with salt and pepper.

DRIED LIMA BEANS WITH HAM

Simmering dried beans in a covered pot gives them a puréed texture. Any leftover beans are a good base for a hummuslike dip (see Leftovers).

(Serves 1)

1 cup dried lima beans	1 piece country ham, trimmed
Water or ham stock	of fat
2 tablespoons chopped celery	1/4–1/2 teaspoon cider vinegar
(optional)	(optional)
1 onion, chopped	

Put the beans in a heavy stove-top pot; cover them with water with 2 inches to spare, bring the water to a boil, and boil for 2 minutes. Cover the pan and let the beans sit for 30 minutes. Rinse the beans, cover once again with water to spare, and bring to a boil. Lower the heat, add the optional celery, the onion, and the country ham, and cover the pan. Simmer for 40–60 minutes, stirring occasionally and checking the water level. Watch carefully toward the end of the cooking time—if the beans get too dry, they will burn. Taste and add vinegar to pick up the flavor if you wish.

VARIATION

Without meat. Omit the ham. Add 2 teaspoons chopped *garlic* and 1 teaspoon chopped *jalapeño pepper* along with the *celery*. Proceed as above.

LEFTOVERS

Broccoli-Lima Dip

Leftover broccoli and lima beans combine to make a tasty snack. If you wish to remove the slightly bitter taste from the curry powder, microwave it with 1 teaspoon olive oil for 45 seconds, and then add to the mixture. This is easiest to make in a food processor. A blender works as well, but you'll need to add the water along with the broccoli and lima beans. Crackers or toasted pita bread make good scoops for the dip.

(Serves 1)

1/2 cup cooked broccoli
1 cup cooked lima beans (with
   ham removed)
1 tablespoon lemon juice
1/4 teaspoon cumin
1/2 teaspoon curry powder
1 teaspoon minced garlic

1/4 cup water
1 tablespoon chopped parsley
   or mint
Salt
Parsley or mint sprigs, for
   garnish

Put the broccoli in a blender or food processor along with the lima beans. Pulse for a few seconds to incorporate them. Add the lemon juice, cumin, curry powder, garlic, water, and parsley. Pulse (or blend) for about 30 seconds or until the ingredients form a purée. Taste and add salt. Let the mixture least 30 minutes before serving to meld the flavors. Garnish with parsley or mint sprigs.

SAUTÉED CARROT AND SQUASH

The vivid colors of the carrot, squash, and basil make this an attractive dish. I like to retain the vegetable juices, but if you prefer a drier vegetable dish, salt the grated zucchini and carrot and let them sit for 30 minutes, then squeeze dry before cooking.

(Serves 1)

1 carrot
1 small zucchini or summer
    squash
2 teaspoons butter
1/2 teaspoon minced garlic (1
    small clove)

1 teaspoon chopped basil
Mild red wine vinegar
Salt and freshly ground black
    pepper

Grate the carrot and zucchini. Heat the butter in a heavy nonreactive frying pan and gently cook the garlic for about 2 minutes, stirring frequently, until it has softened but not browned. Add the carrot and squash and cook, stirring constantly, until the vegetables have exuded all their moisture, about 5 minutes. Stir in the basil and continue stirring for 30 seconds. Then add a dash of red wine vinegar. Cook for a moment or two to combine the flavors, season to taste with salt and pepper, and serve immediately.

VARIATION

Vegetable Stuffing for Fish. Add 2–3 tablespoons fine dry *breadcrumbs* (or more to taste) and use as a stuffing for flounder or sea bass.

OKRA WITH TOMATOES

Throughout much of the South, summer is fresh okra season. People eat it deep-fried in a batter, cook it with black-eyed peas, or use it to thicken and flavor a gumbo. This tropical member of the hibiscus family has a mucilaginous (some would say slimy) texture, which is lessened in this quick version and virtually disappears as it simmers in the gumbo liquid. The bacon variation adds a great deal of flavor.

(Makes 1 cup)

2 teaspoons olive oil
1/3 cup chopped onion
2 teaspoons minced garlic
2/3 cup peeled, seeded, and
　chopped tomatoes

1 cup thinly sliced fresh okra
Salt and freshly ground black
　pepper

Heat the olive oil in a heavy enamel or stainless-steel skillet and sauté the onion and garlic for about 2 minutes, stirring occasionally. Add the tomatoes and cook, stirring frequently, for about 5 minutes. Stir in the okra and continue cooking until it is the consistency you prefer. I like the okra just cooked through (about 5 minutes), so it still has some texture (but this is sacrilege in the South). Season with salt and pepper.

VARIATION

Okra with Bacon and Tomatoes. Omit the olive oil. Thinly slice two meaty pieces of *bacon* and cook them slowly in a heavy pan. Then add the onion and garlic and proceed as above. Use this version to make gumbo.

LEFTOVERS

Okra, Bean, and Rice Soup. Simmer any leftover okra mixture in *stock* (a proportion of 1/2 cup leftovers to 11/2 cups stock is good) for at least 30 minutes. Add fresh or leftover *lima beans* or *black-eyed peas* and continue cooking until cooked through. Add *cooked rice* to taste. Taste and stir in chopped *chives or parsley* just before serving.

Gumbo

Gumbo is a wonderful dish for a solo diner because it improves upon standing—and it utilizes any number of leftovers, such as scraps of meat, shredded greens, or cooked rice. My one caveat is that if you're adding fish or meat (except ham) to the gumbo, wait to do so until it's almost finished cooking. This is particularly important when using fish or shell-

Gumbo (continued)

fish because their texture will be destroyed by overcooking. The flour/fat roux is traditional—as is the filé powder, which is stirred in just before serving. You can find filé powder at many supermarkets or at specialty food stores. But it can be omitted if you wish.

(Makes about 1 1/2 cups)

1 tablespoon butter
1 1/2 tablespoons flour
2 cups stock, approximately
1 cup *Okra with Tomatoes*
    (page 80)

Salt and freshly ground black
    pepper
Filé powder (optional)
1/4 cup cooked rice (optional)

Heat the butter in a heavy pan. Stir in the flour and cook over medium heat, stirring constantly, until it is a nutty-colored brown. This will take at least 10 minutes. Off the heat, stir in the stock, then add the okra-tomato mixture. (If you're using ham, add it now.) Simmer over low heat for at least 45 minutes, adding additional stock if needed. The full flavor of the gumbo will not develop unless it cooks this long. As it cooks, the okra will thicken and flavor the gumbo. Taste and season with salt and pepper, and the filé powder, if using. Stir in the rice before serving.

Note: If you're making a shellfish gumbo, such as a shrimp version, add the raw shrimp directly to the sauce. Small shrimp will cook in about 2 minutes, larger shrimp in 3 or 4 minutes. Oysters will cook through in about 5 minutes; crabmeat in about 2 minutes. Many shellfish or fish gumbo recipes will have you add the shellfish and cook it to death. I prefer to start with a good full-flavored fish or shellfish stock as a base. That way you have great flavor *and* texture. Also, be sure to bring any leftover cooked meats, such as roast chicken, to room temperature and add just before serving. Braised meats may be added sooner, but will lose some texture if cooked for longer than 30 minutes.

SWEET POTATO CORNCAKES

The rich, full flavor of these corncakes contrasts nicely with grilled meats and poultry—or you can eat them alone as a light main course. Try the variation made with banana with maple or cane syrup for breakfast.

(Makes three 3-inch corncakes)

1/4 cup cornmeal (preferably stone-ground)
3–4 tablespoons milk
2/3 cup raw grated sweet potato or yam
1 medium egg, beaten
1 tablespoon chopped herbs, such as parsley or basil

2 tablespoons chopped scallions (optional)
Flour (optional)
1–2 tablespoons butter or olive oil

Place the cornmeal in a large mixing bowl and stir in the milk. The amount of milk varies depending upon how the cornmeal was ground. The cornmeal should be moist, but not soppy. (Let it sit while you grate the sweet potato.) Stir in the egg, herbs, and scallions. Then add the sweet potato. Either drop the batter into the frying pan or form it into cakes with your hands and dust with flour. Heat the butter in a heavy frying pan. Add the corncakes and cook over medium heat for about 1 minute, then turn and cook the other side. The corncakes should be slightly puffy—they will flatten out as they sit. Serve immediately.

VARIATIONS

Sweet Potato, Rutabaga, and Potato Corncakes. **Substitute** 1/4 cup each grated sweet potato, *rutabaga,* and white *potato* for the sweet potato. Use 4 tablespoons milk. Proceed as above.

Banana–Sweet Potato Corncakes. **Substitute** 3 tablespoons *orange juice* for the milk and add about 2 tablespoons mashed *banana* and 1 teaspoon *sugar.* Omit herbs and scallions. The mixture will be soppy. Using a large spoon, drop the batter into the heated butter and smooth out with the bowl of the spoon. The cakes should be about 1/2 inch thick. Proceed as above. Serve with syrup.

ZUCCHINI AND RED PEPPER CAKES

You can whip these up in a matter of minutes either to eat alone or to accompany a main course. The vegetables are easiest to grate on an old-fashioned standing grater. Use the side with the largest holes. As you need only 1 tablespoon of egg—either discard the remainder or cook it in a little oil and thinly slice it for a soup garnish.

(Serves 1)

1/3 cup grated zucchini
1 tablespoon grated onion
1–2 tablespoons grated red
    pepper—either sweet or hot
1 tablespoon beaten egg

1 tablespoon flour
Salt and freshly ground black
    pepper
1/2–1 teaspoon olive oil

Take the zucchini in your hands and squeeze it dry. Put it in a bowl and add the onion, red pepper, egg, flour, and salt and pepper to taste. The mixture will be gloppy. Heat the olive oil in a heavy frying pan. Form the zucchini mixture into 2 cakes. Put them in the pan and spread them out with the tips of your fingers. Cook over medium-high heat until they are browned and cooked through, turning once. This will take 2–3 minutes. Serve immediately because they get soggy if they sit around.

LIMA BEANS AND SUMMER SQUASH SCRAMBLE

This beautifully colored vegetarian main dish relies for its subtle flavor upon garden-fresh vegetables and their juices. If you're stuck with supermarket vegetables of dubious heritage, make the variation, with hot peppers, additional garlic, and olive oil.

(Makes 1 generous serving)

1/4 pound fresh shelled lima
    beans (about 2/3 cup)
1 teaspoon olive oil

1 cup diced summer squash or
    zucchini
1/2 teaspoon minced garlic

Sprig of fresh thyme
1/2 cup peeled, seeded, and
    chopped tomato
1 tablespoon chopped fresh
    basil or tarragon, or 1
teaspoon chopped fresh
    rosemary
Salt and freshly ground black
    pepper

Boil a large pot of water, add the lima beans, and slowly boil for 2–4 minutes. The cooking time will vary depending upon the freshness of the beans. Drain, and set aside.

In a heavy stove-top pan with a cover, heat the olive oil. Stir in the summer squash, garlic, reserved beans, and the sprig of thyme. Cover, and cook over medium-low heat for 5 minutes, or until the vegetables have released some of their juices and the squash is tender, yet slightly crisp. Stir in the tomato and basil. Remove the pan from the heat, cover it, and let sit for 3 minutes. Taste and season with salt and pepper. Serve in a large bowl with crusty French bread to sop up the vegetable juices.

VARIATION

With hot pepper. Add 2 teaspoons peeled, seeded, and minced *hot pepper.* Increase the amount of garlic to 1 teaspoon, and the olive oil to 1 tablespoon. For a slightly different taste, add a generous pinch of *cumin* or *curry powder* along with the garlic.

LEFTOVERS

Any leftover vegetables go well in a salad with cooked *brown or white rice, vinegar,* and *olive oil.* Toss the vegetables and rice with olive oil to taste, then slowly add dashes of vinegar. Add just enough olive oil and vinegar to bind the mixture. Taste and add chopped *scallions or chives* to freshen the flavors if necessary. This looks particularly nice over fresh *chicory.* For a more filling salad, add canned, drained *tuna fish* or leftover scraps of oily fishes such as cooked *mackerel, tuna,* or *swordfish.*

ONION AND SPINACH CUSTARD

This satisfying vegetarian main dish is equally good fixed from scratch or put together with leftover cooked spinach, rice, and scraps of cheese. I use Parmesan here—but you can substitute virtually any flavorful grated cheese. It's quite attractive when unmolded. Any leftovers are good cold or cut into thick slices and sautéed in olive oil.

(Makes a 6-inch custard)

1/3 cup raw rice (or 2/3 cup cooked)
2 teaspoons olive oil
2/3 cup chopped onion
1/3 cup chopped scallion greens (optional)
11/3 cups chopped raw spinach
11/2 tablespoons chopped fresh herbs, such as basil and sweet marjoram—a few leaves of fresh mint are good, too
1/3 cup cottage or ricotta cheese
2 medium eggs
1/2 cup milk
Freshly ground black pepper
1/3 cup freshly grated Parmesan cheese

In a large pot of boiling water, boil the rice for 10 minutes. Drain and set aside. Meanwhile, heat the olive oil in a heavy enameled or stainless-steel frying pan. Add the onion, scallion greens, and spinach. Cook over medium heat, stirring frequently, for 2 minutes, or until the vegetables are slightly wilted. Stir in the herbs.

In a mixing bowl, beat together the cottage cheese, eggs, and milk. Add the vegetable mixture. Season with pepper and stir in the cheese. Spoon into an oiled 6-cup dish (such as a soufflé dish). Cover loosely with a piece of foil. Bake in a preheated 350°F oven for about 1 hour. The custard should be cooked through. Remove the cover and bake another 5 minutes to brown the top. Let sit for 1 minute before unmolding. Serve warm.

Note: You can substitute 1/2 cup chopped cooked spinach for the raw spinach. Add it along with the cottage cheese and proceed as above.

VARIATIONS

Escarole Custard. Substitute chopped *escarole* for the spinach. Omit the mint. Proceed as above.

Asparagus Custard. Substitute 3/4 cup coarsely chopped *asparagus* for the spinach. Use parsley as the herb. Proceed as above.

Spinach and Noodle Custard. Substitute 1 cup leftover *cooked pasta* for the rice. Add 1/4 teaspoon *nutmeg.* Proceed as above.

MASHED POTATO AND ESCAROLE CASSEROLE

Leftover mashed potatoes taste brand-new when you combine them with onions and escarole. This is a hearty vegetarian main dish or a satisfying accompaniment to baked fish or leftover roast chicken. Do not combine the mixture with an electric beater—it makes the texture of the mashed potatoes gooey.

(Serves 1)

2 teaspoons olive oil or butter
3/4 cup chopped onion
2 cups coarsely chopped escarole
1 medium egg

1 1/2 cups mashed potatoes (at
  room temperature)
1/8–1/4 teaspoon nutmeg
2 tablespoons grated Parmesan
  or Romano cheese

Heat 1 teaspoon of the olive oil in a frying pan, add the onion, and cook, stirring constantly, for 1 minute. Add the escarole and cook about 3 minutes longer, stirring frequently.

Beat the egg in a mixing bowl. Stir in the mashed potatoes, onion, escarole, nutmeg, and cheese. Spoon the mixture into an oiled 2-cup casserole and drizzle with remaining 1 teaspoon olive oil. Bake in a preheated 350°F oven for 20 minutes. Serve immediately.

CAULIFLOWER AND POTATO IN A YOGURT SAUCE

You can eat the vegetables and sauce hot for dinner—or use them cold as a sandwich stuffing for whole wheat pita bread. (Whole wheat seems to bring out the flavor of the vegetables.) Thinly sliced spinach, or a mixture of lettuce and mint, is a good sandwich addition. This is a good way to use up leftover cooked potatoes and cauliflower.

(Serves 1)

1 medium potato	1 cup cauliflower florets

Yogurt Sauce

1/3 cup plain yogurt	1/2–1 teaspoon lemon juice
Sugar	2 teaspoons chopped scallion
1/3 cup chopped cucumber	(optional)
1 tablespoon chopped fresh	Freshly ground black pepper
coriander, mint, or basil	1/8 teaspoon ground cumin

Peel the potato, quarter it, and cover with water. Bring the water to a boil and gently boil the potato until cooked through, about 10–15 minutes, depending upon the kind of potato. Drain and set aside, covered with a towel to keep warm.

Meanwhile, boil a pot of water, add the cauliflower, lower the heat, and simmer gently until just cooked through, about 4 minutes. Drain the cauliflower and set it aside.

To make the sauce: Mix together the yogurt, a pinch of sugar, the cucumber, 2 teaspoons of the coriander, the lemon juice, scallion, black pepper, and cumin.

Put the sauce in a bowl. Cut the cauliflower and potato into serving-sized pieces and arrange around the bowl. Sprinkle with the remaining 1 teaspoon coriander. (Or you can mix the sauce together with the vegetables.)

BAKED TOMATOES STUFFED WITH RICE

In much of Italy, stuffed vegetables are served at room temperature as part of either an antipasto or a light meal. Sometimes they're filled with breadcrumbs, herbs, and cheese—other times with rice and/or leftover vegetables and meats. This version, which uses lots of herbs and rice, is good hot or cold. I'm suggesting amounts, but you should feel free to experiment: Add leftover chopped broccoli (or broccoli rabe) or greens such as escarole or spinach, top with grated cheese, and vary the herbs. I cook four tomatoes so that I have enough for a second meal. The sage and cumin add a more complex flavor, but omit them if you wish.

(Makes 4 stuffed tomatoes)

4 large tomatoes
1 tablespoon olive oil
2 tablespoons chopped
parsley—or a combination
of parsley and basil
1/4–1/2 teaspoon chopped fresh
sage (optional)
Ground cumin

1/2 cup chopped onion
1 teaspoon minced garlic
1/2 cup cooked rice
Vegetable or chicken stock
(about 1/4 cup)
Salt and freshly ground black
pepper

Cut a slice off the top of each tomato, remove the seeds, and carefully scoop out the interior flesh. Chop it and set aside. In a large frying pan heat the olive oil and add the parsley, sage, a generous pinch of cumin, the onion, and the garlic. Cook, stirring frequently, for about 3 minutes. Stir in the rice and cook just long enough so the grains are coated with oil. Add the reserved tomato flesh and enough stock to moisten slightly (anywhere from 2 tablespoons to 1/4 cup, depending upon the type of rice). Taste and season with salt and pepper.

Place the tomatoes in an oiled baking dish and stuff each one with the rice mixture. Bake in a preheated 350°F oven for 25–30 minutes, or until the rice is tender. The tomato skins will toughen slightly (but they still taste fine). Baste with the remaining stock if the tomatoes look as if

Baked Tomatoes Stuffed with Rice (continued)
they're getting too dried out. Remove from the oven and let sit for a few minutes before serving.

VARIATIONS

With cheese. Add 1–2 tablespoons grated *Parmesan or Romano* cheese to the rice mixture. Or, sprinkle on top and drizzle with olive oil.

With leftover meat, poultry, or fish. Along with the onion add 1/4 cup chopped leftover meat, such as minced *lamb;* poultry (scraps from a roast *duck* are wonderful); or fish (fresh *tuna* or leftover *shellfish* is excellent).

CHICKPEAS WITH POTATOES

You can toss this together in minutes if you have cans of tomato sauce and chickpeas in your cupboard. Store-bought pita bread provides a handy scoop.

(Makes 1 generous serving)

1 medium potato	1/2 teaspoon curry powder
1 small onion	Freshly ground black pepper
A 15-ounce can chickpeas (garbanzos)	1–2 tablespoons chopped fresh coriander or parsley (or a
An 8-ounce can tomato sauce	combination of both)
1/4 teaspoon cumin	Salt

Peel the potato and cut it into chunks any size you prefer (1/2 inch works well). Cover with water, bring to a boil, and gently boil until cooked through. Peel and coarsely chop the onion. Meanwhile, rinse the chickpeas with water and drain. Place them in a nonreactive pan along with the tomato sauce, cumin, curry powder, a generous amount of black pepper, and the onion. Cook over low heat, stirring occasionally, for 10 minutes. Cover the pan and let sit until the potatoes are cooked through. Drain the potatoes and add them to the mixture along with the herbs. Season with salt to taste.

VARIATIONS

With cauliflower or broccoli. Reduce the chickpeas to 1/2 cup and add 1 cup cooked *cauliflower* or *broccoli* florets along with the potatoes.

With zucchini or summer squash. Add raw diced *zucchini or summer squash* along with the chickpeas. Or, if you have cooked leftovers, add after the chickpeas have been cooking for 5 minutes.

With leftover meat, poultry, or white fish. Coarsely chop leftover *pork, beef, lamb, poultry,* or cut cooked white fish (such as *pollack* or *hake*) into chunks. After the chickpeas have been cooking for 5 minutes, add the leftovers.

LEFTOVERS

This mixture makes a tasty stuffing for a pita bread sandwich. If you have only a little bit left over, stretch it with shredded *lettuce,* chopped *peppers* or *onions*—or maybe some fresh *tomato* chunks. Coarsely chopped raw greens, such as *spinach or escarole,* sprinkled on top, also taste delicious.

STUFFED EGGPLANT

Position the eggplant skin side up while simmering—otherwise the flesh will be undercooked. Use the other half of the eggplant for *Eggplant Gratin* (page 94).

(Serves 1)

A 1-pound eggplant
1–2 tablespoons olive oil
1/4 cup chopped onion
2 teaspoons minced garlic
3 tablespoons minced pepper

1/2 cup chopped peeled and
   seeded tomato
3 tablespoons minced parsley–or
   a combination of parsley and
   basil or parsley and coriander

Halve the eggplant lengthwise. Refrigerate 1/2 for another meal, rubbing the cut surface first with lemon so it doesn't darken. Boil a large pot of water, add the eggplant, and simmer for about 15 minutes, or until the flesh is cooked through. Remove from the heat and cool. Without puncturing the skin of the eggplant, scoop out the flesh and chop coarsely. Set aside. Heat the oil in a heavy frying pan. Add the onion, garlic, and pep-

Stuffed Eggplant (continued)

per. Cook, stirring frequently, for 3 minutes. Add the tomato and re-served eggplant, and cook for another 5 minutes, stirring. Add the herbs, reserving a teaspoon to sprinkle on the cooked eggplant. Place the egg-plant skin in a small, oiled baking dish. Stuff it with the vegetable mix-ture and mound the top. (It's a generous amount of stuffing.) Bake in a preheated 350°F oven for 30 minutes, or until the stuffing is heated through. Sprinkle with the reserved herbs and serve either warm or at room temperature.

VARIATIONS

Stuffed Eggplant with Ground Turkey. Add 2–3 ounces raw ground *turkey* and 1/8 teaspoon ground *cumin* along with the eggplant and tomato. Pro-ceed as above.

Stuffed Eggplant with Mushrooms. Add 1/2 cup chopped *mushrooms* along with the eggplant. Be sure to stir frequently and cook through be-fore stuffing. You may need to add another teaspoon of oil.

EGGPLANT PARMIGIANA

Eggplant parmigiana is a good old-fashioned Italian-American favorite, but it's usually too oily. If you salt the raw eggplant and let it sit for an hour before frying it, it will exude its vegetable juices and absorb less oil while cooking. You can use canned tomato sauce with this recipe—the fresh basil is the primary flavor. Even though this makes 2 servings, it's worth it for the leftovers. Any leftovers make a delicious submarine sand-wich or reheat well in the microwave.

(Makes 2 servings)

A 1-pound eggplant
Salt
1 egg
2 teaspoons water
Flour
2–3 tablespoons olive oil

3 tablespoons chopped fresh
    basil, stems and leaves
1 cup tomato sauce
3 tablespoons grated Parmesan
    or Romano cheese

Slice the eggplant into 1/2-inch-thick pieces, salt them well on both sides, and let sit for about 1 hour. Rinse quickly and blot dry. Beat the egg with 2 teaspoons water, and dip each slice first in this mixture then in flour. Shake off any excess flour.

Heat 2 tablespoons oil in a heavy frying pan. A few slices at a time, sauté the eggplant until just golden, not browned. You may need to wipe out the pan and add additional oil as you go along. Continue until all the slices are cooked. Drain the slices on paper towels. Mix together the basil and tomato sauce. Place a layer of the eggplant slices in a shallow baking dish about 8 inches in diameter. Top with 1/2 the tomato sauce and 1/2 of the cheese. Add the remaining eggplant and then top with the remaining sauce and cheese. Bake in a preheated 350°F oven for 30–40 minutes or until the sauce is bubbling and the eggplant is cooked through.

VARIATIONS

Eggplant with Parmesan and Mozzarella Cheeses. Add 2 ounces grated or sliced *mozzarella* cheese along with the Parmesan cheese and proceed as above.

With hot pepper. Add 1–2 teaspoons chopped *hot pepper* to the tomato sauce and proceed as above.

"When I get home at 7:30 in the evening, after working all day and going to the gym, the last thing I want to do is cook. I head right for the refrigerator and scoff down whatever I find. Usually it's tuna fish sandwiches—or I get take-out. On Sundays I fix pasta. My girlfriend doesn't cook either—she eats the same garbage that I do. I know I should be eating better, but I can't seem to find the time."

Philipp Hoyos, printer

EGGPLANT GRATIN

This easy-to-make main course has a delicate flavor set off by a soft texture that's a cross between a custard and a soufflé. The recipe makes enough for a hearty meal—or you can recycle leftovers with no loss of flavor. As the eggplant mixture looks beige when cooked, set it off with something colorful, such as sliced tomatoes topped with scallion greens or a raw carrot, zucchini, and lettuce salad. The cheeses are salty, so you may wish to omit the salt.

(Makes 1 generous serving)

A 1¹/₄-pound eggplant, stem
  removed
1 tablespoon olive oil
¹/₂ cup cottage cheese
  (preferably low-fat)
¹/₄ cup Parmesan or Romano
  cheese

2 medium eggs, lightly beaten
2 teaspoons chopped fresh
  coriander or basil
Salt (optional)

Halve the eggplant lengthwise. Refrigerate ¹/₂ for use with another recipe. Oil the eggplant. Place a stainless-steel fork in the center to radiate the heat, put in a baking dish, and bake in a preheated 375°F oven for 30–40 minutes, or until just cooked through. (I usually do this in advance. The baked eggplant keeps well in the refrigerator for about 3 days.)

Cut up the eggplant and place in a food processor. Add the olive oil, and the cottage and Parmesan cheeses. Pulse until well combined. The mixture should have some texture, including pieces of skin. Add the eggs and herbs. Pulse again. Season with salt if you like.

Spoon the mixture into a well-greased baking dish about 6 inches in diameter. Bake in a preheated 375°F oven for about 20 minutes. The eggplant mixture will puff up. Remove from the oven when the surface feels firm when you press upon it lightly. If you wait until a knife inserted comes out cleanly, the gratin is overdone and the soft texture will be lost. Let cool for about 10 minutes before serving.

LEFTOVERS

Cut any leftover gratin into ¹/₂-inch slices, dip them first in egg, then in *flour,* and brown in olive oil. Topped with chopped *chives,* the eggplant pieces taste delicious served alone. Or after browning, use them as the base for a *vegetarian submarine sandwich* topped with *tomatoes,* chopped ripe *olives,* and *lettuce.*

VEGETABLE STEW

This stew, which looks as good as it tastes, takes about 15–20 minutes from start to finish. To save time, chop the vegetables and refrigerate them covered with the stock. When you get home from work all you'll need to do is put the pot on the stove. If you cook the vegetables in water rather than vegetable or chicken stock, add herbs to round out the flavor.

(Makes 1 generous serving)

1 1/2 cups chicken or vegetable
stock, or water
1 cup 1/2-inch potato cubes
(about 1 medium potato)
1/2 cup chopped onion
1/2 cup chopped celery

2/3 cup chopped carrot
1 cup thinly sliced cabbage
Freshly ground black pepper
1/4 cup frozen corn kernels
Salt (optional)

Put the stock, potato, onion, celery, and carrot into a stove-top pot. Bring the mixture to a boil, lower the heat to medium-high, and gently boil for 5 minutes. Add the cabbage and a generous sprinkling of black pepper. Cook the mixture 5 minutes longer. Taste to see if the potato is cooked through. (The other vegetables should be cooked through but retain some texture.) Stir in the corn, cover the pan, and let the mixture sit for 2–5 minutes before serving. Taste and season with salt if you wish.

VARIATIONS

With herbs. Add 1 tablespoon chopped *parsley, basil,* or *coriander*—or 2 teaspoons chopped *sweet marjoram, tarragon,* or *dill.*

With chickpeas or cooked beans. Omit the corn. Substitute 1/2–1 cup cooked *chickpeas* or cooked *dried beans,* such as navy. Or use 1/2 cup frozen *lima beans.*

HUNGARIAN PEPPER STEW

This multi-purpose stew is excellent reheated with leftover meats, such as pork, chicken, turkey, sausage, and the like—or densely textured fish, such as monkfish or tuna. Hungarian sweet paprika is sold in the gourmet sections of most supermarkets and specialty shops. Try this stew flanked by a mound of *Mashed Potatoes* (page 66) or noodles. If you're having company (or just feel like fixing a roast), this dish marries well with roasted pork or ham.

(Makes 1 generous serving)

1/3 cup diced bacon
3/4 cup chopped onion (1 medium onion)
1 teaspoon paprika (preferably Hungarian sweet paprika)
2 cups peeled, seeded, and coarsely chopped tomatoes

2 cups seeded and sliced peppers (preferably a combination of red and green)
Salt and freshly ground black pepper (optional)

Slowly cook the bacon in a large frying pan, until the fat is rendered (melted) and the bacon is crisp. Add the onion, and cook, stirring frequently, for 2 minutes. Pour off most of the fat, leaving just enough in the pan to moisten the paprika. Stir in the paprika, and cook for 3 minutes, stirring constantly. Add the tomatoes and peppers. Cover the pan and simmer for another 20–30 minutes, until the peppers are tender. Taste and season with salt and pepper, if you like.

VARIATIONS

Vegetarian. Omit the bacon. Substitute 2–3 teaspoons *butter* and proceed as above. (Hungarians would use lard.)

With sausage. Substitute sliced *hot or smoked sausage* to taste for the bacon.

LEFTOVERS

Pepper Soup. Simmer equal parts of the pepper mixture and vegetable liquid. Add diced *potatoes* and *celery* to taste. (A good ratio would be 1 cup pepper mixture, 1 cup liquid, 1/2 cup diced potatoes, and 1/4 cup diced celery.) Just before serving stir in chopped *parsley* or *sweet marjoram.*

Sour Cream Goulash Stew. Simmer any leftover vegetables and liquid along with thinly sliced leftover *meats* (pork, chicken, turkey, sausage). Just before serving, stir in a tablespoon of *sour cream or yogurt* and correct the seasonings.

SPICY BROWN RICE WITH VEGETABLES

In this vegetarian main dish, you can change the vegetables depending on what's in season (or in your refrigerator). The sweet potato cooks down and gives body to the rice. If you prefer the potato to have texture, add it 15 minutes after the rice starts cooking.

(Makes 1 generous serving)

1/3 cup brown rice
1/8 teaspoon cumin
Cinnamon (optional)
Paprika (optional)
1 cup water
1/2 cup peeled and chopped
    carrot
1/2 cup sweet potato pieces, cut
    at least 1/2 inch wide

1/2 cup peeled, seeded, and
    chopped tomato
1/2 cup raw green beans
Freshly ground black pepper
2 tablespoons chopped scallion
    greens or 2 teaspoons
    chopped coriander or parsley
Salt (optional)

Put the brown rice, cumin, a pinch of cinnamon and a generous pinch of paprika (if using), the water, carrot, and sweet potato in a heavy pot. Bring to a boil over high heat; lower the heat and simmer, covered, for 25 minutes. Stir occasionally and check the water level to be sure that the mixture doesn't burn. Stir in the beans, making sure they are covered by the rice, and sprinkle with a generous amount of black pepper. Continue cooking for 15 minutes, or until the rice is cooked through but still retains some texture. Stir in the scallion greens or herbs. Add salt, if you wish.

Spicy Brown Rice with Vegetables (continued)

VARIATIONS

With zucchini or summer squash. Omit the beans. Add 1/2 cup *zucchini* cut into 1/2-inch slices 15 minutes before the rice is done.

With winter squash. Substitute 3/4 cup 1-inch chunks peeled and seeded *winter squash* for the sweet potato.

FRESH TOMATO SAUCE

During tomato season I keep a bowl of this sauce in the refrigerator as a staple—or freeze it in 1-cup servings for future use. It's important to cook the sauce rapidly; a temperature halfway between a simmer and a slow boil is best because the longer tomatoes cook, the more acidic they become, and the more they lose their fresh garden flavor. I use this sauce in many ingredients in this book. If you've never made a fresh tomato sauce—and don't have a garden—at least try it once. During tomato season at farm stands and farmers' markets you can buy inexpensive super-ripe "canning" tomatoes that need to be used up immediately. You'll be amazed how delicious and subtle-tasting a fresh tomato sauce can be.

(Makes 3 1/2–4 cups sauce)

2 tablespoons olive oil	3 tablespoons chopped basil
1 1/2 cups peeled and chopped	or combined basil and sweet
onions	marjoram
2 teaspoons minced garlic	
4 cups peeled, seeded, and	
chopped tomatoes	

Heat the oil in a heavy stainless-steel or enameled pan and add the onions and garlic. Cook, stirring frequently, over low-medium heat for 10–15 minutes, or until the onions are soft but not browned. Tip the pan and spoon out all but a film of the olive oil. Add the tomatoes, bring to a boil, and boil until the juices are released, stirring frequently. Lower the heat to a rapid simmer, and cook, stirring occasionally, for 20–30 minutes. The sauce should be thick—if not, cook another 10 minutes. Stir in the basil and remove from the heat. Cool the sauce and store in the refrigerator in a covered glass bowl, where it will keep in good condition for 5–7 days. It will also keep in the freezer for up to 10 months.

VARIATION

Tomato Soup. For each serving, heat together 1 cup tomato sauce and 1/2 cup *chicken stock.* Add 3 tablespoons *cream* and 1 teaspoon *butter.* Taste and season with *salt* and freshly ground *black pepper.* You could add 1 teaspoon minced sweet marjoram or *lovage* just before serving.

QUICK MEALS

At the end of a busy day, when you're the only one doing the shopping, cooking, and cleaning up, preparing a meal is often the last thing on your mind. You eat a tuna fish sandwich—or a microwave potato (at least there's no mess)—and get on with the evening. These meals-on-the-fly are fine once in a while, but they're dispiriting as a way of life.

We tend to forget that simply prepared food is the best food. We can do little to improve upon the flavor of a freshly harvested ear of corn or a garden ripe tomato. An absolutely fresh piece of haddock needs no embellishments—nor does a plate of roasted or grilled vegetables. When we buy high-quality primary ingredients and build them into our menus, quick cooking can be as easy as steaming a handful of asparagus or oven-steaming a piece of fish.

Throughout this book you'll find both easy main courses that take less than 20–30 minutes to cook as well as a number of meals-in-one, many of which bake in the oven while you relax. You'll notice that many of the recipes use an oven temperature of 450°F. Baking foods at a high temperature seals in the juices—and they cook faster in less fat. Fat is a quick fix for fast foods. I believe the best-tasting food gains its flavor from a judicious use of vegetables, herbs, and spices rather than fat—that's why even my quick-to-prepare recipes usually include vegetables and herbs, if only as seasonings. I know that you don't always have a wide selection of vegetables and herbs on hand, so in the storage section (see page 12) I've explained how you can use your freezer as a holding station. This cache of home-style convenience food can bail you out on nights when the refrigerator is bare.

Staples

In addition to a well-stocked freezer, certain foods are invaluable when you're cooking in a hurry. I try to keep these on hand at all times:

Black pepper. Freshly ground black pepper adds a jolt of flavor to quick meals cooked in a liquid. And, when they're cracked, not ground, peppercorns can become the predominant (and only) flavor—making your work even easier. You don't even need a pepper mill to crack peppercorns; a heavy bottle will do. (I've used a hammer with great success.) But you will need good-quality peppercorns. To crack: Press down on the peppercorns with the side of a bottle, such as a vinegar or wine bottle, and rock back and forth. The peppercorns will crack in large pieces. Then gather up the peppercorns and grind down on them with the edge of the bottle.

Breadcrumbs. Whether you're baking chicken or fish at a high temperature and want to seal in the juices, or need to stretch a small amount of ground meat a little further, breadcrumbs are indispensable. You can recycle stale bread in seconds in a food processor or blender, but you can also just crumble the bread with your hands, dump it in a paper bag, and roll a bottle back and forth over it to make crumbs. (This works only with dry, stale bread.) Breadcrumbs sautéed with a touch of butter or olive oil and sprinkled over vegetables such as cauliflower or asparagus add a rich, toasted flavor—and an elegant look.

Fresh herbs. I think fresh (or frozen) herbs are the most useful ingredients for last-minute cooking because they add a distinctive flavor to the finished dish while requiring virtually no work along the way. You can make exactly the same recipe, changing only the herbs, and it will taste completely different. Think, for example, of how a piece of cooked salmon would taste sprinkled with mint, and then imagine it with parsley or tarragon. Many supermarkets now stock fresh-herb packages airshipped from California, making the use of herbs such as sweet marjoram a viable choice for someone without a garden. If you store the herbs in a glass, with their stems in water, they will keep for several days in the refrigerator; otherwise, freeze them (see page 14). At virtually any supermarket you can buy fresh parsley and fresh coriander (cilantro). If you're not going to use up the herbs within a few days, you can freeze them. I don't use dried herbs now that fresh herbs are so readily available, but if you need to substitute dried for fresh herbs, use 1/3 the amount. For example, you would substitute 1 teaspoon of dried tarragon for 1 tablespoon of chopped fresh tarragon.

Jalapeño peppers. I never appreciated the diversity of jalapeño peppers until I wrote a salt-free cookbook. I discovered that a touch of something hot compensates for less salt, certainly of interest to anyone on a salt-restricted diet. But for the rest of us, even a small amount of jalapeños rounds out the flavor of a sauce while adding a touch of color. And, if you peel them before cooking (or freezing) they will be easier to digest. Jalapeños freeze well, so you can have them on hand to use at will.

Fresh limes or lemons. Either limes or lemons give the acidity that's often just what's needed to finish off a dish, or to use as a tenderizing marinade for fish, meat, or poultry before cooking. Limes have a full taste that I find more versatile than lemons, but both are easy to find. When you're squeezing limes or lemons, first roll them back and forth on the counter, pressing down with your hands. (Don't be too vigorous or they will split.) This step will substantially increase the amount of juice you obtain when you're squeezing them.

Scallions. Scallions are an excellent ingredient for rapid cooking because they break down quickly in a sauce, releasing their onion flavor immediately. They're also a wonderful garnishing aid: A few sliced scallion greens floating on a bowl of soup, or scattered over a chicken salad, add color (and flavor). The easiest way to prepare scallions is to slice them lengthwise first, and then chop them into pieces. If you want the look of scallion rounds, just cut them crosswise into thin slices.

Starches. With dried beans, pasta, rice, or fresh potatoes on hand you'll never go hungry. What microwave owner hasn't microwaved a potato on occasion? Rice is tremendously versatile: Many single cooks make a pot of rice at the beginning of the week, microwave it one night to go along with poultry or fish, add it to stock with some vegetables to make a quick soup, or use it as a base for salads with leftover vegetables such as peas or broccoli. And with pasta in the cupboard, you can resuscitate just about any leftover in the refrigerator.

Stocks. Stocks come into their own when you're cooking in a hurry. With a supply of frozen stocks, you can make a sauce for a simple pan-fried chicken or for stir-fried vegetables—or put together a quick soup from leftover vegetables. Making stocks is one of those cooking processes that sounds intimidating if you've never done it, but is remarkably easy in practice. Essentially all you're doing is covering your basic ingredients with water and gently cooking them until their flavor is extracted (see pages 250–51). You can make chicken, fish, meat, or vegetable stocks when you get the chance, and strain and freeze them in ice-cube trays. One cube is about 2 tablespoons stock. You can also substitute canned stock (preferably low-sodium) in the recipes.

SEAFOOD

Fish is naturally tender. There's little we can do as cooks to enhance this state—but we can destroy it by over-cooking. Unlike meat, the longer fish cooks, the drier and more tasteless it becomes. That's because its connective tissue is formed in short strands (rather than the long bundles found in meat)—and there's less of it. This means fish doesn't need to cook for a long time to be tender, a bonus for anyone who wants a meal in minutes. That's why I think of it as the ultimate convenience food.

If you're a novice fish cook, a useful guideline was developed by the Canadian Department of Fisheries. After much experimentation the department decided that 10 minutes of cooking time for each inch of thickness is a handy rule of thumb. This method is applicable for steamed, broiled, fried, or poached fish—and fish baked at a high temperature, such as 450°F. A fish fillet is cooked through in 5–15 minutes, depending upon the cooking technique and the kind of fish you're using.

Fish continues to cook after it's been removed from the heat, so you should cook it only to the point when its flesh looks opaque rather than translucent. Too often, people test fish by seeing if the flesh flakes when poked with a fork. That's a poor test: By then, the fish is overdone.

Really fresh fish doesn't need much in the way of embellishments. How you prepare it is often a matter of personal preference. Some people prefer baked fish—others broil it. I'm listing the various cooking techniques I find useful as a single cook. The only techniques I'm not suggesting are deep-fat frying and poaching. (I think it's too much trouble to heat up fat to cook a small portion of fish; likewise, I'd be more likely to oven-steam fish than to poach it.)

In this chapter I'm concentrating on cooking techniques, rather than giving you lots of recipes. Fish tastes best cooked simply. Good-quality fish needs no enhancement. Buy the very best quality you can find and treat it with respect.

COOKING FISH

The texture of a fish is the single most important factor in choosing a cooking method. In general, densely textured fish, such as cusk, monk-fish, or tuna, can be prepared any way, while softer-textured fish, such as sole or cod, may fall apart when they're grilled or steamed. Baking and pan-frying in a crumb mixture are good methods for softer-textured fish, but even a soft-textured fish broils well if it's thick enough. You can oven-steam any fish.

There are no set rules with fish: If you like broiled fish, using the method I've suggested, you can broil just about any species as long as you're careful. The method you use is very much a matter of personal preference. I think most fresh fish is delicious no matter how it's prepared.

Baking

Baking is an excellent way to cook fish. If the fish is naturally fatty, such as salmon, bluefish, or mackerel, you don't need to add additional fat. A leaner fish, such as haddock, benefits from a touch of butter or oil.

If you bake fish between 425 and 450°F, a higher temperature than you might expect, you'll find that the high heat seals in the juices keeping the fish moist. To bake: Place the fish in a lightly buttered pan skin side down (you can add vegetables, such as celery or onions, for flavor), and dot it with butter (1/2 teaspoon for each 3–4 ounces would work well). If you wish to baste the fish as it cooks, you can add a tablespoon or two of white wine (always use a glass dish or enameled pan because of the acids in the wine). Bake at 425–450°F for 8–15 minutes, depending upon the thickness of the fish.

Broiling

You can broil any fish successfully—even thin fillets of flatfish—as long as you take certain precautions: Preheat the broiler at least 20 minutes before you cook the fish; lightly oil the fish first; and cook it about 3–4 inches below the heating element. If you don't want to oil the fish, I'd suggest using another method; coating the surface keeps the fish from burning and holds in the moisture.

To broil: Dry the fish, coat both sides with oil, and place in a broiler pan. (I prefer to line the pan with foil because I dislike cleaning broiler pans—but it's up to you.) Broil the fish about 3–4 inches below the heating element until cooked through. There's no need to turn the fish because the reflected heat from the pan will cook the other side. A thick fish fillet, such as 1-inch swordfish, will be cooked through in about 10 minutes.

Sautéing

If you live in an area where your local fish is flounder—or some other form of flatfish—sautéing is an excellent way to preserve its flavor. (This is also a good method for cooking any thin fish fillets.)

In the sautéed fish recipes in this book, I've cut down the amount of fat traditionally used. In most sautés, the bottom of the cooking pan is generously coated with oil (or butter and oil). You can cook with less fat, as I suggest, but it's essential that you're working with a nonstick frying pan or a heavy one, such as a cast-iron pan. Otherwise, the heat isn't distributed evenly and the fish will burn or stick to the pan. (If you think this will be a problem, add additional butter or oil to my recipes.)

You can soak the fish in milk (or buttermilk) before sautéing and make sure the fat is hot before you add the fish; otherwise it will stick to the pan. If you're cooking fillets, leave space between them—and keep the

"I'm very social and I certainly enjoy dining with friends, but I like cooking (and eating) alone because I don't have to prepare anything that would appeal to someone else. Home cooking is all about simple, comfortable food. When food is fresh it doesn't take much to bring out its flavor. Fishing is my hobby, so I prefer eating fish. I'll grill some tuna and put it together with some grilled vegetables and let the flavors come through."

Jerry Goldstein, businessman

pan uncovered so the coating stays crisp. Cook the fish over medium-high heat until it is a light golden color on both sides. Turn it once. A flounder fillet, for example, will cook in about 4–6 minutes.

Oven-Steaming

I learned this technique from George Berkowitz, the owner of Legal Sea Foods, when we were writing that restaurant chain's cookbook. Oven-steaming is particularly useful for solo cooks because you can eat the fish either hot or cold. You bake fish and thinly sliced vegetables in an envelope of heavy aluminum foil. The fish steams in its own juices, always coming out moist, and creates fish and vegetable juices to spoon over rice or potatoes. You can use whatever local fish is plentiful in your region and whatever vegetables are in season, sliced 1/4 inch thick so that they'll cook as rapidly as the fish.

To oven-steam: Preheat the oven to 450°F. Cut a piece of foil large enough to hold the fish and vegetables without crowding. Place the fish in the middle of the foil and cover with whichever vegetables you fancy, cut no more than 1/4 inch thick. Add seasonings to taste, then dot with about 1/2–1 teaspoon of butter for every 4–6 ounces of fish. Form the foil into an envelope that encloses the fish and vegetables. Put the foil on a cookie sheet. Bake for about 15–20 minutes. The fish will be cooked through, and the vegetables will still retain some of their crunch. Good choices for vegetables include onions, broccoli florets, green beans, fennel, tomatoes, peppers, summer squash—in short, any vegetable that has enough water content to cook through rapidly.

Steamed Shellfish and Fish

I like to steam shellfish and recycle the steaming liquid either as a base for fish soups or as an ingredient in salad dressings when fish is part of the salad. (To freeze: Drain the steaming liquid through coffee filters and freeze it in 1/4-cup amounts.)

This technique works best with a good-quality steamer, available at any restaurant supply store and in many gourmet cooking departments. You can also use the collapsible basket steamers that fit into different-sized pots. To steam: Place about 1 inch of water in the bottom of the pot. Bring the water to a boil, insert the steamer basket holding the fish, cover, and steam until the fish is just cooked through. Thin fillets take about 3 minutes, while a 1-inch-thick fillet will be ready in 8–10 minutes. In steaming, the density of the fish is important: Densely textured fish, such as monkfish, take longer to steam than sole. The fish should sit for a moment before serving.

You should follow the same technique when cooking shellfish, such as shrimp, scallops, or mussels. Remember that shellfish will cook through more rapidly than you might expect; depending upon their size, shrimp, for example, will be done in 1–3 minutes. The cooking time depends upon the size of the shellfish.

BREADED FLOUNDER

This is one of the easiest ways to prepare any fish fillet. The breading, which should be done with fine, dry breadcrumbs (see page 100), seals in the flavor and keeps the fish moist.

(Serves 1)

1 medium egg

1 tablespoon milk

4–6 ounces flounder or sole fillets

3–4 tablespoons fine, dry bread- crumbs

1 teaspoon canola oil

1 teaspoon butter

Salt and freshly ground black pepper (optional)

Beat together the egg and milk in a shallow dish, add the fish, and stir to coat. Let the fillets sit in the mixture for 5 minutes, then dip in the breadcrumbs. The fillets should be thoroughly coated with the crumbs.

Heat the oil and butter together in a medium frying pan, add the fish, and cook it over medium heat for 2 minutes on each side. The bread-crumb coating should brown but not burn. Season with salt and pepper to taste. Serve immediately (the coating gets soggy as it sits).

VARIATION

With herbs. Place the fish fillets on the breadcrumbs and sprinkle with 1 teaspoon minced herbs, such as *sweet marjoram, basil, or parsley.* Press down slightly so that they adhere, spoon a little egg mixture over them, then roll in the crumbs. Proceed as above.

BAKED BLUEFISH WITH BACON

This is a no-fuss way to enjoy fresh bluefish.

(Serves 1)

1 bluefish fillet (4–6 ounces)   Freshly ground black pepper
1 teaspoon Dijon mustard   2 strips bacon

Dry the fillet. Spread both sides with Dijon mustard. Sprinkle generously with black pepper. Cover with the bacon. Bake the fish in a preheated 425°F oven for 12–15 minutes, depending upon the thickness of
the fillet. You can either eat the bacon with the fish, or remove it before
serving.

BAKED BLUEFISH
WITH BROILED TOMATOES

Broiling tomatoes gives them added flavor, which is a particularly useful
technique when all you can buy is out-of-season tomatoes. This recipe
works particularly well with strongly flavored fish, such as bluefish or
mackerel.

(Serves 1)

1/2 teaspoon olive oil   1 tablespoon chopped scallion
1 bluefish fillet (4–6 ounces)   or onion
2 tablespoons roasted Italian   Freshly ground black pepper
   plum tomatoes (see Note) or   1 tablespoon water
   peeled, seeded, and chopped   1 teaspoon chopped parsley,
   ripe tomatoes   basil, or chives (optional)

Lightly oil a small baking pan. Place the bluefish in the pan, top with
the tomatoes, and then the scallion. Sprinkle with the pepper. Add the
water to the pan. Bake the fish in a preheated 450°F oven for 12–15 minutes, or until cooked through, basting occasionally with the pan juices.
Sprinkle with fresh herbs before serving.

Note: Broiled tomatoes have a rich, cooked flavor that's particularly good with oily fish. Just place fresh Italian plum tomatoes on a baking sheet covered with foil and broil them on the top rack of the broiler for about 10 minutes. Their skins will blacken. Remove them from the oven, wrap the foil around them, and let sit for a few minutes. Then lift off the blackened skins and slice the tomatoes. Any leftover tomatoes are good on pizza or in casseroles. Store them covered with olive oil in the refrigerator.

VARIATION

With pepper. Add 1 tablespoon chopped *jalapeño* or *green pepper* along with the tomatoes.

SOUTHERN-STYLE FRIED GROUPER OR CATFISH

The salad dressing flavors the fish. Seasoned fish-fry mix is available at most supermarkets or fish markets.

(Serves 1)

1 grouper or catfish fillet (4–6 ounces)
1 recipe *Sweet-Sour Poppy Seed Dressing* (page 24), omitting the poppy seeds

1 medium egg
1/4–1/3 cup commercial fish-fry mix (made with cornmeal)
Oil (preferably peanut)
Cocktail sauce

Marinate the fish in the dressing for several hours. Remove it from the marinade and set aside. Beat the egg into the marinade and dip the fish into it until thoroughly coated. Put the fish-fry mix into a dish and place the fish in it until coated. Pour oil to 1/4-inch depth into a frying pan and heat it until a piece of the cornmeal coating dropped into the pan sizzles (about 360–375°F). Fry the fish for 3–5 minutes on each side, or until it is cooked through and the coating is browned. Drain on paper towels and serve with cocktail sauce.

EASY BAKED HADDOCK

You can fix any fish fillets following this method. The mayonnaise serves merely to anchor the breadcrumbs.

(Serves 1)

1 haddock fillet (4–6 ounces)
1 teaspoon mayonnaise
1 tablespoon breadcrumbs

1 teaspoon butter (optional)
1 teaspoon chopped parsley

Place the haddock in a buttered baking dish. Spread with the mayonnaise and sprinkle with the breadcrumbs. Dot with butter if you wish. Bake in a preheated 425°F oven for 12–15 minutes or until the fish is cooked through. Sprinkle with parsley before serving.

BAKED HAKE WITH SCALLIONS

You can substitute virtually any fish, such as grouper, haddock, or cod, for the hake. Hake is an exceptionally tasty—and economically priced—fish that's less well known than other white-fleshed fish, but it's equally good.

(Serves 1)

1 fresh hake fillet (4–6 ounces)
About 1 teaspoon fresh lime
   juice ($1/4$ lime)

1 teaspoon chopped basil
2 tablespoons chopped scallion
$1/2$ teaspoon butter

Place the hake in a small, buttered baking dish. Squeeze over about a teaspoon of lime juice, and sprinkle with the basil and scallion. Dot with the butter. Bake in a preheated 425°F oven for 10–12 minutes, basting after 5 minutes.

VARIATIONS

With mushrooms. Sauté $1/4$ cup sliced *mushrooms* in the $1/2$ teaspoon butter. Stir in the scallion and basil. Top the fish with this mixture and proceed as above.

With tomato. Add 1/4 cup peeled, seeded, and chopped *tomato* to the scallion. Proceed as above.

With fennel or celery. Sauté 1/4 cup chopped *fennel or celery* in the 1/2 teaspoon butter until slightly wilted, about 4 minutes. Stir in the scallion and basil and proceed as above.

HALIBUT WITH ASPARAGUS

This is a popular way of serving thick white-fleshed fish in Belgium. And, for solo cooks, it's a good way to use up leftover asparagus stalks.

(Serves 1)

2 teaspoons butter
2 teaspoons vegetable oil, such as canola
Flour
A 4–6 ounce halibut steak, about 1 inch thick

4–6 stalks cooked leftover asparagus, at room temperature
1 hard-boiled egg (see page 32), finely chopped

Heat the butter and the oil together in a large frying pan. Flour the halibut, shake it to remove any excess flour, and sauté for 4 minutes, then turn and cook on the other side. Depending upon the thickness of the fish, it should be cooked through in about 8 minutes.

Remove the fish from the pan. Arrange it on a plate with the asparagus spears fanning out from it. Sprinkle with the finely chopped egg.

VARIATION

With browned asparagus and nuts. While the fish is cooking, quickly reheat the asparagus in 2 teaspoons butter. Brown 1 tablespoon chopped *almonds or cashews* and pour over the fish. Omit the eggs.

BAKED SALMON WITH LEMON

This is one of the easiest, yet most delicious, ways to prepare fish. You can substitute virtually any kind of fish fillet for the salmon. If you have any left over, make Chilled Salmon and Cucumber Soup (page 245).

(Serves 1)

1 lemon
1/2 teaspoon olive oil
1 salmon fillet or steak (4–6 ounces)

Freshly ground black pepper (optional)

Cut the lemon into 1/4-inch-thick slices. Place about 1/2 teaspoon olive oil in the palm of your hand and rub it over the salmon. Place the salmon in an ovenproof dish. Sprinkle with the black pepper and cover with the lemon slices. Bake in a preheated 425°F oven for 8–15 minutes, depending upon whether you're cooking a fillet or a steak. Remove the lemon slices before serving.

VARIATION

Cusk or Monkfish Baked with Lemon. Substitute *cusk* or *monkfish* (or any firm-fleshed white fish) for the salmon.

SOLE WITH BROWNED BUTTER

Sole with browned butter is a classic French way of cooking fish. I'm suggesting a range of butter amounts—even a teaspoon of the browned butter adds a delicious nutty flavor.

(Serves 1)

4–6 ounces sole fillets
Milk
Salt and freshly ground black pepper
Flour

2 teaspoons canola oil
1–3 teaspoons butter
1/2 teaspoon minced parsley
Lemon wedge

Cover the sole fillets with milk and let sit for 15 minutes. Pat dry. Season with salt and freshly ground black pepper, then dip in flour. Shake to remove any excess. In a heavy frying pan heat the oil over high heat. Add the fish and cook until browned on both sides, about 2–3 minutes. Remove it to a plate. Wipe out the pan with a paper towel and add the butter. Cook the butter until it is lightly browned. Pour the browned butter over the fish, sprinkle with the parsley, and serve with a lemon wedge.

VARIATION

With capers and lemon. After you wipe out the pan, lower the heat and melt 1 teaspoon of butter. Add *lemon juice* to taste and stir in 1/2 teaspoon *capers.* Pour over the fish.

SWORDFISH IN A SWEET-SOUR TOMATO SAUCE

The tomato skin and seeds add a marmaladelike consistency to this quick dish inspired by the sweet-sour cooking of Greece. You can substitute virtually any white fish, such as cusk, haddock, hake, pollack, or monkfish for the swordfish.

(Serves 1)

2 teaspoons olive oil	2/3 cup chopped ripe tomato
4–6 ounces swordfish, cut in	(about 1 large tomato)
1/2-inch-thick pieces	Cinnamon
1 teaspoon minced garlic	Salt and freshly ground black
1 teaspoon red wine vinegar	pepper
1 teaspoon honey	

Heat 1 teaspoon of the olive oil in a heavy nonreactive frying pan. Cook the swordfish pieces on both sides until lightly browned, about 3 minutes. Remove the swordfish from the pan and set aside. To the same pan, add the remaining teaspoon of oil and the minced garlic. Raise the heat to medium and, stirring constantly, cook the garlic until it is slightly colored, about 1 minute. Off the heat, stir in the vinegar, honey, tomato,

Swordfish in a Sweet-Sour Tomato Sauce (continued)

and a pinch of cinnamon. Place the pan back on the heat and continue cooking, mashing the tomato occasionally with a fork, until the mixture has thickened, about 3 minutes. Taste and season with salt and pepper. Place the swordfish back in the pan, top with the tomato mixture, and reheat for just a moment.

VARIATION

With grilled chicken or pork medallions. Substitute 1/2-inch-thick *chicken* slices or 1/4-inch-thick *pork* medallions for the fish. Increase the sautéing time to 5 minutes.

SHELLFISH

Shellfish are wonderful choices for the single cook because most types cook in minutes. Shrimp is probably the most popular shellfish, but many markets now stock clams, mussels, oysters, scallops, crabmeat, and lobsters as well.

It's important, however, when you're buying fresh shellfish to find out where it originated. It's insane to take a chance on eating shellfish that might have come from contaminated waters. Bivalve mollusks, such as mussels, clams, and oysters, retain any toxins they ingest, so it's critical to determine where they came from. All shellfish gathered in certified clean areas are tagged by state inspection agencies, and any reputable fishmonger should be able to show you the health tags attached to the packing crates.

Shellfish are even more perishable than fish, so try to use them up immediately. Shellfish overcook easily because their flesh is so tender that they need only a few minutes to cook through. If you cook scallops or shrimp too long, their flesh will become rubbery. Cook them carefully, and you will enjoy the essence of the sea.

FRESH CRAB CAKES

Most commercial crab cakes have so much filler in them that you can barely taste the crab, so it's much better to make your own. Freshly picked crabmeat is usually sold in 8-ounce packages. As you only need half a container for this recipe, try a tasty crabmeat sandwich to use up the rest (see page 117). Unfortunately, crabmeat freezes and stores poorly, so use up any extra crabmeat within a day.

(Makes 2 crab cakes)

3 teaspoons butter
1 tablespoon flour
1/3 cup milk
Dry mustard or cayenne pepper
3 tablespoons breadcrumbs

3/4 cup picked cooked fresh
   crabmeat (about 4 ounces)
Freshly ground black pepper
1/2 lemon or lime

Heat 2 teaspoons of the butter in a small saucepan. Off the heat stir in the flour. Return the pan to the heat and cook over low heat, stirring constantly, for 1 minute. Add the milk and cook, stirring constantly, until the mixture is thick. Remove the pan from the heat and add a pinch of dry mustard or cayenne pepper, 2 tablespoons of the breadcrumbs, the crabmeat, and freshly ground black pepper to taste. Stir until the mixture is incorporated. Wet your hands and form 2 crab cakes. The mixture will be somewhat sticky. Put the remaining breadcrumbs on a plate and dip the cakes in the crumbs to coat both sides.

Heat the remaining 1 teaspoon butter in a pan. Add the crab cakes and cook 1–2 minutes on each side, or until the surfaces are browned. Serve with wedges of lemon or lime on the side.

VARIATION

Crab Cakes Southern-Style. Add 2 tablespoons chopped *bell pepper* or a mixture of bell and *jalapeño* pepper, 1 tablespoon minced *scallion*, and 1/2–1 teaspoon *Creole mustard* along with the crabmeat. Proceed as above.

BOILED LOBSTER

Eating a lobster is definitely an endeavor that's best done at home because it's so messy. Lobster seems expensive, but once you realize that it took 5 to 8 years for a lobster to reach 1 pound, the price seems almost reasonable.

I prefer to eat a slightly larger lobster, and here's why. Lobsters move through the water propelled by their tails. A baby, or "chicken," lobster is always on the move, while an older lobster is more likely to stay put, which means that its flesh is usually more tender. If you have Maine super "hard-shell" lobsters, add about 3 minutes' cooking time.

(Serves 1)

Water	Butter
A 1¹/4–1³/4 pound Maine lobster	Lemon

Fill a large pot with cold water, bring it to a boil, and add the lobster. When the water comes to a *second* boil, lower the heat to a gentle boil. Start timing. A 1¹/4-pound lobster will be done in about 12 minutes; a 1³/4–2-pound lobster will be cooked through in 18 minutes.

Remove the lobster from the water, drain it for a moment or two in the sink, and serve with melted butter, lemon, and plenty of paper or kitchen towels.

LEFTOVERS

Cold Lobster. **Any leftover lobster is wonderful cold sprinkled with fresh *lime juice* and, if you wish, *black pepper*. Or you could make:**

Lobster Roll

(Serves 1)

¹/2 cup coarsely chopped cooked lobster meat	2 tablespoons celery (optional)
2 tablespoons mayonnaise	Butter
	1 hot dog bun

Mix together the lobster, mayonnaise, and celery, if using. Butter the outside of the bun and sauté over medium heat until it is lightly browned. Stuff the bun with the lobster and serve immediately.

Variation

Crabmeat Sandwich. Substitute 2–3 ounces *crabmeat* for the lobster. Before mixing with the mayonnaise, press down slightly on the crabmeat to remove any extra liquid. Proceed as above.

EATING A LOBSTER

If you haven't mastered the art of eating a lobster, here are a few tips. Once the lobster is cooked, drain it in a clean sink for a moment or two, then hold the lobster body with one hand and grab the tail with the other. Bend the tail until it breaks free from the body, remove the tail meat, and put on a serving plate. Now you can head for the table and enjoy the lobster without being drenched with cooking juices. Remove the large claws and crack the shells with a lobster cracker or hammer. Extract the meat. If you are truly a lobster fancier you will also pick out the flesh that's contained between the cartilages in the body cavity, and you'll savor the tomalley, the lobster's liver, the soft green substance found in the cavity. (In Maine, lobster pounds often sell tomalley in small plastic tubs. It's delicious spread on a cracker or dipped in butter.) Although the cooked red coral's texture is dense, it's also good with lime juice, or you could remove it, mash it with mayonnaise, and use it to flavor the dressing in a lobster sandwich or salad. Be sure to have plenty of paper or kitchen towels on hand to wipe your fingers and/or clothes. A bib or a kitchen towel around your shoulders is also handy.

MUSSELS—TWO WAYS

Any leftover steamed mussels can have a new life as a salad or as a sauce for pasta. Save the steaming liquid because it adds flavor to seafood salads or pasta. You can freeze it in ice-cube trays and use as needed.

(Serves 1)

1 pound mussels	3 tablespoons water or
2 tablespoons chopped	white wine
onion	Freshly ground black pepper

Wash each mussel thoroughly under running water and pull down (almost yank) to remove the "beard," the hairlike mass the mussels secrete to anchor themselves. Discard any that have broken shells or feel unusually heavy (they're usually full of mud). Put the mussels in a heavy, nonreactive pan and add the onion, water, and a generous amount of freshly ground black pepper. Put the pot on the stove, bring the water to a boil, cover the pot, and steam the mussels until open, depending upon their size. Do not overcook or the mussels will rapidly lose flavor.

Lift the mussels into a serving bowl. Strain the broth through coffee filters and serve with the mussels. (Or freeze to use as a liquid for cooking fish.)

With a slotted spoon, transfer the mussels and their shells to a serving bowl.

LEFTOVERS

Mussel Salad

(Serves 1)

1/3 cup whole leftover mussels	Salt and freshly ground black
removed from their shells	pepper (optional)
1 tablespoon chopped tomato	Boston lettuce or fresh baby
1 tablespoon chopped scallion	spinach leaves
3 tablespoons liquor from	1 ripe tomato
mussels	1/2 teaspoon minced chives

Mix together the mussels, tomato, scallion, and mussel liquor. Taste and season with salt and pepper, if you wish. Mound on washed and dried Boston lettuce leaves. Cut the tomato into wedges and arrange around the mussels. Sprinkle the mussels with the chives.

Variation

Mussels and Pasta. Toss the above mixture with 3 ounces fresh cooked *pasta.* Season with salt and pepper. Serve with 2 tablespoons grated *Parmesan* cheese (optional).

BAKED OYSTERS WITH GARLIC BUTTER

A major advantage of cooking for one is that you can occasionally treat yourself to a food that would be prohibitively expensive if you were feeding a family. In much of the country, oysters fall into that category. Yet savoring the briny flavor of truly fresh oysters (that haven't been excessively washed, a reason so many "fresh" oysters taste insipid) turns a simple meal into an occasion. Even if you think you don't like oysters (or are hesitant to eat them raw), try baking them in their shells—a quick and easy method that accentuates their sweet flavor and delicate texture. When they're done, the oysters' shells will be slightly opened. It's handy to have an oyster knife to finish opening them, but if you can't locate one (found in many fish shops or kitchen stores), use the blade of a well-washed thin screwdriver to finish opening the baked oysters. Just insert it at the hinged section of each shell and twist.

(Serves 1)

8–12 raw oysters
1 clove garlic, finely minced

1 tablespoon butter

Place the raw oysters in their shells on a cookie sheet and bake in a preheated 375°F oven for 20–25 minutes, or until the shells open slightly or the liquids start oozing out. Do not overbake or the oysters' flesh will toughen. Meanwhile, simmer the garlic and butter together in a small pot on the stove for a minute or two, or microwave for 30 seconds, to mingle the flavors. Do not let the garlic brown. Dip the cooked oysters in the butter—and enjoy.

BAKED SCALLOPS WITH PESTO

This sauce works wonders with any kind of scallops.

(Serves 1)

2 tablespoons *Pesto* (page 202)   4 ounces fresh scallops
3 tablespoons breadcrumbs

Mix the pesto with 2 tablespoons of the breadcrumbs. Toss with the scallops. Place in a buttered baking dish just large enough to hold the scallops in one layer and sprinkle with the remaining tablespoon of crumbs. Bake in a preheated 450°F oven for 10–12 minutes, or until the scallops are cooked through and the crumbs are browned.

SCALLOP AND CELERY STEW

This is an excellent way to round out the flavor of less-than-perfect scallops, such as the Calico scallops found in many supermarkets in the South, which are slightly steamed before they're sold.

(Serves 1)

1 tablespoon butter   2 cups milk
1 cup thinly sliced onions   Salt and freshly ground black
1/2 cup chopped celery or fennel   pepper
1/4 pound scallops   1 teaspoon minced parsley

Heat the butter in a heavy pot and stir in the onions. Cook them over low heat, stirring frequently, for about 10 minutes. Add the celery, and continue cooking another 10 minutes. Add the scallops and cook 2–3 minutes, stirring constantly. Pour in the milk and slowly heat. Do not let boil. Taste and season with salt and pepper. Sprinkle with parsley before serving.

VARIATIONS

Oyster Stew. Reduce the onions to 1/2 cup. Substitute 6–8 shucked *oysters* for the scallops.

With shrimp. Garnish with 2 *shrimp*.

"My cooking is pretty primitive. I eat out mostly. I have a small repertoire of dishes, such as tuna melt or hamburgers. I fix a lot of salads and vegetables. I'll buy a prepared pizza dough and put on my own toppings, or I fix pasta because it's easy and I can come home from work and put together a meal fast. I like eating alone. I sit with the paper over dinner and relax."

Gil Anav, lawyer

BOILED SHRIMP

"I never get enough shrimp," a friend laments about standard shrimp cocktails. Most of us can eat 1/4 to 1/2 pound cooked shrimp quite easily (the amount listed below is only a guide). Remember that the larger the shrimp, the more expensive the price and the longer the cooking time. For shrimp cocktail, ask for medium-sized shrimp.

Previously frozen shrimp are the norm at the market. It's rare to find fresh shrimp except in the Gulf of Mexico ports of the Southern coast. If you have a source for fresh shrimp, count yourself lucky for they have a sweet flavor that can't be duplicated. Regardless of whether they're fresh or defrosted, shrimp should be cooked only for a minute or two. You can tell when shrimp are done because they turn pink and have a firm texture. If their texture is flaccid and soft, throw away the shrimp. They're too old (or overcooked) to eat.

(Serves 1)

Water
1/2 lemon, thinly sliced
Peppercorns
2 bay leaves (optional)

1 onion, sliced
4–6 ounces raw shrimp in shells,
    heads removed

Fill a large nonaluminum pot with enough water to cover the shrimp. Add the lemon, about 8 peppercorns, the bay leaves (if using), and the onion. Bring the mixture to a boil, turn the heat down, and simmer for

Boiled Shrimp (continued)

about 10 minutes. Bring again to a boil, add the shrimp, and gently boil for 1–2 minutes, depending upon their size.

Drain the shrimp, either run under cold water or plunge into ice water to stop the cooking process, and drain again. Serve with commercial cocktail sauce into which you could add grated horseradish to taste and fresh lemon juice.

VARIATIONS

Hot Shrimp with Garlic Butter. **Drain the shrimp as above. Serve warm with 2–3 tablespoons of** *butter* **microwaved for 30–40 seconds with a dash of** *hot pepper sauce* **and 1 clove minced** *garlic.* **Dip the shrimp into the butter.**

With soy-sesame sauce. **Drain the shrimp as above. Mix together 1 tablespoon** *soy sauce,* **1 teaspoon minced** *garlic,* **and dashes of** *Oriental sesame oil* **and** *balsamic vinegar* **to taste. Dip the shrimp into the sauce.**

SAUTÉED SHRIMP WITH GARLIC AND SCALLIONS

This recipe takes about 6 minutes to prepare. Do try the variation with lemongrass if you can track down this delicious herb, which is used frequently in Thai cooking; it provides a distinctive counterpoint to the shrimp. (Oriental markets stock fresh lemongrass in the produce department. Or, if you live in a warm climate, plant some in your garden, where it will thrive year-round.)

(Serves 1)

2 teaspoons butter
1 scallion, thinly sliced, both
  green and white portions
  (about 2 tablespoons)
1 clove garlic, minced (about
  1 teaspoon)

3–4 ounces peeled shrimp
1 tablespoon freshly squeezed
  lime, orange, lemon, or
  grapefruit juice

Heat the butter in a large frying pan, add the scallion and garlic, and cook over medium-high heat for 1 minute, stirring constantly. Add the shrimp, lower the heat slightly, and cook for 2 minutes longer, stirring frequently. Add the citrus juice, stir to coat the shrimp, and serve immediately with rice and a salad.

VARIATION

Shrimp with Lemongrass. Add 1–2 teaspoons minced *lemongrass* and a pinch of *cayenne pepper* along with the shrimp. Proceed as above.

BAKED SHRIMP WITH BREADCRUMBS

This easy recipe is delicious enough for company. Use fresh breadcrumbs (not packaged) and fresh basil. The breadcrumbs keep the shrimp from drying out and add textural contrast. You can assemble this in the morning before you head for work and pop it in the oven while you relax at the end of the day.

(Serves 1)

3 ounces peeled raw shrimp	3 tablespoons dry breadcrumbs
2 teaspoons melted butter	1 tablespoon chopped basil

Toss the shrimp with the melted butter and spread them out in a single layer in a small baking dish. Mix the breadcrumbs and basil together (a blender is handy—but not essential). Sprinkle the breadcrumb mixture over the shrimp and top with any remaining melted butter. Bake in a preheated 350°F oven for about 15–20 minutes, or until the shrimp turn pink and are cooked through. Do not overcook or the shrimp will toughen.

VARIATIONS

Shrimp with Garlic and Parsley Breadcrumbs. Add 2 teaspoons minced *garlic* to the breadcrumbs, and substitute *parsley* for the basil. Proceed as above.

Shrimp with Tarragon Breadcrumbs. Substitute 2 teaspoons chopped *fresh tarragon* for the basil.

THE CONVENIENCE FOOD TRAP

An insidious aspect of living alone is how quickly (and painlessly) you can slide into the take-out food trap. When you need to cook only for yourself, it's so easy to opt for convenience—to buy a pastry and a coffee for breakfast, grab a sandwich and soft drink for lunch, and then pick up a taco or chef's salad for dinner. Many convenience foods taste just fine. Unfortunately, they're often chock-full of preservatives and fat. And, thanks to the need for uniformity, they always taste the same.

However, when you're in the mood to eat fast, you're willing to overlook these drawbacks. You tell yourself that you're too tired to cook after working hard all day. Or that you don't even have time to talk with your friends, let alone cook a meal. When life calms down, you'll start preparing dinner.

Sound familiar?

I used all these arguments when I was in my convenience-food phase. One day I just got tired of the heavy taste of prepared foods. I had dribbled away a *lot* of money. But, above all, I wanted my own cooking.

I was hungry for chicken with vegetables, mashed potatoes, and a basil and tomato salad. I wanted leftovers to make a hefty club sandwich or a fresh chicken noodle soup. I craved a simple stir-fry of broccoli that wasn't dripping with oil—or a tender biscuit that tasted homemade. I hoped never again to see another container of pasta tossed with sundried tomatoes, or greasy fried chicken. It was time to get out of the take-out line and back into the kitchen.

I was ready to cook for myself.

POULTRY

Many single cooks roast a chicken, then gnaw on it on and off for days until they're heartily sick of facing even one more morsel. Roast chicken is delicious (and you'll find a master recipe in this chapter), but it's not the most useful way to cook a whole chicken when you're alone. Instead, if you want chicken for leftovers, you could try braising it, a method that keeps leftover chicken moist because it's cooked and stored in liquid.

Chances are, however, that you're more likely to prepare smaller amounts of chicken. Virtually all markets sell chicken parts, allowing you to purchase exactly what you need in small quantities. Or, if you prefer, you can buy a whole chicken and divide it up yourself, which costs far less. That's what I do (see *Chicken Management*, page 126). Out of one chicken, I'll end up with at least four meals. Sliced chicken from a whole breast stuffed under the skin with garlic or sliced lemons and roasted at a high temperature has a wonderful flavor. Roasting a smaller portion gives me a portion of chicken for dinner with just enough left over for sandwiches. Another night, I might barbecue the thighs or braise the legs in a Basque-style sauce—two festive inexpensive entrées. I'll store the wings in the freezer until I have enough to cook in a hot, spicy sauce, along with the other chicken parts I'm not cooking within a day or two.

Now even in small towns you can find ground turkey, turkey cutlets, and turkey wings. I usually ask the butcher to repackage the ground turkey into 1/2-pound portions to use for chili or meatballs. Cutlets are particularly good smothered in vegetables, while the wings make an inexpensive main course with leftovers for soup.

I've given you a wide sampling of poultry recipes. Poultry is one of the most versatile and inexpensive foods available today—yet it's one of the easiest for the single cook to handle.

CHICKEN MANAGEMENT

One of the advantages of the solo state is buying exactly what you want to eat. For many poultry fanciers this means purchasing only cut-up chicken, such as boneless chicken breasts. When you're cooking for one, even when boneless chicken breast costs almost $5 a pound, the final sum isn't that outrageous.

But, if you happen to like eating both the white and the dark meat— and you don't cringe at the thought of cutting up a carcass—you can save a lot of money. Whole chickens are frequently sold as "loss leaders" (rock-bottom prices where the market sells the item virtually at cost to bring customers into the store). By dividing up the chicken, you end up with several meals and can freeze any portions you don't want to use immediately.

I prefer to separate the dark meat from the white, because when you're cooking solo, you often use them in different recipes. My method leaves the breast attached to some of the backbone (making a natural "rack" for roasting), and the legs and thighs attached to each other—in case you want to grill them or cook them as one piece. Cutting up a chicken sounds very anatomical, but, once you have the chicken in front of you, you'll see how easy it is to do. It takes me less than a minute to cut up a chicken (but I've had years of practice: count on five minutes the first try). You must have a sharp knife.

Cutting a chicken into pieces. Put the chicken in the sink. Reach into the cavity and remove both the bag containing the chicken innards and any fat. Rinse the chicken, inside and out, under cold running water. Dry the chicken and place it on a flat surface, breast side down. Press down as hard as you can on the backbone to flatten it.

Turn over the chicken so that it is now breast side up. (I'm right-handed, so I work left to right; if you're left-handed, reverse the directions.) Pull the left leg slightly away from the body and slice down through the skin. Pull the leg farther away from the body so that you can see the natural junction of the thigh and breast. Simultaneously, pull the leg and thigh away from the breast with one hand and slice down to the beginning of the backbone with the other. Repeat this step with the remaining leg and thigh. At this point, the chicken is held together only by its backbone.

Turn the chicken over onto its breast and press down hard on the center of the back. This will break the backbone.

Cut through the broken backbone at the break point. Now all the white meat is separated from the dark meat. You have two portions: a breast and wings with some of the backbone attached, and the legs and thighs held together with the remaining backbone.

To cut off the wings, pull a wing back toward the backbone. This will show you where the socket is (the easiest place to detach the wing). Cut around the socket and remove the wing. Repeat with the other wing. Remove the wing tips and set them aside with the chicken innards. Divide each wing in two at the second joint and set aside.

If you want to separate the dark meat further, cut down where the leg joins the thigh and remove the leg. Repeat with the other leg and thigh. The thighs are still attached in one piece. If you like roasted dark meat, press down on the backbone to flatten the thighs and roast them as one piece. Or, to separate, place the thighs skin side down on the counter and, to the left of the tail, slice down, dividing into two thighs. You will end up with one portion that has the backbone attached to it. If you'd prefer to use it for stock, cut away the backbone.

You now have the potential for several meals. You should wash and dry the chicken innards (and the wing tips) that are in the plastic or paper wrap. You can put them into a heavy resealable plastic bag and freeze until you have enough to make a stock. If you're feeling particularly frugal, you can store the chicken livers in a recycled plastic container (such as a yogurt or cottage cheese container) and put them in the freezer to make *Chicken Livers Sautéed with Herbs* (page 155), once you've accumulated about 6. Or, you can sauté them and add to tomato sauce (bottled is fine) and serve over pasta as they do in central Italy.

After cutting up a few chickens you'll be a pro—and you'll congratulate yourself on how much money you're saving every time you pass up a package of cut-up chicken.

POACHED CHICKEN BREAST WITH TARRAGON

Cooling the chicken breast in the liquid keeps it moist and adds extra flavor to this low-calorie, low-fat meal. If you prefer chicken with a sauce, make one of the variations.

(Makes 1–2 servings)

2 cups chicken stock or water
1 whole chicken breast
3 sprigs tarragon
3 sprigs parsley

2 tablespoons chopped celery
  (optional)
Salt and freshly ground black
  pepper

Put the chicken stock and chicken breast in a small pot, bring the liquid to a boil, and lower the heat. Add the tarragon, parsley, and celery, if using, and gently simmer the chicken for 15 minutes. Remove the pan from the heat and let the chicken cool in the stock. To serve, skin and bone the chicken, slice the meat, and spoon over some of the stock. Season with salt and pepper to taste.

LEFTOVERS

Chicken in a Mushroom Sauce

(Serves 1)

2 teaspoons butter
1 tablespoon chopped scallion
2 teaspoons flour
1/2 cup hot tarragon-flavored
  poaching stock (see above)

1/2 cup thinly sliced mushrooms
  (about 5)
1 cup sliced cooked chicken
Salt and freshly ground black
  pepper

Heat the butter in a small saucepan. Add the scallion and cook for 1 minute over medium heat, stirring frequently, or until slightly wilted. Off the heat stir in the flour. Return the pan to the heat and cook the flour mixture for 1 minute, stirring constantly. Add the stock and stir rapidly until it is incorporated. (This is easiest with a whisk.) Then, cook the sauce for 3 minutes, stirring frequently. It will be lightly thickened. Stir in the mushrooms and cook 2–3 minutes longer or until they are cooked through. Add the sliced chicken and continue cooking until it is reheated. Season with salt and pepper to taste. If you wish add 1 teaspoon of sliced scallion greens or chopped tomatoes for color.

NEW-STYLE CHICKEN PAPRIKASH

Leftover chicken works well in this flavorful one-pot recipe. Sour cream is traditional, but you can substitute yogurt if you wish. Hungarian sweet paprika is sold in the gourmet sections of most large supermarkets and at specialty food stores. In Hungary this would be served with a sliced cucumber or pepper salad and noodles.

(Serves 1)

2 teaspoons butter
1/3 cup chopped onion
1/3 cup seeded and chopped
   green pepper
1 tablespoon flour
2–3 teaspoons sweet Hungarian
   paprika
1/3–1/2 cup homemade or
   canned chicken stock, at
   room temperature

1/3 cup peeled, seeded, and
   chopped tomato
3/4–1 cup coarsely chopped or
   shredded cooked chicken
2 tablespoons sour cream or
   yogurt
Salt and/or freshly ground black
   pepper

Heat the butter in a small stove-top pot. Stir in the onion and green pepper and cook for 1 minute over medium heat. Cover the pan and cook 5 minutes longer, stirring frequently. Remove the cover, add the flour and paprika, and cook 2 minutes longer, stirring constantly. Off the heat stir in the stock, and return to the heat. Cook, stirring occasionally, for 3 minutes. Add the tomato and chicken, and slowly cook just long enough to reheat the chicken (about 2 minutes). Stir in the sour cream. Season to taste with salt and/or pepper. Serve immediately.

VARIATION

Chicken Curry. Substitute 2 teaspoons chopped *jalapeño peppers* for the

New-Style Chicken Paprikash (continued)
bell pepper, a good-quality *curry powder* for the paprika, and yogurt for the sour cream. Add 1 tablespoon chopped *basil* just before serving. Serve over rice.

CRUNCHY CHICKEN

This exceptionally easy method can also be used for boneless pork, turkey cutlets—and even vegetables, such as eggplant and zucchini. All are equally tasty. I like to vary the cheeses, but Parmesan is always a safe choice. The breadcrumbs should be fine and dry.

(Serves 1)

2 tablespoons grated cheese,
    such as Parmesan, Swiss, or
    cheddar
3 tablespoons breadcrumbs
1 medium egg
1 teaspoon soy sauce

1 teaspoon water
Flour
1 boneless chicken breast,
    halved lengthwise (about 3
    ounces)
1–2 teaspoons butter

Mix together the cheese and breadcrumbs in a shallow bowl. In a separate bowl, beat the egg with the soy sauce and water. Spread the flour on a piece of waxed paper or a plate, and dip the chicken breast first in the flour, then the egg, and turn over and over in the cheese-and-breadcrumb mixture until it is completely coated. Gently shake off any excess crumbs.

Put the butter in a medium-sized baking dish and place it in a preheated 450°F oven just long enough so the butter melts. Tilt the dish to coat it with butter. Put the chicken in the dish, and bake in the oven for about 20 minutes, or until the coating browns and the chicken is cooked through. Turn once. (The coating encases the chicken and keeps it moist.)

VARIATIONS

With herbs. Add 1 tablespoon chopped fresh herbs, such as a mixture of *basil and tarragon, sweet marjoram*—or, if you can locate it, *lemongrass* or *lovage.*

With mustard. Add 1 teaspoon Dijon or whole seed *mustard* to the egg mixture. Proceed as above.

With cornmeal. Omit the breadcrumbs and cheese. Use the variation with *mustard* and roll the chicken in *cornmeal* rather than breadcrumbs. (When this bakes, it's similar to a fried food but without the fat. It's a good technique for fish.)

Crunchy Eggplant. Omit the chicken. Slice a 1/2–3/4 pound *eggplant* into 1/2-inch-thick pieces. *Salt* lightly, and let sit for about 10 minutes (you want to leave some moisture). Blot dry. Add 1/3 teaspoon salt to the cheese-and-breadcrumb mixture. Substitute *olive oil* for the butter and use 1–2 tablespoons oil. Proceed as above.

Crunchy Double-Thick Pork Chop. Squeeze *lemon juice* over both sides of a thick *pork chop* (about 1 inch thick), then sprinkle lightly with a good-quality *curry powder.* Proceed as above, baking for 40 minutes.

Note: You'll probably have some leftover egg mixture. If you cut a thick slice or two of a *sweet onion,* dip it in the egg (preferably the version with mustard) and then in the breadcrumbs—or cornmeal—and bake along with the chicken, you end up with a tasty onion side dish vaguely reminiscent of fried onion rings.

SAUTÉED CHICKEN BREAST WITH BASIL

This recipe takes about 15 minutes from start to finish. It needs color—so serve it with a vivid side dish such as a tomato salad (especially nice made with both yellow and red tomatoes) or a sliced orange and onion salad.

(Serves 1)

3 ounces boned and skinned
   chicken breast
Flour
1–2 teaspoons butter
3 tablespoons shredded basil
2 cloves garlic, crushed and
   chopped

1/2 cup thinly sliced sweet
   onion (about 1/2 onion)
1/2–3/4 cup chicken stock
Salt and freshly ground black
   pepper
1 teaspoon mustard with mustard seeds (optional)

Sautéed Chicken Breast with Basil (continued)

Cut the chicken breast into 1/2-inch-thick slices. Dip in flour and shake to remove any excess. Heat 1 teaspoon of the butter in a heavy frying pan and cook the chicken, stirring frequently, over medium heat until it is lightly browned, about 2 minutes. Remove from the pan and add the remaining butter if necessary. Stir in 2 tablespoons of the basil, the garlic, and the onion. Cook for 1 minute, stirring constantly, then add 1/2 cup of the stock, scraping up any brown particles in the pan. Return the chicken to the pan, and cook, uncovered, for 5 minutes, stirring frequently. Add the rest of the stock or water if needed. Taste and season with salt and pepper. Stir in the mustard, if using, and sprinkle with the remaining basil.

PIQUANT BONELESS CHICKEN BREAST

This chicken is ready in 10 minutes. If your chicken stock is frozen in cubes (see page 17), add them to the pan while still frozen. They'll defrost immediately. Frozen juice concentrate also works well. An opened can will hold in the refrigerator for about 5 days—or you can refreeze the concentrate in ice cube trays and use in the first variation.

(Serves 1)

1 skinned, boneless chicken breast (about 3 ounces)	1 teaspoon minced garlic
Freshly ground black pepper	3 tablespoons chicken stock
Dry mustard or cayenne pepper	1 teaspoon lemon or lime juice
Flour	Salt (optional)
2 teaspoons butter or olive oil	Lemon slice

Halve the chicken lengthwise. Sprinkle with black pepper and a pinch of dry mustard or cayenne pepper. Place about 1 tablespoon flour in a paper bag and shake the chicken pieces in it. Heat the butter in a heavy frying pan. Shake the chicken pieces to remove any excess flour and place them in the pan. Cook over medium-high heat for 4–5 minutes, or until browned and cooked through, turning once. Set the pieces aside loosely covered by a kitchen towel to keep warm. Tip the pan, blot out the fat with a paper towel, leaving just a film. Add the garlic and cook for 30 seconds over medium heat, stirring constantly. Add the chicken stock, lemon or lime juice, and salt (if desired) and cook 30 seconds longer. Pour the sauce over the chicken and garnish with a halved lemon slice.

VARIATIONS

With pineapple-orange concentrate. Proceed as above, omitting the garlic and lemon juice. Add 1 tablespoon *frozen pineapple-orange concentrate* along with the chicken stock and 1 tablespoon sliced *scallion.* Cook over high heat, stirring constantly, until the sauce almost forms a glaze, about 2 minutes. (If you let it reduce too far, the sauce will burn.) Put the chicken back in the pan and roll in the glaze before serving.

With tarragon. Add 1 teaspoon chopped *tarragon* along with the garlic.

With capers. Add 1/2 teaspoon chopped *capers* along with the chicken stock.

BAKED CHICKEN WITH COUNTRY-STYLE MILK GRAVY

This simple recipe for baked chicken was my mother's favorite way of cooking chicken when she was in a hurry. I vary the accompaniments depending upon the contents of the refrigerator, but in this version, the juices from the cherry tomatoes and mushrooms flavor the gravy. Halving the pieces speeds up the cooking time.

(Serves 1)

2 pieces chicken, halved	2 teaspoons butter
1/2 lemon	4 cherry tomatoes
2 tablespoons flour	4–6 large mushrooms
1/4 teaspoon dry mustard	1 small onion, peeled and quartered
Salt and freshly ground black pepper	1/3 cup milk

Place the chicken pieces on a flat surface and squeeze lemon juice over their surfaces. Put the flour, dry mustard, salt, and a generous amount of

Baked Chicken with Country-Style Milk Gravy (continued)

black pepper into a small plastic or paper bag. Hold the bag shut and shake it. Add the chicken pieces and shake until they are thoroughly coated with flour. Remove them from the bag, shake off any excess flour, and place in a stove-top baking dish. Dot them with butter. Use a corner of the butter wrapper to lightly butter the tomatoes and mushrooms. Scatter them around the chicken along with the onion.

Bake the chicken in a preheated 425°F oven for 20–25 minutes, basting everything once. The cooking time depends upon whether you're preparing white or dark meat. Remove the pan from the oven and place the contents on a plate. Pour off all but 1 teaspoon of the fat from the pan and stir in 1 teaspoon of the flour remaining in the bag, making sure that all the pan juices are incorporated. Cook the mixture on top of the stove over medium heat for 1–2 minutes to remove any raw taste. Off the heat, stir in the milk. Cook over low heat for 3 minutes, stirring constantly and adding a tablespoon of water if the gravy is too thick. Taste and season with additional salt and pepper if necessary. Pour over the chicken.

VARIATIONS

With chicken stock. Substitute *chicken stock* for the milk.

With zucchini and celery. Omit the tomatoes and mushrooms. Substitute 1/2 cup thickly sliced *zucchini* and 2 stalks *celery,* cut into 1-inch lengths.

BONELESS CHICKEN SAUTÉED WITH PEARS

This specialty of northern Spain is a flavorful way to use up any extra pears you may have on hand. Either rice or noodles would go well with the chicken.

(Serves 1)

2 teaspoons butter or canola oil
4–6 ounces boned and skinned
    chicken breast, cut into
    1/2-inch-wide slices

1/3 cup thinly sliced scallions
1 cup peeled, seeded, and sliced
    pears (about 1–11/2 pears)

3/4 cup chicken stock	1/4 teaspoon red wine vinegar
1 teaspoon minced parsley	(optional)
(optional)	Salt

Heat the fat in a heavy nonreactive frying pan with a cover. Over high heat, quickly sear the sliced chicken. Lift from the pan and set aside.

Add the scallions and pears to the pan, and cook over high heat, stirring constantly, for 1 minute. The pears will be lightly seared. Place the chicken back in the pan, lower the heat, and add the stock. Cover the pan and cook over medium heat for 5 minutes. Taste. The pears should be cooked through but retain some texture. If you prefer a thick sauce that will coat the pears and chicken, remove them with a slotted spoon and boil the sauce, stirring constantly, until it is the consistency you prefer. (It usually takes 1–2 minutes to reduce to a coating consistency, but this depends upon the juiciness of the pears.) If you like, add the parsley and red wine vinegar to the sauce. Season to taste with salt.

VARIATIONS

With celery. Add 1/4 cup chopped *celery* along with the pears.

With apples. Substitute slices of a firm-textured *apple* (such as Cortland) for the pears. Proceed as above.

With white wine and cream. Omit the vinegar. Just before boiling the stock, add 2 teaspoons dry *white wine* (*or* 1 teaspoon dry *sherry*). Reduce (boil down) the stock and stir in 1 tablespoon *heavy cream.* Reheat the sauce without boiling. Taste and season with salt.

Meal-in-One. Add 1 peeled and sliced *carrot* along with the pears. After the pears are cooked through, stir in 3/4–1 cup cooked *rice, barley, or pasta* such as shells. Cover the pan and cook over low heat until the rice is reheated, about 3 minutes.

BACK-TO-THE-SIXTIES CHICKEN BREAST

Baking chicken with frozen juice concentrates was big in the 1960s, but we didn't have exotic combinations such as pineapple-orange. This is vaguely reminiscent of the Hawaiian chicken of that era—and takes about 2 minutes to put together.

(Serves 1)

1 boned half chicken breast
1 tablespoon pineapple-orange
    juice concentrate
1 teaspoon soy sauce
3/4–1 cup thinly sliced green
    pepper

3/4 cup thinly sliced onion
1 teaspoon chopped garlic
2 tablespoons water or a dry
    sherry/water combination
Salt (optional)

Skin the breast and put it in a small baking dish just large enough to hold the chicken and vegetables. Top with the pineapple-orange juice concentrate and the soy sauce. Scatter the green pepper, onion, and garlic around the chicken. Add the water to the pan.

Bake in a preheated 450°F oven for about 15–20 minutes, basting occasionally. Toward the end of the cooking time, you may need to add additional water. (The water keeps the concentrate from scorching on the bottom of the pan.) The chicken will be browned and have a slight glaze from the concentrate. Season with salt, if you wish.

CHICKEN WITH CELERY AND LEEKS

You get two meals with this easy meal-in-one: A baked chicken dinner and a flavorful soup that's like a lighter version of vichyssoise, made with yogurt. This meal lacks color, so you might want to serve it with a tomato salad.

(Serves 1)

1 chicken leg and thigh
3 small potatoes
1 cup thinly sliced celery
1 cup sliced leeks

Freshly ground black pepper
1–1 1/4 cups chicken stock or
    water, approximately
Salt

Skin the chicken, if you wish. Put it in a small, deep, ovenproof casserole. Peel and halve the potatoes. Scatter them over the chicken along with the celery and leeks and a liberal sprinkling of black pepper. Cover with the chicken stock, adding additional stock or water if necessary.

Bake the chicken in a preheated 425°F oven for about 40 minutes, or until the chicken and potatoes are cooked through, basting occasionally and adding water if needed. Remove the pan from the oven and taste the sauce. Season to taste with salt. If it is watery, pour it into a saucepan and rapidly boil it down until it has the intensity of flavor you prefer. (Loosely cover the chicken to keep it warm.) Taste and season with salt. Serve the chicken pieces surrounded by the vegetables.

LEFTOVERS

Cold Leek and Potato Soup. Purée every 1¹/4 cups of leftover vegetable and stock mixture with ¹/4 cup nonfat *yogurt*. If you have less vegetables and stock, adjust the amount of yogurt accordingly. Add a pinch of *cayenne pepper* and salt to taste. Chill before serving with a garnish of chopped *chives* or *scallion greens*.

CHICKEN BREAST BAKED WITH GARLIC

The garlic imparts a subtle flavor to the chicken, making it an excellent choice to eat as is—or in sandwiches or composed salads for lunches at work.

(Makes 1–2 servings)

1 whole chicken breast
1–2 teaspoons cold butter,
  thinly sliced
2 teaspoons finely chopped
  garlic

Salt and freshly ground black
  pepper

Loosen the skin on the chicken breast and lift it up. Cover the flesh with the thin slices of butter, then sprinkle with the garlic. Lightly sprinkle with salt and grind a generous amount of black pepper over the flesh. Replace and smooth out the skin, place breast in an ovenproof pan, and

Chicken Breast Baked with Garlic (continued)
bake in a preheated 450°F oven for 25–30 minutes or until cooked through. Remove from the oven and let the chicken sit for at least 20 minutes. Discard the skin and garlic pieces before serving. (If you're making a stock, add them to the broth.)

VARIATIONS

Chicken with Bread Stuffing

You either can stuff the chicken breast under its skin (omitting the butter and the garlic), or you can fill the cavity between the breast and the backbone. You don't need the egg, but it binds the stuffing together.

(Makes 1–2 servings)

1 teaspoon butter
3–4 tablespoons chopped onion
    or scallions
1/2 cup chopped celery
1 cup shredded stale bread
3 tablespoons chicken stock or
    water

Salt and freshly ground black
    pepper
2 teaspoons chopped parsley or
    sweet marjoram (optional)
1 medium egg (optional)
1 whole chicken breast

Put the butter in a frying pan, add the onion and celery and cook over medium heat, stirring frequently, for 5 minutes. Add the bread, toss to distribute the onion and celery, and stir for 1 minute. Stir in the stock or water. Season with salt, pepper, and parsley, if using. Remove the mixture from the stove and combine, if you like, with the egg. Stuff the chicken and proceed as above.

With lemons. Place *lemon* slices over the surface before roasting.

SAVORY CHICKEN WINGS

If you cut up chickens and store the wings in the freezer, you soon accumulate enough wings for a supper. (Or you can buy 1/2 pound of chicken wings at the supermarket.) These wings taste equally good served at room temperature.

(Serves 1)

1/4 teaspoon dry mustard
1 tablespoon sherry (either sweet or dry)
2 tablespoons soy or teriyaki sauce
1/8 teaspoon cayenne pepper

1 teaspoon minced garlic
1/4 teaspoon coarsely ground black pepper
1/2 teaspoon cocktail bitters (optional; see Note)
4–6 chicken wings

In a small baking dish, mix together the mustard, sherry, soy sauce, cayenne pepper, garlic, black pepper, and bitters, if using. Add the chicken wings and turn them in the sauce. Bake in a preheated 425°F oven for 20–25 minutes, or until cooked through, turning occasionally.

VARIATION

Savory Chicken Livers. This sauce is equally good with *chicken livers.* Substitute 4 ounces chicken livers for the wings. Proceed as above, checking after 15 minutes to see if the livers are done. They should be cooked through, but still pink in the center.

Note: Cocktail bitters, such as Angostura, are sold in liquor stores and some supermarkets.

HOT SAUCE CHICKEN WINGS

The proportions I'm suggesting for the marinade are only a guideline. All you need to do is put the wings in a glass bowl, squeeze over some lime juice, add the sauces, and stir in the honey and garlic. I prefer to cut the wings into individual pieces, but that's up to you. You can marinate the wings in the refrigerator all day and broil them when you're ready. These wings are also good served cold for picnics.

(Serves 1)

3–5 chicken wings, tips removed
1/4–1/3 cup freshly squeezed lime juice
1 teaspoon hot pepper sauce (such as Tabasco)

1/4 teaspoon Worcestershire sauce
1/2–1 teaspoon soy sauce
1 teaspoon honey
1 teaspoon finely minced garlic
Freshly ground black pepper

Hot Sauce Chicken Wings (continued)

Put the chicken wings in a glass bowl. Add the lime juice, hot pepper sauce, Worcestershire sauce, soy sauce, honey, garlic, and a generous sprinkling of black pepper. Marinate from 30 minutes at room temperature to 24 hours in the refrigerator. Remove the wings from the marinade, place them on a broiler pan, and spoon over some of the marinade. Broil in a preheated oven for 5 minutes, turn the wings, spoon over some of the marinade, and cook another 5–8 minutes, turning once. The flavor is better if you let them cool slightly before serving.

VARIATION

Hot Sauce Spareribs. This sauce is equally good with *spareribs or pork chops.* Simmer the ribs in water until they are cooked through, dry them, then marinate them for 15 minutes before broiling.

GLAZED CHICKEN WITH CARROTS

The frozen orange juice concentrate cooks together with the vegetables and stock to form a flavorful sauce for the chicken. Count on about 5 minutes of preparation and 30 minutes in the oven.

(Serves 1)

1 chicken leg and thigh (or
   1 chicken breast)
1 carrot
2 tablespoons chopped celery
3 tablespoons chopped scallions
1 teaspoon chopped garlic
1/2 teaspoon Dijon mustard or
   mustard made with mustard
   seeds

1 tablespoon frozen orange
   juice concentrate
2 teaspoons lime juice
   (optional)
Freshly ground black pepper
1/4 cup chicken stock or water

Put the chicken in a small, shallow ovenproof pan just large enough to hold it and the vegetables in one layer. Peel the carrot, halve it lengthwise, and cut it into diagonal slices about 1/2 inch wide. Scatter it around the chicken along with the celery and scallions. Sprinkle with the garlic. With your fingertips spread the mustard over the skin of the chicken, and top with the frozen orange juice concentrate and optional lime juice. Generously grind black pepper over the surface and pour the stock around the chicken.

Bake in a preheated 450°F oven for 30 minutes, basting occasionally.

Note: To bake a potato quickly, halve a baking potato, brush with oil, and cut an X in the tops so that the steam can escape. Place the potato halves on the oven rack and bake along with the chicken. The potato and chicken will be done at approximately the same time.

BASQUE-STYLE CHICKEN

The vegetable juices flavor the sauce, giving this easy-to-make chicken a subtle, yet full, flavor. If you can locate both red and yellow tomatoes, it makes for a more colorful sauce. There is enough sauce to cook a larger amount of chicken if you wish.

(Makes 1–2 servings)

2 tablespoons olive oil
2 chicken thighs—or 2 thighs
    and 2 legs
2 teaspoons minced garlic
1 bell pepper, seeded and
    thinly sliced

3/4 cup chopped onion
2 cups peeled, seeded, and
    chopped tomatoes
Salt and freshly ground black
    pepper

Heat the olive oil in a heavy frying pan with a cover. Over medium heat, brown the chicken pieces in the oil for about 10 minutes. Remove them and set aside. To the same pan, add the garlic, and cook over medium heat for 1 minute, stirring constantly. Add the pepper and onion, and cook 2 minutes longer, stirring frequently. Pour off the fat. Add the tomatoes and cook, stirring frequently, for about 3 minutes, or until the tomatoes are slightly cooked.

Place the chicken in a heavy stove-top casserole and top with the tomato mixture. Cover and simmer over low heat for about 25–30 minutes, or until cooked through. Season to taste with salt and freshly ground pepper. Serve over rice or pasta shells.

Baroque-Style Chicken (continued)

Note: The cooking fat is flavorful. Pour it into a small bowl and refrigerate it for future use.

VARIATIONS

Chicken with Capers. Add 1–2 teaspoons chopped *capers* about 5 minutes before the chicken is cooked through. Taste and season with *lemon juice* and additional black pepper if you like.

Chicken with Olives. Add 1/2 cup rinsed good-quality *green or black olives* about 10 minutes before the chicken is cooked through.

LEFTOVERS

Use any leftovers to make an omelet filling or tortilla stuffing. Skin and bone the chicken and coarsely chop it. Cover with the sauce and refrigerate for no longer than 3 days.

SMOTHERED CHICKEN WITH GREEN BEANS

This is a satisfying dish on a cool winter night served with mashed potatoes or rice and a tossed salad with tomatoes. Skin the chicken if you wish.

(Serves 1)

2 chicken thighs (or breasts), halved	1–1 1/4 cups chicken stock
1/2 juicy lemon	1 cup thinly sliced mushrooms
Freshly ground black pepper	1 sprig fresh thyme
Flour	2 ounces trimmed fresh green beans (about 1 cup)
Oil	Salt
1 teaspoon chopped garlic	1–2 teaspoons minced parsley

Place the chicken pieces on a flat surface and sprinkle with the lemon juice and black pepper. Dip in flour, shake to remove any excess, and set aside. In a small stove-top casserole, heat enough oil to cover the bottom of the pan about 1/4 inch deep. Brown the chicken pieces. Remove them from the pan and spoon out all but 2 teaspoons of the oil. Add the garlic and cook, stirring, for 30 seconds. Do not let the garlic brown. Off the heat, add 1 tablespoon flour. Stir in the chicken stock, and continue cooking, stirring constantly, until the gravy thickens slightly.

Place the chicken pieces in the gravy. Add the mushrooms and thyme. Cover the pan and simmer, turning the chicken once, for about 10 minutes. Add the beans, making sure they are submerged in the gravy. You may need to add about 1/4 cup stock. Raise the heat slightly, and cook the mixture for 5 minutes, or until the beans are barely cooked through. They should still be quite crunchy. Taste and season with salt and pepper. Stir in the parsley.

VARIATIONS

With snow peas and scallions. Substitute *snow peas* for the green beans. Add 3/4 cup stringed snow peas and 2 tablespoons chopped *scallions* after the chicken has cooked for 10 minutes. Remove the cover from the pan and cook about 3 minutes, or until the peas are barely cooked through.

With carrots and sweet marjoram. Substitute 1 cup thinly sliced young *carrots* for the green beans. Just before serving, stir in 1–2 teaspoons *sweet marjoram.*

TWO-WAY ROAST CHICKEN

Cooked this way, a frying chicken gives you two totally different flavors and styles of cooking—one a vegetable-stuffed breast, the other, barbecued dark meat that's great for a picnic or lunch at work. Both recipes create plenty of leftovers.

Split a 3 1/2- to 4-pound frying chicken along the back and flatten it out to a butterfly shape. Remove the legs and thighs, leaving a heart-shaped whole breast with the wings attached. Refrigerate or freeze the dark meat for *Barbecued Chicken Legs and Thighs* (page 145). Gently loosen the skin from the breast by lifting it and cutting any tendons with a paring knife. You will be placing a zucchini–cottage cheese stuffing between the skin and the flesh. (The stuffing serves a double purpose—it keeps the flesh moist while flavoring it.) You're now ready to proceed with stuffing

Two-Way Roast Chicken (continued)

the breast. Your butcher can prepare the chicken if you don't want to bother with this step; even supermarket personnel are willing to cut up the chicken if you explain exactly what you want.

Chicken Breast Stuffed with Zucchini

(Makes 2 servings)

1¹/2 tablespoons olive oil
³/4 cup chopped onion or scallions (including green stems)
2 tablespoons chopped fresh herbs, such as a mixture of tarragon and parsley—or sweet marjoram
³/4 cup zucchini that has been coarsely grated and squeezed dry, then measured (about 1 small zucchini)
³/4 cup dry-curd cottage cheese
1 egg, beaten
1 whole chicken breast, skin attached, about 2 pounds
¹/2 lemon

Heat 1 tablespoon of the olive oil in a frying pan, add the onion, and cook, stirring frequently, for about 1 minute. Add the herbs and cook 30 seconds longer. Spoon the mixture into a bowl and stir in the zucchini, cottage cheese, and egg. (The stuffing may be a little gloppy, but it dries out as it bakes.) Place the chicken breast in a small ovenproof dish. Lift the skin and squeeze lemon juice over the flesh, then spoon over the stuffing mixture. Place the skin back down over the stuffing. If you have any extra stuffing, place it under the chicken.

Drizzle the remaining olive oil over the skin and bake the chicken in a preheated 425°F oven for 25–30 minutes, or until it is cooked through and the skin is browned. Occasionally baste with the pan juices. Let the chicken sit for at least 15 minutes before slicing into pieces. Serve with tomatoes marinated in a vinaigrette sauce or blanched broccoli.

Variation

Chicken Breast Stuffed with Escarole. Use 1 cup raw thinly sliced *escarole* for the zucchini and sauté it with the onion, adding additional oil if necessary. Add 2 or 3 chopped *mushrooms* and a tablespoon of chopped *ham* (optional). Cook for 2 minutes, then proceed as above, adding the escarole mixture to the cottage cheese.

Barbecued Chicken Legs and Thighs

This version of barbecued chicken uses a commercial sauce as a base—preferably one minus the ingredient of liquid smoke. If you're grilling the chicken, marinate it overnight in the sauce (or lime juice), oil the pieces, and baste with the marinade. The type of citrus juice you use depends upon how tart you'd like the barbecued chicken. The orange juice gives a sweeter aftertaste than the lime and grapefruit juices. There's plenty for leftovers—or if you prefer, cook up either the legs or the thighs.

(Makes 2 servings)

2 teaspoons vegetable oil	1/2–1 teaspoon Dijon mustard
2 chicken legs and thighs	1/4 cup citrus juice (freshly
Freshly ground black pepper	squeezed orange, lime, lemon,
1/2 cup commercial barbecue	or grapefruit)
sauce	1 tablespoon brown sugar or
Worcestershire sauce	molasses

Rub oil on the chicken, place in an ovenproof pan, and sprinkle with black pepper. Cook the chicken in a preheated 400°F oven for 20 minutes. Remove, and lower the heat to 350°F.

Meanwhile, make the barbecue sauce. Most commercial sauces are improved by some mustard, citrus juice, and a touch of sugar or molasses. The amounts I suggest work well with most sauces, but you should adjust the amount of citrus juice and sugar to suit your taste. Stir together the barbecue sauce, a dash of Worcestershire sauce, the mustard, citrus juice, and brown sugar. Pour over the partially baked chicken. Return to the oven and bake another 25 minutes. Let the chicken cool for 10 minutes before serving. Any leftover sauce freezes well.

Variation

With curry powder. Omit the black pepper and rub with a good-quality *curry powder* before baking.

Leftovers

Barbecued Chicken Sandwich. Skin the chicken and remove it from the

Barbecued Chicken Legs and Thighs (continued)
bones. Coarsely chop it. For each cup of cooked chicken, add 2 table-spoons chopped *onion* and 1/4 cup chopped raw *celery, fennel, or celeriac.* Cook the vegetables in about 1/2 cup leftover barbecue sauce until they are cooked through but still have some texture. Add the chicken and continue cooking until the chicken is heated through. Serve on a toasted roll or a small loaf of French bread.

ROCK CORNISH GAME HEN MEAL-IN-ONE

A Rock Cornish game hen is just the right size for a hungry solo cook. Roasting it at a high temperature keeps it moist and cooks the vegetables quickly. If you prefer a baked potato, cook it on the rack alongside. This may seem like a generous amount, but leftovers are good for another dinner or lunch at work.

(Makes 1 generous serving)

A 11/4–11/2 pound Rock Cornish
   game hen
1 teaspoon olive oil
1 teaspoon minced garlic
1/2 teaspoon chopped fresh sage
   (optional)
1 teaspoon chopped tarragon
1 tablespoon citrus juice, such
   as lemon, orange, lime, or
   grapefruit

2 small carrots, peeled and cut
   into 2-inch-long pieces
1 medium baking potato
   (russet), cut lengthwise into
   sixths
1 small sweet onion, peeled and
   quartered
Freshly ground black pepper

Cut the hen along the backbone lengthwise, turn and press down on the breastbone to flatten it. Coat the hen with the olive oil, and place in a large baking pan. Sprinkle with the garlic, sage, if using, and tarragon. Pour over the citrus juice. Surround with the carrots, potato, and onion (cut sides down). Generously sprinkle with black pepper.

Roast in a preheated 450°F oven for 40–50 minutes, until the hen is browned and the vegetables are cooked through, basting with the pan juices occasionally. After 25 minutes, turn the carrots and potato pieces to coat with the juices. Remove from the oven and let sit for at least 10 minutes before serving.

VARIATIONS

With zucchini. After the hen has been baking 20 minutes, add half a small *zucchini* that's been quartered and cut into 2-inch-long pieces.

With turnips. Add 1 small *turnip,* quartered, along with the carrots.

With scallions and fennel. Omit the carrots and onion. Add 1 cup *fennel* (or celery) stems, cut into 2-inch-long pieces, and 1 bunch *scallions,* white parts only, trimmed, along with the potato.

With cabbage, celery, and carrots. Omit the tarragon and sage. For the vegetables use 2–3 cups sliced *cabbage,* 1/2 cup sliced *carrots,* and 3/4 cup chopped *celery.*

Roasted Whole Rock Cornish Game Hen. Omit the vegetables. Put half a quartered *lemon* in the cavity of the hen along with a stem of sage. Coat the hen with the olive oil, garlic, and tarragon and pour over the citrus juice. Sprinkle generously with black pepper. Bake as above, basting with the pan juices occasionally. Serve hot or cold.

Roasted Chicken Leg and Thigh. Substitute a *chicken leg and thigh* for the Rock Cornish game hen.

ROAST CHICKEN

Virtually everyone likes roast chicken, particularly this version, flavored with fresh herbs and lemon. Usually I'll cook smaller amounts of chicken, but there are times when it's handy to have a roast chicken in the refrigerator so that cooking can be kept to a minimum. I prefer to roast chicken breast side down (which keeps it moist) over a bed of vegetables, which I save and add to the chicken carcass along with water to make a flavorful chicken broth. Use the leftovers for salads, soups, casseroles—or just eat the chicken cold. But however you recycle it, store the chicken in a covered glass bowl and use it up within two or three days.

Roast Chicken (continued)

(Makes 1 roast chicken)

A 3¹/2-pound chicken
Sprigs of fresh herbs, such as
    parsley, sweet marjoram,
    sage, and thyme
1 lemon, quartered
Peppercorns

4 cloves garlic, smashed
2 carrots, washed and thickly
    sliced
1 onion, peeled and thickly
    sliced
2 celery stalks, sliced

Remove any fat from the cavity of the chicken, wash the chicken under warm running water, and dry it. Stuff the cavity with several sprigs of fresh herbs, the lemon quarters, about 10 peppercorns, and the garlic. Place the carrots, onion, and celery in a roasting pan. If you have a meat rack, place it in the pan and put the chicken breast side down in the rack. (Otherwise, put it in the pan and press down slightly on the backbone, then scatter the vegetables around the chicken.) Place any chicken fat on the backbone.

Roast the chicken in a preheated 425°F oven for 30 minutes. Lower the heat to 350 and cook another 30–45 minutes, or until it is cooked through. Remove from the oven and let stand for at least 20 minutes before serving.

VARIATION

Chicken Stuffed with Sage and Tarragon. Stuff the chicken with 2 sprigs of fresh sage (about 6 leaves) and 1 sprig of *tarragon*. Loosen the skin of the chicken breast and place dabs of *butter* (about 1 tablespoon) under the skin. (This will keep the flesh from drying out.) Rub the surface with a cut lemon, then grind fresh pepper over the entire chicken. Be generous. The roasted black pepper flavor is essential. Place the chicken, breast side up, in a roasting pan. Proceed as above, omitting the basting.

LEFTOVERS

Once roast chicken is refrigerated, it loses its fresh taste somewhat. For this reason, I'll often strip the meat from the bones immediately after finishing the meal and make a *stock* with the pan juices and vegetables, skin, and bones (after first discarding the lemon). Then I'll cover the leftover meat with stock while refrigerating it.

Chicken Salad

The most delicately flavored chicken salad is made with breast meat (sometimes I'll simmer chicken breasts and cool them in stock for an extra-moist chicken salad). To add extra flavor to leftover roasted chicken, toss the chicken pieces in the lemon juice and pepper in the morning, refrigerate, and then assemble the salad in the evening when you get ready for dinner.

(Serves 1)

1–1 1/3 cups cooked boneless chicken, cut into 3/4-inch pieces
1 tablespoon lemon juice
Freshly ground black pepper
Cayenne pepper or dry mustard (optional)
1/4 cup minced scallions or sweet onion (optional)
1/2 cup diced celery

1/4 cup mayonnaise—or equal parts mayonnaise and nonfat yogurt
1/2 teaspoon Creole or Dijon mustard
1 tablespoon minced parsley or chervil, or 2 teaspoons minced tarragon or lovage
Salt

Toss the chicken with the lemon juice, a generous amount of black pepper and, if you like, a pinch of cayenne pepper or dry mustard. Let sit for at least 30 minutes in a glass bowl. Tilt the bowl and remove any juices if you wish. Add the optional scallions and the celery, mayonnaise, mustard, and herbs. Taste and season with salt.

Variations

With curry or cumin. Add 1/2 teaspoon good-quality *curry powder or* 1/4 teaspoon *cumin* to the mayonnaise.

With mango chutney. Substitute *lime juice* for the lemon juice. Add 1 tablespoon chopped *mango chutney* to the salad.

With roasted red pepper. Omit the scallions. Add 1–2 tablespoons chopped *roasted red pepper* to the salad.

BRAISED CHICKEN WITH VEGETABLES

This is by far the most versatile way to cook chicken. You can vary the vegetables depending upon the season—and because the poultry is simmered (and stored) in a liquid, leftovers taste brand-new. This version with rutabaga, potatoes, and carrots is a flavorful winter choice, while in summer you could try a lighter version made with baby turnips, pattypan squash, baby carrots, and whole new potatoes. Whatever you do, don't omit the rutabagas or turnips, because they add a rich, mellow flavor to the completed dish. I remove the legs and thighs for another meal, but braise the chicken whole if you prefer. You can save the leftover cooking fat for another meal.

(Makes 2–3 servings)

A 3-pound chicken, either whole or with legs and thighs set aside

2 tablespoons fat, such as melted salt pork or olive oil

1 cup 3/4-inch pieces peeled rutabaga

1 cup 3/4-inch pieces peeled carrots

1 cup 3/4-inch pieces peeled potatoes

1 cup 3-inch-long slices scallions (or 1 cup chopped onions)

2 teaspoons minced garlic

1 1/2–2 cups chicken stock

2 tablespoons minced fresh herbs, such as parsley, tarragon, sweet marjoram, or lovage (optional)

Rinse and dry the chicken. Heat the fat in a large frying pan and brown the chicken. Remove it to a stove-top casserole just large enough to hold it and the chopped vegetables. In the same fat brown the rutabaga for 5 minutes, stir in the carrots, potatoes, and scallions, and cook another 5 minutes, or until the vegetables are lightly browned. (If your frying pan is small, you may have to do this in 2 batches.) Stir in the garlic, and cook another minute. Either remove the vegetables from the pan with a slotted spoon and scatter around the chicken, or put them in a colander to drain the fat and then place them around the chicken. Add the chicken stock. Bring the mixture to a boil, lower the heat, cover the pan, and cook, stirring occasionally, over low-medium heat for about 45 minutes. Let the chicken cool slightly before serving. Just before serving, stir in the herbs.

Note: *Lovage* is an amalgamating herb. Therefore, if you can locate lovage, unlike most herbs, which should be added just before serving, it should be added along with the chicken broth. Farmers' markets often carry bunches of lovage.

VARIATIONS

With summer squash and red peppers. Add 1 cup chopped *summer squash* and 1/2 cup seeded and chopped *red peppers* along with the potatoes. Proceed as above.

With mushrooms. Add 2 cups sliced *mushrooms* along with the rutabaga and omit the potatoes.

LEFTOVERS

Purée any leftover vegetables and broth as a base for soups. (Or you can freeze the purée as a base for beef or lamb stew.)

Carrot Soup. In a covered pot, simmer together for 20 minutes 1 1/2 cups *broth,* any leftover vegetables, 1 cup peeled and sliced carrots, and 1/4 cup peeled and chopped *parsnips* (optional). Blend or put through a food processor. If the purée is too thick, add water or *milk* to taste. Garnish with chopped *chives or scallions.* Sometimes I add thinly sliced raw *asparagus* cut on the diagonal to add color and texture. You can also omit the chives or scallions and stir in 1 teaspoon minced *sweet marjoram* for every cup.

Puréed Vegetable Soup. Purée the leftover vegetables with 1 1/2 cups *broth.* Add chopped *sweet marjoram or parsley* to taste along with strips of fresh *tomato.*

The chicken tastes particularly nice in a composed salad or in *Chicken Curry* (page 129). Or you could make:

Chicken Croquettes

These colorful chicken patties are a far cry from those gummy croquettes served in some English-tearoom-style restaurants. Using an egg white to bind together the ingredients gives a more delicate flavor than a whole

Chicken Croquettes (continued)

egg, but the croquettes need gentle handling so that they don't fall apart while cooking. (When this happens to me, I just press them back together.) But if you prefer, use half of a whole beaten egg instead of the white. Peeling the red pepper with a vegetable peeler makes it easier to digest.

(Serves 1)

1/2 cup chopped cooked skinned and boned chicken
1/4 cup chopped leftover vegetables, drained
1 tablespoon chopped scallion greens
1 tablespoon peeled and chopped red pepper

Salt
1 medium egg white, lightly beaten with a fork
3 tablespoons fresh breadcrumbs
1 tablespoon butter or olive oil

Mix together the chicken, vegetables, scallions, red pepper, salt to taste, and the egg white. Add 1 tablespoon of the breadcrumbs. The mixture will barely hold together. Using the palms of your hands, form 2 patties and dip them into the remaining breadcrumbs. Heat the butter in a heavy frying pan and brown the patties on both sides over medium heat, turning once. This will take about 6–8 minutes. Serve hot.

CHICKEN BAKED WITH SWEET POTATOES AND ONIONS

If you like to have plenty of leftovers on hand to eat throughout the week but don't want to taste the same flavors day after day, this is an easy, inexpensive choice. The baked chicken is good, but the soup you make with the leftover sweet potatoes and onions is even better—rich tasting with an elusive hint of sherry and ginger. By inserting the lemon slices under the skin of the breast, you flavor the white meat for a composed salad or sandwiches. If you make the jambalaya (see Leftovers) with the leftovers, use some of the soup for flavoring.

(Makes 3 meals)

A 3 1/2-pound chicken

1 lemon, thinly sliced

A $1/2$-pound sweet potato
2–3 sweet onions (about
  $1/2$ pound)

$1/4$ cup dry sherry, approximately
Ground ginger
Freshly ground black pepper

Either butterfly the chicken yourself or ask your butcher to do it. (To butterfly, just cut along the backbone, place the chicken breast side up, and press down on the breastbone to flatten it.) Loosen the breast skin, lift it up, and cover the flesh with the lemon slices. Peel the sweet potato and cut into 1-inch-thick wedges. Place the sweet potato wedges in the center of a large baking dish and cover with the chicken. Peel and halve the onions, and place them cut sides down around the chicken. Pour the sherry over the chicken, generously sprinkle it with ground ginger (about $1/4$ teaspoon), and then grind black pepper over the surface.

Place in a preheated 400°F oven for about 45 minutes. Remove the chicken from the oven, lift it, and arrange the sweet potato slices around the chicken (they will be flavored by the chicken juices). Place the chicken back in the oven and cook 30 minutes longer, basting frequently with the pan juices, adding 2–3 tablespoons water or sherry if necessary. Remove the chicken from the oven and let it sit for at least 20 minutes before serving. Check to make sure the sweet potatoes are cooked through. If not, baste them and place back in the oven to cook further while the chicken rests. Reserve the chicken breast for another meal. Serve the legs and thighs with some of the sweet potato slices and onions, and a tossed green salad with a tart marinade.

LEFTOVERS

Sweet Potato and Onion Soup

(Makes about 1³/4 cups soup)

1 cup leftover chopped sweet
  potato
$1/2$ cup leftover baked onion
2 cups chicken stock

Salt and freshly ground black
  pepper
Chopped fresh sage, tarragon, or
  rosemary

Place the sweet potato, onion, and stock in a large pot and simmer over medium heat for at least 30 minutes. Mash the sweet potatoes and

Sweet Potato and Onion Soup (continued)

cook for another 10 minutes. Purée in a blender or food processor. (If you are using the food processor, omit mashing the sweet potatoes and pulse them with a little broth, then add to the remaining broth.) Taste and season with salt and pepper. Serve with a garnish of chopped fresh sage, tarragon, or rosemary.

Variation

With vegetables. To 1³/4 cups puréed soup, add ¹/2 cup chopped *tomatoes* and ¹/3 cup *lima beans* and cook for 10 minutes. Stir in ¹/4–¹/2 cup leftover cooked *corn* kernels, and ¹/4 cup chopped raw *celery;* reheat for 2 minutes. Garnish with chopped *chives* or *scallion tops.* Or, add chopped *ham* and sliced *okra* to taste along with the beans.

Note: The puréed version of this soup adds flavor to braised beef or pork dishes—or other soups. Freeze in ¹/2-cup amounts and use as you wish.

Chicken with Ham, Rice, and Vegetables

This is inspired by jambalaya, the rice dish found throughout Louisiana and other parts of the South. The list of ingredients is lengthy, but once you've chopped the vegetables, there's little left to do but stir the rice. I prefer my rice and vegetables cooked for a shorter time than is traditional, so I cook this dish on top of the stove, rather than baking it in the oven. For a more complex flavor, add some of the leftover soup: Use ¹/3 cup and decrease the stock to ³/4 cup.

(Serves 1)

2 teaspoons olive oil or butter
1–2 teaspoons minced garlic
¹/3 cup chopped onion or scallions (green stems only)
¹/4–¹/3 cup chopped pepper
¹/4–¹/3 cup chopped ham or Cajun-style sausage
¹/2 cup chopped cooked chicken
1 cup chicken stock
¹/2 teaspoon minced fresh thyme
¹/2 teaspoon chopped rosemary (optional)
¹/2 cup long-grain rice, such as basmati
¹/4 cup peeled, seeded, and chopped tomato
1–2 tablespoons minced parsley
Salt and freshly ground black pepper

Heat the fat in a large frying pan, add the garlic, and cook, stirring constantly, for 1 minute. Stir in the onion, pepper, ham, and chicken, and continue cooking, stirring frequently, for 3 minutes. Add the chicken stock, thyme, optional rosemary, and rice. Cook, stirring frequently, for about 15 minutes, or until the rice is barely cooked through. Add additional water, stock, or soup if necessary. (Rice varies in its absorption qualities.) Stir in the tomato and parsley and season with salt and pepper.

Leftovers

The rice tends to get mushy if reheated for any length of time. I prefer to use any leftovers as soup ingredients. Just add stock to taste. (A ham stock is tasty.) With the addition of shredded greens, such as *kale* or *escarole,* cooked in the stock for 5 minutes, you end up with a robust meal-in-one. Or combine any leftover sweet potato soup with the leftover jambalaya. Either way, add the leftover jambalaya just before serving. You want only to reheat the ingredients, not cook them further.

CHICKEN LIVERS SAUTÉED WITH HERBS

Chicken livers have the twin virtues of being inexpensive and providing a good source of iron. Unfortunately, they're usually sold in 1-pound containers, and are highly perishable, so if you fancy livers, either ask the butcher to sell you less—or freeze the extra raw livers.

(Serves 1)

4 ounces chicken livers
2 tablespoons butter
1/4 cup chopped scallions (white portions only) or sweet onion
1–2 teaspoons chopped tarragon or parsley

Salt and freshly ground black pepper
1/2 lime (optional)

Clean the chicken livers, cutting away the membranes with a sharp paring knife and removing any fat. Wash and dry the livers. Heat the but-

Chicken Livers Sautéed with Herbs (continued)

ter in a heavy frying pan and add the scallions. Cook over medium heat for 3 minutes. Add the chicken livers, and continue cooking, turning them frequently, until they are barely cooked through, about 4 minutes. They should still be slightly pink inside. (If you overcook the livers, they become virtually indigestible and tough.) Stir in the tarragon and cook 1 minute longer. Tip the pan and remove most of the browned butter. Season the livers with salt and pepper and serve with a half lime to squeeze over them if you wish.

VARIATION

*Chicken Livers Sautéed with Bacon.*Omit the butter and tarragon and use an equal amount of parsley. Cook 1–2 strips *bacon* slowly until crisp. Remove the bacon and all but 1 tablespoon of the bacon fat from the pan. Proceed as above. Just before serving, crumble the reserved bacon over the livers.

TURKEY SAUTÉED WITH RED PEPPERS

Many supermarkets sell turkey cutlets in small quantities. You can either opt for the cutlets or ask a butcher to slice a boneless breast portion and freeze the remainder in meal-sized quantities. The sweet flavor of red pepper complements turkey. In this recipe you can choose either roasted red pepper or pimientos (which add a more complex flavor and a soft texture) or sautéed raw pepper (which gives texture). Peeling the red pepper before cooking makes it easy to digest.

(Serves 1)

3–4 ounces thinly sliced raw turkey
2 teaspoons lime juice
1/4 teaspoon paprika (preferably sweet Hungarian) or black pepper
2 teaspoons olive oil
2 teaspoons minced garlic
1/3 cup sliced roasted red peppers (see page 63), diced canned pimientos, or thinly sliced seeded raw pepper
1 teaspoon minced fresh tarragon (optional)
Salt and freshly ground pepper (optional)
1 tablespoon sliced scallion greens

Place the turkey in a glass bowl, and toss with the lime juice and paprika. (You can assemble the turkey to this point in the morning before you go to work, and need only sauté it at night.)

Heat the olive oil in a heavy frying pan. Add the turkey and sauté it over medium-high heat, stirring constantly, until it is barely cooked through. This will take 2–3 minutes. Stir in the garlic, roasted peppers, and tarragon, if using, and cook, stirring frequently, 2 minutes longer. Taste and season with salt and pepper if you wish. Sprinkle with the scallions before serving.

VARIATION

Meal-in-One. Increase the garlic to 1 tablespoon and the scallion greens to 1/3 cup. Use either a roasted or raw red pepper. Once the turkey and the peppers are cooked, add 2/3–1 cup cooked *white or brown rice,* preferably at room temperature, and the scallion greens. Cook, stirring constantly, until the rice is heated through. You can also add 1/4 cup cooked *corn,* either leftover or defrosted, and a peeled, raw, chopped *tomato.*

Note: Leek greens (rather than scallions) are especially good sautéed along with the rice.

TURKEY CUTLET WITH MUSHROOMS

There's just enough cream to moisten the mushrooms. This is particularly nice served with rice and a cucumber salad.

(Serves 1)

A 3-ounce turkey cutlet, sliced thin
1/2 lime (about 2 teaspoons lime juice)
Freshly ground black pepper
Flour
2–3 teaspoons butter
1 teaspoon minced garlic

1 cup sliced mushrooms
1 tablespoon cream or sour cream (or more for a creamier sauce)
1 teaspoon minced chives (optional)
Worcestershire sauce

Place the cutlet on the counter and squeeze lime juice over both sides.

Turkey Cutlet with Mushrooms (continued)

Sprinkle with black pepper. Dip in flour and shake off any excess.

Heat 2 teaspoons butter in a small, heavy frying pan and add the turkey cutlet. Brown quickly on both sides, and remove from the pan. Add the 1 teaspoon additional butter if necessary. Stir in the garlic and cook, stirring constantly, for 1 minute. Add the mushrooms and cook, stirring, for 3 minutes, or until they wilt slightly. Return the cutlet to the pan and continue cooking it until it is cooked through, about 3 minutes. Stir in the cream, chives, if using, and a dash of Worcestershire sauce.

TURKEY CUTLET SMOTHERED IN VEGETABLES

Turkey cutlets may be low in fat and calories, but they need a bit of zip to avoid tasting bland. In this recipe, the flavor comes from the vegetable juices. If you don't have a meat pounder, get the butcher to flatten the cutlet for you (or use a heavy bottle).

(Serves 1)

Freshly ground black pepper
A 3–4 ounce turkey cutlet,
　pounded thin
Flour
1 tablespoon butter or olive
　oil
3 tablespoons chopped onion
1/2 teaspoon chopped garlic
1/3 cup seeded and sliced

pepper (preferably a thin-
　skinned type such as Banana)
1/2 cup peeled, seeded, and
　chopped tomato
1/2 cup coarsely chopped yellow
　summer squash
1–2 tablespoons chopped celery
　leaves or parsley
Salt

Generously pepper the turkey cutlet. Dip it in flour, shaking off excess, and set it aside. Heat the butter in a large frying pan. Add the onion, garlic, and sliced pepper. Cook over medium heat, stirring constantly, for 2 minutes. Move the vegetables to one side, tilt the pan so the fat runs into the center, and brown the turkey cutlet on both sides. Remove from the pan and set aside. Spoon out all but a film of fat. Add the tomato, summer squash, and celery. Cook, stirring frequently, for 3 minutes, or until the vegetables cook down slightly. You may need to add 1 tablespoon of water or stock. Return the cutlet to the pan, and cook another 3–5 minutes or until it is cooked through. Taste and season with salt if you wish. Place the cutlet on a plate and top with the vegetables.

VARIATION

With capers. Add 1/2 teaspoon chopped *capers* along with the tomatoes. Proceed as above.

GROUND TURKEY CHILI

You'll never miss the fat in this easy-to-make chili that tastes fresh for days because it has no salt. Simmering the beans with onion and garlic and adding a touch of cider vinegar just before serving deepens the flavor of the chili.

(Makes 3 cups)

1 cup dried pinto beans
1 cup chopped onion (about 1)
2 teaspoons minced garlic
Freshly ground black pepper
A 15-ounce can of tomato sauce
1 green pepper
Worcestershire sauce

2 tablespoons good-quality chili powder, such as Gebhardt's
4 ounces ground turkey
2 tablespoons catsup or cocktail sauce (optional)
1 teaspoon cider vinegar

Put the beans in a pot, cover with 5 cups of water, bring to a boil and boil for 5 minutes. Let sit for 30 minutes. Drain, cover again with water, and bring the beans to a boil. Add the onion, garlic, and black pepper to taste. Simmer, stirring occasionally and adding more water if needed, for 11/2–2 hours. The beans should be cooked through, but retain some texture. Stir in the tomato sauce and cook over medium heat, stirring occasionally, for 20 minutes. Seed the pepper, cut it into chunks, and add to the chili. (The size doesn't matter, but 1-inch pieces are easy to eat.) Add a dash of Worcestershire sauce, 2 tablespoons chili powder, and the ground turkey. Simmer, breaking up the ground turkey, until it is cooked through, about 10–15 minutes. Taste and add catsup or cocktail sauce, if you wish. Just before serving stir in the cider vinegar.

VARIATIONS

With beef. Substitute 4 ounces ground or chopped beef for the turkey.

Ground Turkey Chili (continued)

With mushrooms. Add 1 cup sliced *mushrooms* along with the turkey.

With olives. Add 1/4 cup seeded and coarsely chopped *black olives* along with the turkey.

With corn. Add 1 cup cooked *corn* along with the turkey.

Vegetarian. Omit the turkey.

LEFTOVERS

This chili stays in good condition in the refrigerator for at least 5 days if stored in a covered glass bowl. It also freezes well—even the pepper retains its texture. There's no need to defrost the chili if you have a microwave—just reheat it while still frozen.

TURKEY MEATBALLS WITH MUSHROOMS

Simmering the browned meatballs and mushrooms in a liquid creates a flavorful sauce to spoon over rice, potatoes, or pasta. You can freeze any leftover sauce as a soup base and slice the meatballs for a sandwich (see Leftovers).

(Makes 2 meals)

1 medium egg	1/2 cup chopped scallions
1 1/2 cups water or chicken stock	1/2 teaspoon coarsely ground
1/2 pound ground turkey	black pepper
1/2 cup fine, dry breadcrumbs	Worcestershire sauce (optional)
2–2 1/2 teaspoons olive oil	Salt
1/2 cup chopped celery	Flour
1/4 cup peeled, seeded, and	2 cups sliced mushrooms
finely chopped fresh or	
frozen red pepper	

In a bowl, beat the egg and mix with 1/4 cup of the water, the ground turkey, and the breadcrumbs. Cover the mixture and let it sit while you cook the vegetables. (The breadcrumbs will absorb the liquid, resulting in moister meatballs.) In a small stove-top pot, heat 1/2 teaspoon of the olive oil. Stir in the celery, red pepper, 1/4 cup of the scallions and cook over medium heat, stirring constantly, for 2 minutes. Stir in another 1/4 cup water, the black pepper, and a dash of Worcestershire, if using. Lower the heat and cook slowly, stirring occasionally, for 10 minutes, or until the vegetables have absorbed the water and are slightly wilted.

Stir the vegetables into the turkey mixture and season with salt. Place about 1/3 cup flour in a bowl. Using either a large spoon or your hands (moisten them first with water) form 6–8 large meatballs, roll them in the flour, and shake to remove any excess flour.

Heat the remaining 1 1/2 teaspoons olive oil in a heavy stove-top casserole and brown the meatballs on all sides. This will take about 2 minutes. (Depending upon the size and heft of your pan, you may need to brown them in 2 batches, and you may need to add the remaining 1/2 teaspoon oil.) Remove the meatballs from the pan with a slotted spoon and set them aside. Add the mushrooms to the pan and, over high heat, stir and toss them back and forth with a wooden spoon until they have wilted slightly, about 1–2 minutes. Put the meatballs back in the pan and add 1 cup water or stock. The water should cover the meatballs; add more if necessary. Cover the pan and gently simmer the meatballs over low heat, stirring and turning them occasionally, for 25 minutes. Stir in the 1/4 cup remaining scallions, cover the pan, and let the mixture sit for at least 5 minutes before serving.

VARIATIONS

With herbs.   Add 2–3 teaspoons chopped *sweet marjoram, parsley,* or *basil,* or 1 teaspoon chopped *tarragon,* or 1/2 teaspoon chopped *rosemary* along with the scallions. Proceed as above.

With spices.   Add 1/4 teaspoon *curry powder or paprika* along with the 1/2 teaspoon olive oil. Or, season the meatball mixture with a generous pinch of *nutmeg or cardamom.*

With fennel.   Substitute 1/2 cup chopped *fennel* for the celery. Proceed as above.

LEFTOVERS

Any leftover meatballs reheat well either in a microwave or gently simmered on top of the stove. You can also separate the mixture—freezing the sauce in 1-cup increments for soups and slicing the meatballs for sandwiches.

Turkey Meatballs (continued)

Turkey-Meatball Sauerkraut Sandwich. Slice 2–3 leftover meatballs and arrange in a toasted *sandwich bun* spread with *mustard.* Top with 2–4 tablespoons drained *sauerkraut* or shredded fresh *cabbage* and *carrots.*

Turkey-Meatball Grinder. Slice 2–3 leftover meatballs and place them in a toasted *sandwich bun* spread with *mayonnaise.* Top with shredded *lettuce* to taste (about 1/4 cup is good), 2–3 slices *tomato,* and sliced *onion* or *sweet pickles* to taste (optional). If you have a jar of opened *olives,* add a few sliced olives to the mixture. And, if you want cheese, a slice of *provolone* goes well.

BRAISED TURKEY WINGS

You end up with 2 main dishes out of one economically priced staple—less than $1 a pound at any market I've ever frequented. Don't omit the salt pork; it's essential for the flavor of the dish. The easiest way to render salt pork is in a microwave for 2 minutes—or you can slowly cook it on top of the stove until the amount of fat needed melts.

(Makes 1 serving)

2 tablespoons rendered salt-pork fat	1 cup sliced carrots
3 pounds turkey wings, skin on	1 1/2 cups chopped onions
	2 cups rich chicken stock

Heat the salt pork in a heavy frying pan, add the turkey, and brown on all sides, about 5 minutes. Remove the turkey and set in an ovenproof casserole. Add the carrots and onions to the pan, and cook, stirring frequently, for about 5 minutes. Remove them with a slotted spoon, and scatter in the casserole. Add the chicken stock, cover the pan, and bake in a preheated 325°F oven for 1 1/4 hours or until cooked through. Check occasionally, and add additional liquid if needed.

VARIATION

Braised Turkey with Fresh Peas. Remove the leftover turkey from the stock and vegetables. Skin and bone the meat and cut it into chunks. Reheat the casserole liquid and vegetables, adding additional stock or water if necessary. Stir in 1 cup shelled fresh *peas,* and cook for about 3 minutes. Add the turkey and 1 tablespoon chopped fresh *sweet marjoram.* Cook just until the chicken is heated through. Serve over brown rice or noodles.

Note: There's still some flavor left in the turkey skin and bones. Either simmer them in water to make a thin stock, or freeze them to use in future stocks.

TURKEY BREAST BRAISED WITH FENNEL AND CARROTS

I make this recipe when fresh turkey breast is on sale at the market. I ask the supermarket butcher to halve the breast and repackage it. I freeze one of the portions and braise the other half to serve immediately. The size of the turkey breast is of less importance than the gender. If possible, get a hen turkey breast, which will be meatier with a smaller amount of bone. Store the leftover braised turkey in the stock to keep it moist and use in salads or stir-fries. (The bacon imparts a smoky taste, but if you prefer a more subtle flavor, either blanch the bacon strips for 4 minutes in boiling water, or substitute 3 tablespoons oil.) *(Makes 2 meals)*

4 tablespoons bacon strips made by slicing raw bacon into 1/4-inch-thick pieces (about 4 slices)
1 tablespoon vegetable or olive oil
About 3 pounds turkey breast, bone in

2 cups sliced fennel
2 cups chopped carrots
1 onion, chopped (about 2/3 cup)
2 cloves garlic, minced
3–4 cups chicken or turkey stock

Heat a large frying pan and render the bacon strips in the oil. Remove them with a slotted spoon to a casserole. In the rendered fat, brown the turkey breast for 5 minutes, turn, and brown on the other side. Remove from the pan and add the fennel, carrots, onion, and garlic. Sauté for 3–4 minutes, remove the vegetables with a slotted spoon, and place around the turkey breast in the casserole. Cover with the stock, place on the

Turkey Breast Braised with Fennel and Carrots (continued)

stove, and heat just to the boiling point. Cover the pan and bake in a pre-heated 325°F oven for 1 hour, or until turkey is cooked through. Skim off any fat from the cooking juices. Slice some of the turkey breast and surround with some of the fennel and carrots. Serve with a starch such as brown rice or mashed potatoes and accompany with a tossed green salad.

LEFTOVERS

Fennel Soup. Use oil rather than bacon. Purée the leftover vegetables and stock. Heat the mixture and add about 1/4 cup diced *fresh fennel* and minced *sweet marjoram or basil* to taste. Cook for 1 minute and serve.

TURKEY POT PIE WITH HERBS

Pot pies are a foolproof way to make refrigerated cooked poultry taste fresh once again. You can use chunks of either cooked turkey or cooked chicken in this recipe, but don't skip the yellow turnip—it adds a rich flavor. If you don't have homemade chicken stock, commercial double-strength broth works well; however, as it tends to be salty, taste before adding more salt. You can substitute frozen commercial puff pastry for the piecrust if you prefer.

(Makes 1 generous serving)

1/2 cup peeled and diced yellow turnip (rutabaga) (1/2-inch pieces)
2/3 cup peeled and diced waxy potatoes (1/2-inch pieces)
2/3 cup peeled and diced carrots (1/2-inch pieces)
2 teaspoons butter
1/3–1/2 cup chopped onion or leeks (white part only)
1/8 teaspoon minced fresh sage (optional)
1/8–1/4 teaspoon minced fresh thyme leaves

1/2 teaspoon minced fresh garlic
2 teaspoons flour
3/4 cup chicken stock, at room temperature or heated through
1/2–2/3 cup cooked turkey chunks (3/4-inch pieces)
1 teaspoon minced sweet marjoram
Salt
Cayenne pepper (optional)
1/2 recipe *Piecrust* (page 294)

Place the turnip and potatoes in a pot of water, bring to a boil, and lower the heat slightly. Slowly boil for 5 minutes. Add the carrots and boil 3 minutes longer. Remove the pan from the stove and let the vegetables sit in the water while you assemble the pie.

Melt the butter in a heavy saucepan and add the onion, optional sage, and thyme. Cook, stirring frequently, for about 3 minutes. Stir in the garlic and cook another 2 minutes. Off the heat, stir in the flour. Place back on the stove to cook for a minute to remove the floury taste, then pour in the chicken stock, stirring constantly. The sauce will be only slightly thickened. Add the turkey and sweet marjoram. Drain the reserved vegetables and add to the sauce. The mixture may look a little dry, but the vegetables will continue to exude moisture as they bake. Taste and season with salt and a dash of cayenne pepper, if you like. Put the mixture into a 2-cup ovenproof dish, such as an oval au gratin or a small soufflé dish.

Roll out the piecrust and cover the pie. With a knife, cut out a circle for the steam to escape and poke slits in the surface. Place on a baking sheet (in case the sauce drips) and bake in a preheated 425°F oven for 25 minutes, or until the crust is lightly browned and the filling is bubbling. Let sit for 5 minutes before serving.

Note: You can refrigerate any leftover raw piecrust for up to 5 days, or freeze it.

VARIATION

With biscuits. Substitute 2–3 *Biscuits* (page 265) for the piecrust. Bake at 400°F for 15 minutes, or until the biscuits are browned. You can cook the rest of the biscuit recipe on the baking sheet and freeze for shortcakes or breakfast.

THE PLEASURES OF EATING ALONE

Often, eating alone has as much to do with our psyches as our stomachs. A friend of mine claims she's an expert on sink cuisine. When I asked what that meant, she said, "You know. That's when you grab something from the refrigerator and eat it standing up over the sink." This particular friend hates to eat alone so she gets the experience out of the way as quickly as possible.

The absence of a companion to talk with at mealtime bothers some people more than others. When you're used to the sociability of an evening spent with another—or the bustle of family life—it may take a while to adjust to the rhythm of eating by yourself and to focus on the positive aspects of solitary dining. "When I was single," a married friend reminisces, "I came home from a bad day at work, changed into my old clothes, and ate a light supper, such as a bowl of soup or some steamed vegetables. Not that I ever did it, but if I wanted dinner to be a whole lemon meringue pie, that was my choice. I loved experimenting with unusual vegetables my husband won't touch. Actually, I didn't realize it then, but I had a lot more choices than I do now."

When you stop to think about it, many of the choices we take for granted as solitary diners would be viewed as inconsiderate—or even selfish—if we were eating with others. Alone, we can eat whatever, whenever, and wherever we like. We don't have to fit into someone else's schedule: If we get hungry at 6 p.m. that's when we eat—not at 8 p.m., when we're ravenous. If we feel like slurping soup while lolling on the bed watching reruns of "Star Trek," that's our business. And we don't need to converse when we're not in the mood.

Making our mealtimes exactly what we want is a small—but significant—way to build pleasure into our lives. Sometimes we may opt for "sink cuisine," or a snack on a tray table in front of the TV—other evenings we might prefer the ritual of setting the table, lighting some candles, and savoring dinner while listening to music. Taking a few minutes to switch gears and to create a pleasant atmosphere sets a cap on the day and establishes a more leisurely tone for the evening ahead.

MEATS

I was braising a brisket one day when a single acquaintance dropped by. "I'm sorry," she said. "I didn't know you were expecting company." "I'm not," I replied. "This is for me." As she watched me cook, she told me how much she missed eating the old-fashioned meat dishes she had enjoyed as a child, such as the brisket I was making. But she didn't know how to convert her favorite recipes to single-portion size.

In this chapter you'll find many of these old-time favorites, such as the brisket, meat loaf, and roast pork, that are so delicious both as do-ahead main courses and as second-chance leftovers. However, I've cut down the ingredients so that you end up with only two or three meals for one (rather than a standard two meals for four or six), and I've given you recipes—and ideas—for the leftovers. You'll notice a number of braised dishes, where the meat is cooked and stored in a liquid, rather than roasts. That's because braised meats taste fresher once they're cooked than the same cuts do when roasted and refrigerated. You also won't find many stews. Stews taste best made in quantity: Single cooks can make the large-portion stew recipes found in any standard cookbook and freeze the leftovers for another meal. These do-ahead dishes not only taste good, but they save you time during the work week because you need only add a few ingredients to make them taste virtually new.

However, most nights you're going to want to eat something that goes together rapidly, so you'll find numerous "quick and easy" recipes. Flavoring with chopped vegetables and herbs, rather than fat, saves calories and your heart. Also, if you're trying to eat more vegetables and less protein, you can choose recipes where the meat is more of a "trace element" rather than the main event. And, as in the Poultry and Vegetables chapters, you'll find several meals-in-one.

Meat continues to be a wonderful source of protein. The less-expensive cuts have tough connective tissue that is transformed by long, slow cooking. If you eat meat, it's worth designing your menus so that you can enjoy some of the old-time favorites as well as the quick standbys. You'll save money and eat a more varied diet.

STEAK WITH PEPPERCORNS

Adjust the amount of peppercorns to suit your taste. To coarsely crack peppercorns, place them in a small paper bag and crush them with a wine bottle or rolling pin. As steak usually is sold in 8–12-ounce pieces, cut the size portion you wish and freeze the remainder for another meal.

(Serves 1)

1/2 lime (optional)
4–8 ounces steak, such as sirloin, club, or strip

2 teaspoons coarsely cracked
   peppercorns
1–11/2 teaspoons butter

Squeeze the juice of half a lime, if using, over the steak and let sit for a few minutes. Pat dry. Press the peppercorns into the surface of both sides of the steak. Heat the butter in a heavy frying pan, sear the steak on one side, lower the heat slightly, and cook for 1–2 minutes. Turn the steak and repeat the process until it is cooked to the degree you prefer. If you wish, dot with butter before serving.

VARIATIONS

With Worcestershire sauce. Substitute *Worcestershire sauce* for the lime juice. Rub a dash of Worcestershire sauce into each side of the steak.

With gherkins. Serve with a garnish of *gherkins* (small pickled cucumbers) on the side, which you have sliced almost through and arranged in a fan shape.

SAUTÉED BEEF WITH MUSHROOMS

This quick-to-prepare meal is inspired by beef stroganoff, a dish flavored with sour cream. Yogurt gives a lighter touch—you can always substitute sour cream if you wish.

(Serves 1)

1 teaspoon oil, such as canola
1 teaspoon butter
1/4 cup diced onion
1 teaspoon flour
4 ounces thinly sliced raw beef,
  such as sirloin or tenderloin
1 cup sliced white mushrooms
  (about 4 large)
1/4 cup chicken or beef stock,
  tomato juice, or water

1/2 teaspoon Dijon or
  Creole mustard
1 teaspoon catsup, or 2
  tablespoons chopped
  tomato (optional)
Salt and freshly ground
  black pepper
2 tablespoons yogurt or
  sour cream (optional)

Heat the oil and butter in a large frying pan, add the onion, and cook for 1 minute. Meanwhile, sprinkle the flour over the beef, and shake to remove any excess. Move the onion aside and add the beef. Cook, stirring constantly, for 1 minute. Stir in the mushrooms, and continue stirring for 1 minute or until the mushrooms are slightly wilted. Add the liquid, mustard, and catsup, if using. Cook 1 minute longer, scraping up any browned bits on the bottom of the pan. Taste and season with salt and pepper. Stir in the yogurt, if you wish.

CITRUS MARINADE

Try this marinade for meat or poultry that you intend to grill or broil. Vary the citrus juices—grapefruit works well, as does lime juice.

(Makes 1/2 cup marinade)

1/4 cup lemon juice
1/4 cup olive oil
11/2 tablespoons soy sauce
1/2 teaspoon dry mustard

1 teaspoon Dijon mustard
1 tablespoon minced garlic
  (about 4 cloves)

Whisk together the lemon juice, olive oil, soy sauce, mustards, and garlic. Use for poultry, such as duck or chicken; meats, such as lamb; or even fatty fish, such as mackerel. Stored in a glass jar in the refrigerator, the mixture will last for at least 5 days.

STIR-FRIED BEEF WITH PEPPERS

Flank steak is traditional for beef stir-fries, but I prefer the flavor and texture of sirloin—or even rump steak. Slice the beef as thinly as possible (easy to do when it's partially frozen). You can vary this dish by adding sliced raw broccoli or whole pea pods. Try to keep the slices uniform. This is particularly nice served over reheated leftover brown rice. The soy sauce is salty, so you probably won't need salt. The amount of oil is sufficient if your pan is heavy enough.

(Serves 1)

2 teaspoons peanut or canola oil
3–4 ounces steak, thinly sliced
  on the bias
1/2 onion, cut into slivers (about
  3/4 cup)
1/2 large red pepper, cut into
  slivers (3/4–1 cup)

1/4 green pepper, cut into
  slivers (about 1/2 cup)
1 tablespoon light soy or
  teriyaki sauce
1/4 cup beef stock
Freshly ground black pepper

Heat the oil in a heavy frying pan, add the steak, and cook for 30 seconds, over high heat, stirring constantly. Lift the meat out with a slotted spoon, and add the onion and peppers. Fry, stirring constantly, for 2 minutes. Add the soy and beef stock and cook for another minute or two. Stir in the beef, and continue stirring until done. Season with pepper. Serve over rice.

VARIATIONS

With coriander. Add 2 tablespoons chopped *coriander* with the beef, making sure it cooks in the oil.

With mushrooms. Add four thinly sliced *mushrooms* along with the stock.

With broccoli or pea pods. Replace the green peppers with 3/4 cup thinly sliced *broccoli* or whole *pea pods.* (Sugar snap peas, when in season, are a delicious addition.)

With chili peppers. Add 2 teaspoons chopped *hot pepper* along with the red and green peppers.

Stir-Fried Chicken with Peppers. Substitute 2–3 ounces thinly sliced raw boneless *chicken* for the beef and add 2 tablespoons chopped basil. Proceed as above.

Stir-Fried Pork with Peppers. Substitute 2–3 ounces raw *pork* tenderloin for the beef, and add 2–3 teaspoons grated *fresh gingerroot* along with the onions. Proceed as above.

POUNDED STEAK LOUISIANA-STYLE

Vegetables, not stock, give flavor to this beef dish inspired by the grillades of Louisiana (thin veal cutlets simmered in a vegetable sauce). Cubed steak (an inexpensive cut, such as chuck, that is put through the meat-tenderizing machine at the supermarket) is usually sold by the pound; wrap the remaining pieces of meat individually in plastic wrap and freeze them in a heavy plastic bag for future use. You can serve this over plain grits or rice.

(Serves 1)

3–4 ounces cubed steak	1 cup peeled, seeded,
Worcestershire sauce (about	and chopped tomato
$1/2$ teaspoon)	$1/2$ cup chopped green
Freshly ground black pepper	pepper
Flour	$1/2$ cup chopped onion or
2–3 teaspoons canola or	scallions
olive oil	1 teaspoon thyme leaves
$2/3$ cup hot water	Salt

Pound the steak with a meat pounder or a bottle to flatten it as much as possible. Moisten with Worcestershire sauce on both sides and generously sprinkle with freshly ground black pepper. Dip in flour and shake to remove any excess.

Heat the canola oil in a heavy stove-top casserole. Over medium-high heat, brown the meat on both sides, about 30 seconds per side. Remove the meat from the pan and set aside. Off the heat, stir in 2 teaspoons flour. Place the pan back on the heat, lower the temperature, and cook, stirring occasionally, for 1–2 minutes or until the flour is cooked through. Stir in the water, and cook, stirring constantly, until the sauce is

Pounded Steak Louisiana-Style (continued)
smooth, about 2 minutes. (The vegetables will thicken the sauce, but at this point it looks thin.) Add the tomato, green pepper, onion, and thyme. Cook over medium-low heat, stirring occasionally, for 20 minutes, adding additional water if needed.

Thinly slice the beef, put it back in the pan, and cook 5 minutes longer, stirring occasionally. Taste the sauce and season with salt and additional black pepper. Pour it over grits or rice.

VARIATIONS

With mushrooms. Add 3–4 *mushrooms* that have been thinly sliced after the sauce has cooked for 20 minutes.

With bitters. A touch of *bitters* deepens the flavor of the sauce. Just before serving, stir in a dash or two.

Note: You can always substitute a more expensive cut of meat for the cubed steak, but you will need to lightly score the meat and pound it before cooking.

MEAT LOAF

This meat loaf uses cracker crumbs rather than breadcrumbs as the binder. It's a good way to use up soggy crackers, dribs of catsup or cocktail sauce, and mushroom stems. Cold meat loaf makes a hearty rye bread sandwich—or substitute it as the filling in *Eggplant Slices Stuffed with Meatballs* (page 218) or *Green Peppers Stuffed with Beef and Rice* (page 180). This mixture should be well seasoned with salt and pepper. (If you're omitting salt, add 1 tablespoon Dijon mustard.)

(Makes one 7 × 3-inch loaf)

1 cup crushed cracker crumbs (such as saltines)	1/2 cup chopped onion
1/2 cup milk	2/3 cup chopped mushrooms
1 tablespoon olive oil	1 medium egg
1/2 cup chopped red pepper (about 1)	2 tablespoons cocktail sauce or catsup

1 pound ground beef or a mixture of beef, pork, and veal	Salt and freshly ground black pepper

Place the cracker crumbs in a large bowl, cover with the milk, and let sit for at least 10 minutes. In a stove-top casserole, heat the olive oil, add the red pepper and onion, and cook over medium heat, stirring frequently, for 3 minutes. Add the mushrooms and cook another minute, then cover the pan, lower the heat, and cook 5 minutes longer.

Beat the egg with the cracker crumbs and milk. Add the cocktail sauce, ground beef, and vegetable/mushroom mixture. Stir together gently until all the ingredients are combined. Season with salt and pepper.

Place the mixture in a small oiled loaf pan approximately 7 × 3 × 2 inches and brush the top with olive oil. Bake in a preheated 350°F oven for 45–60 minutes, or until cooked through. Let sit for at least 20 minutes, pouring off any fat that has accumulated in the pan before serving.

BRAISED BEEF WITH ONIONS

This recipe, which is designed for two meals, is proof positive that you don't need a lot of fancy ingredients to have a delicious main course. Virtually any cut works fine, but rump steak is particularly flavorful. If you're using a more tender cut, such as sirloin, reduce the cooking time in the oven to 40 to 50 minutes. The technique of cooking the onions over high heat makes them virtually melt away while cooking. Be sure to bake the ingredients in a small, deep casserole.

(Makes 2 meals)

8–12 ounces steak, cut into serving pieces	2 cups thinly sliced onions
Flour	1¹/₂ cups sliced carrots
Freshly ground black pepper	1 tablespoon chopped garlic
1–2 tablespoons fat (such as fat rendered from the beef)	³/₄–1 cup beef stock
	Cayenne pepper
	Salt

Toss the beef in the flour, sprinkle with freshly ground black pepper, and pound with a meat-tenderizing mallet until the meat is flattened and

Braised Beef with Onions (continued)

the flour and pepper are embedded in the flesh. If you don't own a mallet, use the side of an unopened metal can. Set the meat aside.

Heat 1 tablespoon fat in a deep-frying pan or casserole, add the onions, and cook over high heat, stirring constantly, for 5 minutes. The onions should reduce significantly in volume. Add the carrots and garlic and cook, stirring frequently, for another 3 minutes. Remove the vegetables from the pan with a slotted spoon.

Add additional fat if necessary, heat, and brown the meat on both sides. Remove the meat from the pan, drain the fat, add the stock, and scrape up any browned bits. Boil for 1 minute, stirring constantly. Place the meat in a small, deep casserole, cover with the vegetables, and top with the stock. It should almost cover the meat and vegetables. Cover and bake in a preheated 350°F oven for 1–1¼ hours, or until the meat is tender. Taste and add cayenne pepper and salt to taste. Serve with *Mashed Potatoes* (page 66) and a tossed green salad or sautéed zucchini.

LEFTOVERS

This is delicious reheated on top of the stove or in a microwave. (Add a little water if necessary.) Or stir in ½ cup fresh *tomato sauce* (or ⅓ cup bottled), 4 sliced fresh *mushrooms,* and 1 tablespoon chopped herbs such as *parsley, lovage, or basil.* You could also make:

Burritos with Leftover Beef

Homemade burritos, which are far more delicious—and less greasy—than most restaurant versions, are easy to assemble. You can vary the amount of filling depending upon your appetite. I've suggested enough filling for 2 burritos. Serve with plenty of paper towels or napkins.

(Makes filling for 2 burritos)

¼–½ peeled ripe avocado	1–2 teaspoons seeded
Lime juice	and chopped hot pepper
1 cup peeled, seeded, and diced	Salt and freshly ground black
ripe tomatoes	pepper
⅓ cup chopped onion or	2 cooked store-bought or home-
scallions	made *Flour Tortillas* (page 267)

2–4 tablespoons leftover *Red Beans* (page 76) or canned refried beans, at room temperature

1/2 cup thinly sliced drained leftover beef, at room temperature

Lettuce leaves

2–4 tablespoons freshly grated Monterey Jack or cheddar cheese

Place the avocado in a bowl, mash it with a fork, and mix with lime juice to taste. Set aside.

Mix together the tomatoes, onion, hot pepper, and salt and pepper. Set aside.

Assemble the burritos: Spread each tortilla with refried beans and avocado to taste. Top with the tomato mixture, beef, lettuce, and cheese. Fold over (or roll) the tortilla to enclose the filling.

Variations

Vegetarian Burrito. Omit the meat. Substitute chopped raw *cabbage* for the lettuce if you wish. Serve with 1–2 tablespoons *sour cream.*

With chicken or pork. Substitute leftover shredded *chicken or pork* for the beef.

Note: Use the other half of the avocado in salads or sandwiches, or make *Hurry-Up Guacamole* (page 44).

EASY BAKED BEEF

I buy the smallest rump roast that's practical (about 2¹/2 pounds), halve it, and use one portion for this baked beef and freeze the other half for another meal—or cut it into cubes for beef stew. Even though the vegetables cook for almost 3 hours, they retain a great deal of texture. The secret is to cook them in a pot that's not too large: the meat and vegetables should just fit, and the liquid should come up to the cover of the pot. The leftover vegetables and liquid make a satisfying and flavorful soup. During tomato season I save the juice from the seeded tomatoes and put it

Easy Baked Beef (continued)

through a food mill along with the skins and pieces salvaged from less-than-perfect tomatoes, and use this juice as the cooking liquid. (Otherwise use canned tomato or V-8 juice.) Use the leftover beef in sandwiches or salads.

(Makes 1–2 servings)

3/4 cup chopped peeled carrots (about 2)	chopped tomatoes, or use canned whole tomatoes
1/2 cup chopped celery	1 1/4 pounds beef rump roast
1 1/4 cups chopped onions	1 cup tomato juice
1 cup peeled, seeded, and	Freshly ground black pepper

Mix together the vegetables; put 1/2 the mixture in a 6–8-cup ovenproof casserole. Add the meat, surround with the remaining vegetables, and pour over the tomato juice. Season with black pepper to taste.

Bake in a preheated 300°F oven for 2 1/2 hours, checking occasionally to make sure the meat is covered with the vegetables and cooking juices. Add water if necessary. Turn it once during cooking. Remove from the heat and let sit for at least 20 minutes before serving. Cut into thin slices and spoon over some of the vegetables, reserving the remaining vegetables and broth for soup. Serve with boiled potatoes or rice.

LEFTOVERS

Vegetables and Beef Soup

The leftover broth and vegetables make a flavorful vegetable soup. You can chop up some beef to add to the soup or leave it strictly vegetables if you wish. You may add any number of leftover cooked vegetables, such as diced potatoes or cooked beans. By far my favorite variation is as follows. The almost-raw corn adds texture.

(Serves 1)

1/3 cup uncooked macaroni	1/3 cup cooked kidney or pinto beans (canned are OK, but they're soft), or use 1/2 cup sliced leftover fresh green beans
3 cups leftover casserole vegetables and juice	
1 cup raw corn kernels (about 1 ear)	

| 2 tablespoons chopped fresh basil | Chopped cooked beef (optional) |

Heat the macaroni in a large pot of boiling water until cooked through but still tender (al dente). Drain and set aside. Place the casserole mixture in a pot, heat it, and add the corn kernels. Simmer for about 3 minutes, or until the corn is barely cooked through. Add the beans, macaroni, basil, and optional beef. Cook 2 minutes longer before serving.

OVEN-BRAISED POT ROAST

Pot roast is an eminently satisfying meat dish for a solo cook because the leftovers taste as good on day four as the pot roast did on day one. I consider rump the most flavorful cut, but use brisket or chuck if you wish (be sure to trim the fat thoroughly).

(Makes 2 meals)

Vegetable oil	1/3 cup chopped celery
A 2-pound piece of beef rump, brisket, or chuck	Freshly ground black pepper
2 cups peeled and chopped onions	3 cups chicken or beef stock, or a combination of water and tomato juice
2/3 cup peeled and coarsely chopped rutabaga or white turnips	11/2 cups blanched green beans
1 cup peeled and coarsely chopped carrots	2 tablespoons minced parsley, sweet marjoram, or lovage

Heat enough vegetable oil to film the bottom of a large, heavy frying pan. (The amount isn't critical, as you're going to drain off all the fat anyway.) Slowly brown the beef on all sides; this will take about 10 minutes. Remove the roast to an ovenproof casserole just large enough to hold the meat and vegetables comfortably.

In the same fat, over medium heat, cook the onions for 2 minutes, stirring frequently. Remove them from the pan with a slotted spoon and scatter around the meat. Add the rutabaga, carrots, celery, and a generous grinding of black pepper and cook for 5 minutes, stirring frequently, or

Oven-Braised Pot Roast (continued)

until the carrots and rutabaga are barely browned. Put the vegetables in a colander and let the fat drain off.

Pour the stock over the meat and onions; it should cover them with about 1 inch to spare. (If you're using lovage, add it now.) Cover the pan, place it in a preheated 325°F oven, and cook for 1¹/2 hours, adding more water if necessary. Add the reserved vegetables, making sure that they are covered with liquid. Return to the oven and cook for 1–1¹/4 hours, or until the meat is tender. Stir in the green beans and parsley and let the casserole sit, covered, for at least 15 minutes before serving. Skim off any fat. Serve with noodles, potatoes, or rice.

VARIATIONS

With paprika. Along with the onions, stir in 2 tablespoons *sweet Hungarian paprika.*

With tomatoes. Stir in 1 cup peeled, seeded, and chopped *tomatoes* along with the reserved vegetables.

With peppers. Stir in 1 cup peeled, seeded, and sliced *bell peppers* about 20 minutes before the end of the cooking time.

LEFTOVERS

• Reheat any leftover meat and vegetables and serve over rice.

• Thinly cut the meat and use for sandwiches, such as pot roast, horseradish, and onion on rye bread, or pot roast on whole wheat with lettuce, tomato, and mustard.

SWEET-AND-SOUR BRISKET

Brisket is an excellent weeknight main course because it tastes better upon standing. You can prepare this on the weekend and come home to a ready-made dinner with the bonus of leftover brisket for sandwiches or hash. After you assemble the ingredients, there's little to do but turn the meat once in a while as it bakes in the oven. Serve the brisket and vegetables with *Mashed Potatoes* (page 66), baked barley, or noodles and a green vegetable such as sautéed brussels sprouts or broccoli. Any leftovers freeze well.

(Makes 2–3 servings)

2 tablespoons canola or olive oil

1¹/2 pounds beef brisket

1 cup commercial barbecue sauce (made without liquid smoke)

Worcestershire sauce

1/4 cup orange juice

2 teaspoons chopped garlic

1 teaspoon dry mustard

2 teaspoons prepared horseradish

1–2 tablespoons brown sugar

2 cups chopped onions or sliced leek greens

1/2 cup chopped celery

1/3 cup chopped rutabaga (optional)

3/4 cup chopped carrots

Heat the oil in a frying pan and brown the brisket. Remove it to an ovenproof casserole that's just large enough to hold the meat, vegetables, and liquid. Mix together the barbecue sauce, a dash of Worcestershire sauce, the orange juice, garlic, dry mustard, horseradish, brown sugar, onions, celery, optional rutabaga, and carrots. Pour over the brisket. Cover the pan and place it in a preheated 325°F oven. Bake for 2¹/2 hours, basting every 1/2 hour or so. Remove the casserole from the oven and let the meat sit for 15 minutes before serving.

Note: Even a small whole brisket provides too much meat unless I'm planning to freeze several meals. The portion listed above is about one quarter of a standard-sized brisket. I ask the supermarket butcher to sell me half a brisket (about 4 pounds) which I then halve once again, cooking one half and freezing the other. If you prefer, cook the entire 4 pounds of brisket and freeze any leftovers. You won't need to change the quantity of vegetables, but you may need to add a little more liquid so that the brisket is covered.

VARIATION

With peppers and mushrooms. Omit the celery, rutabaga, and carrots. Add 1 cup chopped *green peppers* and 2 cups sliced fresh *mushrooms*.

LEFTOVERS

Barbecued Brisket Sandwich. Thinly slice the meat and reheat in the sauce. Place on a hamburger *bun,* sprinkle with freshly ground *black pepper,* and serve hot. Or first line the bun with *pickles* and sliced raw *onions*.

Brisket Hash

Try this for a hearty breakfast or a satisfying supper. If you're in a rush to cook the potatoes, microwave them.

(Serves 1)

1 tablespoon olive oil or butter	1/2 cup chopped cooked brisket
1/3 cup seeded and chopped	(page 178)
peppers (preferably a mix of	1 cup coarsely chopped cooked
red and green)	potatoes
2 tablespoons minced jalapeño	1/2 teaspoon minced rosemary
peppers (optional)	(optional)
1/3 cup chopped onion	Freshly ground black pepper
3 tablespoons chopped celery	Salt
Cumin	

Heat the oil in a heavy frying pan. Add the peppers (jalapeño, if using), onion, celery, and a pinch of cumin. Cook over medium heat, stirring frequently, for 3 minutes. Stir in the brisket, and cook, stirring constantly, for another 2 minutes. Add the potatoes, toss to distribute the vegetables and meat evenly, and pat into a single layer. Sprinkle with the rosemary, if you like, and black pepper. Cook over medium heat for about 10 minutes, turning once. The potatoes should be lightly browned. Season with salt. Serve with hot sauce or catsup.

GREEN PEPPERS STUFFED WITH BEEF AND RICE

Stuffing peppers is an old-fashioned, yet tasty, way to use up leftover rice and cooked meats and vegetables. The summer squash cooks in the stuffing, but retains some texture, making the stuffing taste fresher.

(Serves 1)

1 large bell pepper, halved and	2 tablespoons peeled, seeded,
seeded	and chopped red pepper
1 teaspoon olive oil	3 tablespoons chopped onion

1 tablespoon chopped celery
(including leaves)

3/4 cup cooked rice

1/3–1/2 cup chopped leftover *Pot
Roast* (page 177) or *Meat Loaf*
(page 172)

1/2 cup chopped leftover vegetables from *Pot Roast* (or use
other vegetables, such as

chopped broccoli, cooked
corn kernels, or spinach)

2–3 tablespoons stock from *Pot
Roast*

1/2 cup chopped raw summer
squash

1 tablespoon chopped dill, basil,
or parsley

Salt

Place the pepper in a large bowl, cover with boiling water, and let sit
while you prepare the stuffing.

Heat the oil in a heavy frying pan. Stir in the red pepper and onion,
and cook for 2 minutes. Add the celery, rice, beef, and vegetables. Cook,
stirring, for 1 minute, until the mixture is combined. Moisten with stock
to taste. Stir in the summer squash and herbs. Taste and season with salt.

Drain the pepper and dry it. Place the halves in a small greased baking
dish. Loosely pack the cavities with stuffing (it will expand slightly as it
cooks). Mound the tops. Lay a piece of buttered aluminum foil over the
tops of the peppers to keep the rice on top from drying out and bake the
pepper halves in a preheated 350°F oven for 25–30 minutes, or until they
are cooked through. Remove the foil the last 10 minutes. Let sit for 15
minutes before serving.

BAKED OXTAILS

Eating certain foods, such as oxtails (and lobster), really ought to be a solitary endeavor because they're so messy to handle. Save any leftover broth
for recipes where you'd like a deep, rich beef flavor. The best pot to use is
a small, deep one just large enough to hold the oxtails and vegetables.

(Serves 1)

2 tablespoons coarsely chopped
raw bacon

1 1/2 cups chopped onions
(about 2 medium)

1 1/2 cups chopped carrots

1 cup chopped celery,
leaves and stalks (or fennel
stalks)

1 teaspoon chopped garlic

1 1/2 pounds oxtails

Baked Oxtails (continued)

1 cup liquid (stock, beer, wine,
   vegetable juice, or water)
3 sprigs fresh thyme

Salt and freshly ground black
   pepper
Lemon juice (optional)

Place the bacon pieces in a heavy stove-top casserole. Cook over low
heat for about 5 minutes to partially render the fat, then stir in the
onions, carrots, celery, and garlic. Continue cooking, stirring frequently,
for about 5 minutes—or until the vegetables are barely wilted. Add the
oxtails, liquid, and thyme. The liquid should cover the oxtails.

Cover and bake in a preheated 325°F oven for 2 hours, or until the oxtails are tender. Add additional liquid if needed. Skim off any fat from the
surface. Taste and season with salt, pepper, and the optional lemon juice.

VARIATION

With tomatoes. **Add 1 cup chopped** *tomatoes.*

LAMB CHOPS WITH TARRAGON

Try these with pilaf and sautéed cherry tomatoes—or a tomato and
sweet-onion salad. Add 2 minutes to the cooking time if the chops are
refrigerated.

(Serves 1)

2 loin lamb chops (about 5
   ounces)
Freshly ground black pepper
1 1/2 teaspoons vegetable oil,
   such as canola
2–3 tablespoons chicken, beef,
   or lamb stock

1 tablespoon dry sherry or
   bourbon
1 tablespoon chopped fresh
   tarragon

Rinse and dry the lamb chops and generously coat with black pepper.
Heat the oil in a heavy frying pan and sear the chops on both sides.
Lower the heat slightly and cook the lamb chops to the degree of done-
ness you prefer. Rare is about 3 minutes on each side. Set them aside,
loosely covered with a towel to keep warm.

Spoon off the fat in the pan, retaining any cooking juices. Add the stock and sherry. Raise the heat and stir for about 30 seconds. Add the tarragon.

Pour the sauce over the lamb chops and serve.

VARIATION

With fresh ginger. Replace 1 tablespoon of the stock with freshly squeezed *orange juice.* Add 2 teaspoons chopped *fresh gingerroot* along with the stock and sherry. Strain and add the fresh tarragon just before serving.

BROILED LAMB CHOPS WITH A MANGO SALSA

The texture of ripe mangoes contrasts nicely with lamb. You can prepare the salsa in the morning and need only broil the lamb chops at night. (If you've never prepared mangoes from scratch, use rubber gloves while peeling them: Some people end up with a poison-ivylike reaction to mango skin.) Adjust the quantity of scallions and herbs to your taste.

(Serves 1)

2 loin lamb chops (about 5 ounces)	1–3 tablespoons minced scallion
1/2 teaspoon vegetable oil	1 tablespoon lime juice
1/2 cup peeled and chopped fresh mango	1–2 teaspoons minced basil or mint
	Basil or mint sprig, for garnish

Preheat the broiler to 500°F. Brush the chops with the oil, place on a broiler pan, and broil for about 3–5 minutes on the first side. Turn the chops and broil 2 minutes longer—just enough to sear the flesh. The chops will be medium rare. The broiling time depends upon how well done you like lamb.

Meanwhile mix together the mango, scallion, lime juice, and basil. Arrange in a line on a plate and flank with the lamb chops. Garnish with a sprig of basil or mint.

VARIATION

Grilled Chops. Grill the chops on a barbecue grill—preferably at the

Broiled Lamb Chops with a Mango Salsa (continued)
same time that you are grilling something else, such as ribs or vegetables for another meal, so you're not heating up the grill just for 2 chops.

STIR-FRIED LAMB WITH BROCCOLI

Serve this with rice. It's similar to a Chinese stir-fry without the cornstarch sauce.

(Serves 1)

3 ounces raw lamb, thinly sliced (about 1 cup)
1 teaspoon cider vinegar
1 teaspoon minced garlic
1 tablespoon peeled and minced fresh gingerroot
Freshly ground black pepper
1 tablespoon vegetable oil
1/4 cup sliced scallions, both green and white portions
1 1/2 cups sliced broccoli stems
1 cup sliced mushrooms
1/4 cup chicken or beef stock
1 tablespoon chopped coriander
Salt (optional)

Mix together the lamb, vinegar, garlic, gingerroot, and black pepper. Marinate for 30 minutes. Heat the vegetable oil in a heavy nonreactive pan. Add the scallions and broccoli, and cook over high heat, stirring constantly, for 2 minutes. Remove from the pan with a slotted spoon, and set aside. Add the lamb mixture to the same pan, and cook over high heat, stirring constantly, until it is barely cooked through, about 1–2 minutes. Lower the heat, add the mushrooms, and cook 2 minutes longer, stirring constantly, or until the mushrooms are cooked through. Put the broccoli and scallions back in the pan along with the stock. Cook, stirring constantly, for 1 minute. Add the coriander.

Taste to see that all the ingredients are cooked through, and add salt if necessary. Serve with brown or white rice.

VARIATIONS

With red pepper. Add 1/2 cup peeled, seeded, and thinly sliced *red pepper* along with the lamb mixture.

With sesame oil. Proceed as above. Just before serving, taste and stir in 1/2 teaspoon *Oriental sesame oil.*

With beef, chicken, or pork. Substitute for the lamb.

PORK SCHNITZEL

Most supermarket meat departments carry boneless pork cutlets by the pound. You can either ask a butcher to sell you less (which most butchers are willing to do), or you can repackage and freeze the extra meat for future meals. Dipping the meat in egg white rather than a whole egg gives it a more delicate flavor. No matter where you head in Switzerland, Germany, Austria, or Hungary you can sample some version of schnitzel. This version is equally good made with veal, turkey, or chicken cutlets. You can bread the cutlet in the morning, refrigerate it, and then cook it when you arrive home from work.

(Serves 1)

1 egg white
Dry mustard
1/4 teaspoon soy sauce
   (optional)
A 4-ounce boneless pork cutlet,
   pounded thin

3 tablespoons fine dry breadcrumbs
2 teaspoons butter or olive oil
1 lime

In a mixing bowl, beat the egg white until it starts to foam. Stir in a pinch of dry mustard and the optional soy sauce. Dip the pork cutlet in the mixture, coating thoroughly, and then in the breadcrumbs. Be sure that both sides are covered well. Set aside, or refrigerate, covered by a piece of waxed paper or plastic wrap.

Heat the butter in a heavy frying pan until hot. Add the cutlet, lower the heat slightly, and cook for about 2 minutes. Turn with a spatula, and brown the other side. Continue cooking, turning once again if necessary, until the pork is cooked through, about 5 minutes in total. When done, the flesh will be white. Drain on a paper bag. Serve with lime quarters.

VARIATION

Chicken, Veal, or Turkey Schnitzel. Substitute pounded *chicken, veal,* or *turkey* for the pork, marinating the meat for at least 2 hours in 3 tablespoons freshly squeezed lemon or lime juice. Dry and proceed as above, omitting the soy sauce. You could also add 1 tablespoon minced herbs to the breadcrumbs, such as *sweet marjoram, parsley,* or *tarragon.*

Pork Schnitzel (continued)

LEFTOVERS

Any leftover meat makes a delicious sandwich. Toast a *bun*, spread with a combination of *Dijon mustard* and *mayonnaise*, top with the leftover pork, a sliced *tomato*, and, if you like, *pimientos* or raw *green peppers*. Season with plenty of freshly ground *black pepper*.

BONELESS PORK CUTLETS WITH MUSTARD AND VINEGAR

The mustard and vinegar serve merely to flavor the pork, not to create a sauce.

(Serves 1)

3–4 ounces boneless pork cutlets, pounded thin	Freshly ground black pepper
1^1/2–2 teaspoons Dijon mustard	Flour
	2 teaspoons canola oil
	1 teaspoon sherry vinegar

Place the cutlets on a flat surface. Lightly spread on both sides with Dijon mustard and sprinkle with black pepper. Dip in flour and shake off excess. Set aside.

In a heavy stove-top pan, heat the oil and brown the cutlets. Lower the heat and cook for 5–10 minutes or until cooked through. (The time varies depending upon the thickness of the cutlets.) Pour off any fat, add the sherry vinegar, quickly swishing the cutlets in the vinegar before it evaporates. Serve immediately. *Mashed Potatoes* (page 66) and pickled red cabbage go well with this—or you could sauté shredded cabbage with apples.

VARIATION

With sour cream. Increase the vinegar to 2 teaspoons, and add 2 tablespoons *sour or heavy cream.* Pour the sauce over the cutlets.

Note: Be sure to use a pan, such as enamel or stainless-steel, that won't react to the vinegar.

BONELESS PORK CUTLETS WITH SUMMER SQUASH

When baby summer squash is in season, this is a delicious way to enjoy its delicate flavor. The amount of pork depends upon how much meat you fancy. I like a lot of vegetables with a little meat—you might prefer a heartier version. If the squash is freshly picked, it will be full of vegetable juices and you probably won't need to add water. Otherwise, add 1–2 tablespoons of water. It's not necessary to peel and seed the tomato.

(Serves 1)

2–3 teaspoons olive oil
2–4 ounces boneless pork cutlets
 (1 or 2)
1 small yellow squash or
 zucchini, washed, quartered,
 and cut into 1/2-inch slices
 (about 1 cup)
1/3 cup chopped onion
1/3 cup chopped tomato

1/3 cup corn kernels (frozen
 is fine)
Freshly ground black pepper
1–2 teaspoons chopped
 herbs, such as a mixture
 of chives, sweet marjoram,
 and parsley
Water, if needed
Salt

Heat the oil in a stove-top casserole with a lid. Add the pork and brown on both sides over medium-high heat. Remove from the pan and set aside. Add the squash and onion and cook over medium heat, stirring frequently, for 2 minutes. Stir in the tomato and corn, and then return the pork to the pot along with any of its juices. Sprinkle generously with black pepper and add the herbs. Add water if the mixture looks dry. Cover the pan and cook over low heat until the vegetables are soft but still have some texture, and the pork is cooked through, about 5–8 minutes. Taste and season with salt.

VARIATION

With mushrooms and garlic. Substitute 1/2 cup sliced *mushrooms* for the corn and add 1/2 teaspoon chopped *garlic* along with the onion.

STUFFED PORK CHOP

You can stuff a pork chop with virtually any bread stuffing, but a corn-bread stuffing is tasty—particularly one made with leftover *Cornbread with Vegetables* (page 270). Ask the butcher to cut a "pocket," an opening along the edge opposite the bone. You can assemble the meal in a jiffy and relax, or go for a walk, while the chop is baking. Save this meal for a night when you have a trencherman's appetite. It's hearty.

(Makes 1 stuffed double pork chop)

1–2 teaspoons butter or olive oil
A 1³/₄-inch-thick pork chop cut
    with a pocket (4–6 ounces)
¹/₂ cup chopped sweet onion
1 tablespoon chopped fresh
    herbs, such as parsley, basil,
    sweet marjoram, or chervil

¹/₃ cup chopped mushrooms
1 cup crumbled leftover corn-
    bread crumbs
Milk or stock
1 egg, beaten

Heat 1 teaspoon butter in a heavy frying pan and quickly sear the pork chop on both sides. Set the chop aside. If necessary, add additional fat to the pan. Sauté the onion and herbs in the fat for about 2 minutes, then stir in the mushrooms and cornbread crumbs. Put the mixture into a bowl and add just enough milk or stock to moisten it, but not make it soppy. Mix in the egg.

Stuff the pork chop with ¹/₂ of the cornbread mixture. Take any remaining stuffing and place it in a small oiled oven-proof dish. Top with the pork chop. Bake the chop in a preheated 350°F oven for 50–60 minutes, or until the chop is cooked through. Serve with apple-sauce or *Pear Sauce* (page 290) and blanched broccoli or asparagus.

STUFFED PORK CHOP
WITH APPLES AND SQUASH

This is a hearty meal-in-one just right for a cold winter night. If you pre-fer, rather than stuffing a thick pork chop, top 2 pork chops with the stuffing and reduce the cooking time by 10 minutes. There's no need for salt because the bacon is salty. Save the mushroom caps for another meal. This is a good way to use up fresh pieces of winter squash.

(Serves 1)

1 strip raw bacon, cut into
  $1/4$-inch pieces (or 2
  teaspoons butter)
$1/3$ cup diced onion (about
  $1/2$ medium onion)
1 tablespoon finely diced red
  pepper
1 tablespoon chopped scallion
  stems (optional)
3 tablespoons chopped mushroom stems
$3/4$–1 cup coarsely shredded
  breadcrumbs

Freshly ground black pepper
1 medium egg, lightly beaten
A 1-inch-thick pork chop
  (about 5 ounces), halved to
  the bone to make a pocket
  for stuffing
1 apple, cored and cut into
  thick slices
Winter squash, seeded, peeled,
  and thickly sliced (4–6 slices)
$1/3$–$1/2$ cup stock or water

Place the bacon in a heavy skillet and render the fat slowly. Remove the bacon bits with a slotted spoon and place them in a large mixing bowl. To the fat in the pan add the onion, pepper, optional scallions, and mushrooms, and cook over medium heat, stirring frequently, for 3 min-utes. Stir in the breadcrumbs and cook 2 minutes longer, stirring con-stantly. Add to the mixing bowl and toss with the bacon. Let cool slightly, then moisten with the egg and a tablespoon or two of stock or water. (The amount of liquid you add depends upon how moist you like stuffing to be.) Taste and season with black pepper.

Sear the pork shop on both sides in a hot pan. Fill the pocket with the stuffing. If there's any leftover stuffing arrange it around the chop. Place

Stuffed Pork Chop with Apples and Squash (continued)

in a small baking dish about 6 inches in diameter. Surround with alternating slices of apple and winter squash and pour the remaining stock over them.

Cover the pan with foil and bake in a preheated 350°F oven for 30 minutes. Remove the foil, raise the heat to 400, and bake 10 minutes longer, adding more stock or water if necessary. Serve with a tossed green salad.

VARIATIONS

Herb Stuffing. Omit the pepper and scallions and add 1 tablespoon chopped fresh *sweet marjoram* or 1 tablespoon chopped *parsley.* Season with a pinch of *cayenne pepper* and proceed as above.

Stuffed Chicken Breast. Flatten a whole *chicken breast.* Loosen the skin from the flesh and stuff with the stuffing from the above recipe, adding 1 teaspoon minced fresh *thyme.* Moisten with 1 tablespoon water or stock if necessary. Dot skin with 1 tablespoon *butter* or dot with *chicken fat.* Baste occasionally with the fat from the pan.

DRIED LIMA BEAN AND PORK CHOP CASSEROLE

Dried lima beans are particularly tasty baked with a pork chop. The cooking time varies, depending upon the age of the beans. If you cook 1/3 cup extra dried beans, you can make a hummuslike dip.

(Serves 1)

1/3 cup dried lima beans
1/2 cup coarsely chopped onion
1 teaspoon minced garlic
1–2 teaspoons chopped fresh or
  frozen jalapeño pepper
1/2 cup *Tomato Sauce* (page 98)
  or commercial sauce made
  with chunks of tomatoes

3/4–1 cup water
1 pork chop (about 4 ounces)
Chili powder
Curry powder
Salt and freshly ground black
  pepper

Cover the lima beans with water, bring to a boil, and boil for 2 minutes. Let the beans sit in the water while you chop the vegetables. Drain the beans, and place them in a small, deep ovenproof casserole with a cover. Mix with the onion, garlic, jalapeño pepper, tomato sauce, and water. Place in a preheated 450°F oven for 25 minutes.

Rub the pork chop with chili powder and/or curry powder to taste. Set it aside. Remove the beans from the oven, check to make sure they are covered with liquid, and add additional water if necessary. Top with the pork chop. Cover and bake for 25–35 minutes, or until the pork chop is cooked through and the beans are soft. Add salt and pepper to taste.

VARIATIONS

With corn. Add 1/2 cup frozen *corn* kernels along with the pork chop. Proceed as above.

With ham. Omit the pork chop. Cube 1/2–3/4 cup of good quality *ham*. Add it to the casserole along with the lima beans.

LEFTOVERS

Lima Bean Dip

This is similar to hummus but with a more complex flavor and a sweeter aftertaste. Defrosted frozen tahini works well in this recipe.

(Makes about 3/4 cup)

3/4 cup leftover lima bean mixture
1/2 teaspoon chopped garlic
Scant 1/8 teaspoon salt
3 tablespoons lime or lemon juice

2 tablespoons tahini (sesame seed paste)
Cumin
2–3 tablespoons water

Place the lima bean mixture in the container of a blender or food processor. Put the garlic on a flat surface, top with the salt, and with your knife held at an angle push down and scrape at the garlic and salt until the garlic has a purée-like texture. Add it to the blender, along with the lime juice, tahini, a generous pinch of cumin, and 2–3 tablespoons water. Purée the mixture for 15–30 seconds, or until the ingredients are com-

Lima Bean Dip (continued)

bined. The mixture should still have some texture. Taste and adjust seasonings.

Variation

With sesame oil. Add 1/4 teaspoon *Oriental sesame oil* along with the lima bean mixture. Proceed as above.

PORK CHOP BAKED WITH BROWN RICE AND ZUCCHINI

You can omit the spices, but they add a lot of flavor to this one-step casserole. If you use a commercial sauce, one with chunks of tomato tastes better.

(Serves 1)

1/3 cup brown rice
1/2 cup water
2/3 cup tomato sauce, either homemade (page 98) or store-bought
1/2 cup thickly sliced onion
Salt
1/2 zucchini

4 mushrooms (optional)
1 pork chop (about 4 ounces)
Ground ginger
Ground cloves
Ground cumin
Freshly ground black pepper
Lemon juice (optional)

Place the brown rice in a small ovenproof casserole. Stir in the water, 1/3 cup of the tomato sauce, the onion, and salt to taste. Quarter the zucchini and place it along the edges of the pan. Scatter the mushrooms, if using, in the center. Rub the pork chop with pinches of ginger, cloves, and cumin. Place it on top of the mushrooms and top with the remaining tomato sauce. Cover the pan and bake it in a preheated 450°F oven for 35 minutes. Uncover the pan, stir the tomato sauce covering the pork chop into the rice, and spoon some of the pan liquid over the pork chop. Bake another 15 minutes, adding additional water if needed. The rice should be cooked through and the pork chop browned. Taste and season with salt and pepper, and add a squeeze of lemon juice if you wish.

VARIATION

With coriander or basil. Omit the spices and substitute 1 tablespoon chopped *coriander or basil*. Stir into the rice after the mixture has cooked for 35 minutes.

CHINESE-STYLE PORK MEATBALLS

I enjoy eating "Lion's Head," a ground pork and cabbage dish from eastern China. But most versions, even in restaurants, are too greasy for my taste. This recipe isn't the least bit authentic—but it tastes great, and reheats beautifully.

(Makes 1–2 servings)

1/2 pound lean ground pork
2 teaspoons dry sherry
11/2–2 tablespoons soy sauce
1/2 teaspoon sugar
1 tablespoon minced garlic
   (optional)
1/4 cup cold water
1 tablespoon cornstarch

Vegetable oil
3 cups bok choy (Chinese
   cabbage) or cabbage
1 tablespoon chopped coriander
1 cup chicken or vegetable
   stock
1/3 cup shredded carrot
Salt (optional)

Place the ground pork in a bowl, and gently mix in the sherry, soy sauce, sugar, and garlic, if using. Stir together the water and cornstarch and stir it into the meat mixture. Cover the bowl and let the mixture sit for at least 20 minutes.

Heat about 3 tablespoons oil in a large frying pan. Using a 1/3-cup measure, scoop out the meat mixture and put it in the oil. Continue until all the meat is formed into balls. You should have 3 or 4. Turn them, flattening slightly with a spatula, and brown on the other sides. Remove from the pan with a slotted spoon.

In the same pan, stir-fry the cabbage and coriander for 3 minutes, stirring constantly. Remove from the pan with a slotted spoon and put the cabbage in a heavy stove-top casserole. Top with the pork patties, and pour over the stock. Cover, and slowly simmer for about 20 minutes. Stir

Chinese-Style Pork Meatballs (continued)
in the carrot, re-cover the pan, and simmer about 5 minutes longer. You want the carrots to retain some crunch to contrast with the cooked texture of the cabbage. Sprinkle lightly with salt if you wish. Serve with boiled white or brown rice.

LEFTOVERS

Any leftovers reheat well on top of the stove or in a microwave.

This is a tasty, easy meal-in-one. If you wish, substitute turkey sausage, but since it's less fatty, you'll probably need to coat it with olive oil before baking. Either way, pour off the oil before serving. If you can buy Italian sausages only by the pound, individually wrap them in plastic wrap, and freeze them. Then all you need to do is defrost one in the refrigerator the night before cooking.

(Serves 1)

1 Italian sausage (or turkey sausage), about 1/4 pound	1 pepper, seeded
	1 onion, peeled
1 baking potato (russet or Idaho)	Freshly ground black pepper

Halve the sausage lengthwise, and cut the potato, pepper, and onion into sixths. Sprinkle with freshly ground black pepper. Bake in a preheated 400°F oven for 40–50 minutes, basting occasionally, or until the sausage and vegetables are cooked through.

VARIATIONS

With fennel. Cut a small fresh *fennel* crosswise into 1-inch pieces. Lightly coat with *olive oil* before baking.

With zucchini or summer squash. Trim 1 *squash* and quarter it lengthwise. Lightly coat with *olive oil* before baking.

"Cooking brings out my imagination. Just because food is fuel for the body doesn't mean that cooking it has to be practical. It can be fun: You actually can take a bunch of different ingredients and throw them together and voilà!—something happens. I enjoy preparing stir-fries, spicy shrimp—and Caesar salad. I don't mind eating alone because I can fix exactly what I want. Opening a bottle of wine is as close to setting the table as I get."

Dan Garlick, ecologist

BONUS ROAST PORK

Both the roast pork and its bonus of a totally different-tasting leftover, barbecued shredded pork, are easy to make. This recipe works well with a standard pork roast as well as a cut such as Boston butt.

(Makes at least 2 meals)

1 1/2–2 pounds pork butt or roast
2 cloves garlic
1 tablespoon Dijon mustard

Freshly ground black pepper
1/2 onion, thinly sliced
2 strips bacon

Place the pork on a flat surface. Peel and sliver the garlic cloves. With a sharp knife, poke holes in the flesh of the pork about 1 inch deep, and insert the slivers. Smear the roast with the mustard, and sprinkle with black pepper. Press the onion slices into the mustard-coated flesh. Cut the bacon slices into thirds and lay over the onion. Roast the pork in a preheated 350°F oven for at least 1 hour, basting occasionally. (The bacon will cook and may fall into the pan. That's fine, it's already basted the meat. You can discard it now.) Raise the heat to 400°F, and cook the roast for 20 minutes or so to brown the surface of the onions. Do not let them burn. Remove the roast from the oven and let it sit for at least 20 minutes before slicing. Serve with *Accordion Baked Potato* (page 64) or *Mashed Potatoes* (page 66) and a marinated cucumber or green pepper salad.

Bonus Roast Pork (continued)

LEFTOVERS

Barbecued Pork. Put any leftover meat in a pot and cover with water. Add 1/3 cup *cider vinegar* and 1/3 cup *barbecue sauce.* Stir to combine. Cover the pan and bake in a preheated 325°F oven for at least 2 hours, or until the meat shreds when pulled apart with a fork. Remove the meat from the sauce and set aside. Place the sauce in a pan and boil it rapidly until it is the consistency you prefer. Taste and correct the seasonings. (I favor a vinegar-based barbecue. If you'd like it sweeter, add 1 tablespoon *brown sugar* and a dab of *mustard.* Simmer to meld the ingredients.) Shred the pork and stir it into the sauce. Serve with corn on the cob, mashed potatoes or rice, and a tossed lettuce and tomato salad.

Pulled Pork Sandwich. Proceed as directly above. Moisten the shredded pork with the sauce and use as filling in a *hamburger bun.* Customarily, the bun is not toasted, but pan-toasting the bun gives a better textural contrast.

LIME-MARINATED ROAST PORK

Lime juice makes an excellent marinade, cutting the rich taste of the pork. Marinate it all day while you're at work, or in the refrigerator overnight.

(Makes 2 meals)

A 1½-pound pork roast
½ cup freshly squeezed lime
   juice
2 tablespoons barbecue sauce
   (preferably one without
   liquid smoke)
2 cloves peeled garlic

1 slice raw bacon, cut into
   pieces
1 small onion, sliced
1 large potato, peeled and
   thinly sliced
Freshly ground black pepper
Salt (optional)

Place the pork roast in a glass bowl just large enough to hold the meat and sauce. Mix together the lime juice and barbecue sauce and pour over the pork. Cover the bowl and marinate for at least 8 hours.

Remove the pork from the marinade, and pat dry. (Reserve the marinade.) Cut the garlic into slivers, and, using a sharp knife, insert them in the flesh of the pork. In a medium-sized baking dish (about 6 inches) scatter some of the bacon pieces, then alternately layer the onion and potato. Top with the roast, then grind black pepper on the surface. Bake in a preheated 350°F oven. After 30 minutes, start basting with the reserved marinade. After 1 hour shift the pork roast to one side of the vegetables, and continue basting. The roast should be done after about 1 1/4 hours. Remove and let sit for at least 20 minutes before serving. Taste a potato to make sure it is cooked through. If not, raise the oven temperature to 400°F and bake another 15 minutes, basting with the pan juices occasionally. Season with salt if you wish.

LEFTOVERS

Thinly slice the pork and use in a sandwich on toasted *whole wheat bread* with *Creole mustard* and shredded *cabbage* and sliced *tomato*. Or make:

Egg Rolls

These Chinese-American egg rolls use vegetables that are easy to find. I buy commercial egg-roll skins, divide them into serving portions, and freeze any extra skins for future use. Then all I need to do is defrost and fill them before frying.

(Serves 1)

Oil (preferably peanut)
1/2–1 teaspoon minced fresh
   gingerroot
1/2 teaspoon minced garlic
3–4 tablespoons finely chopped
   leftover pork
2 tablespoons shredded raw
   carrot
2 tablespoons chopped scallions

3/4 cup finely shredded fresh
   cabbage
1 teaspoon soy sauce
1/4 teaspoon Oriental sesame oil
1 teaspoon dry sherry (optional)
1 teaspoon flour
1 teaspoon water
3–4 commercial egg-roll skins

Heat 2 teaspoons oil in a heavy frying pan or wok. Add the gingerroot, garlic, and pork. Cook, stirring constantly, for 30 seconds. Stir in the car-

Egg Rolls (continued)

rot, scallions, and cabbage, and continue cooking, stirring constantly, for 2–3 minutes or until the vegetables are wilted. Add the soy sauce, sesame oil, and sherry, if using, and stir only until incorporated. Set the mixture aside to cool slightly.

Mix together the flour and water until it forms a paste. Take the egg-roll filling and divide it into 3–4 portions. Squeeze the filling between your palms to extract extra moisture and some of the fat. (Or you could roll it in a dishtowel and press down before dividing into portions.)

Take the egg-roll skins and place on a flat surface in a row. They should be catty-corner with their edges facing north and south. Place a portion of filling in the middle of each roll, then fold over the lower third of the egg roll skin. Fold in the two ends, enclosing the filling. Moisten the top edge of the egg roll with the water-flour paste and press down. Continue until all the egg rolls are formed.

Pour enough oil to cover the egg rolls into a deep pot or wok. Heat it until a piece of egg-roll skin dropped into the oil sizzles and immediately starts to cook, about 350°F. Deep-fry the rolls for about 3–4 minutes and drain them on a kitchen towel or paper bags. Depending upon the size of the pot, you may wish to fry the rolls in more than 1 batch. Serve immediately with a dipping sauce made of equal parts soy sauce and white vinegar into which you've stirred minced gingerroot to taste. (Cool the oil, strain it into a bottle, and reuse it.)

PASTA, GRAINS, AND EGGS

Many solo cooks who will try nothing else are willing to risk pasta. "It's my favorite food," they say. "I eat it once or twice a week. It's easy. It cooks in minutes."

It's true that pasta provides instant gratification. It's also a wonderful pantry food: a pouch of frozen tortellini stashed in the freezer needs only to be boiled and tossed with herbs and a touch of butter or oil. Or you can boil dried pasta and open a jar of commercial tomato sauce, zap its flavor with some fresh basil and grated Parmesan cheese, and dinner is ready.

For something that seems so straightforward, however, there are still a few techniques to keep in mind when cooking pasta. It's important to cook it in boiling salted water in a large pot so the pasta has plenty of room to move. You'll also need to watch the cooking time: the only way to tell when pasta is done is to taste it. Even two packages of the same brand of dried pasta can vary in cooking time up to 5 minutes, depending on their shelf life. Fresh pasta always cooks faster than dried.

Regardless of the kind of pasta, when it's done it should be cooked through, but still slightly firm (al dente).

It's also important to drain the pasta immediately in a colander before tossing with the sauce. You should serve it as soon as possible. If you wait, the pasta continues to cook and becomes overcooked and mushy or gummy.

Rice is almost as versatile as pasta. It's an excellent starch to accompany virtually any main dish, but it's also good on its own, in dishes such as risotto. Or you can combine cold leftover rice with leftover vegetables, poultry, or meat and make a flavorful salad. Fresh herbs, such as parsley, basil, and sweet marjoram, perk up leftover rice salads.

Finally, when there's an egg in the refrigerator you need never go hungry. For years we were told to avoid eggs, but the current thinking is that four eggs a week is just fine. You can make an omelet, a tart—or just enjoy them scrambled with a piece of toast.

These may be basic foods, but there's nothing simple about the way they taste.

> *"I like to cook for myself—but not every day. But even when I'm eating take-out, I try to make eating dinner something special. I'll light the candles, put on classical music, and pour myself a glass of wine. I never eat with the TV on, I never eat fast, and I try to avoid taking phone calls during dinner. Taking the time to do this gives me a sense of peace. I think that people make their lives so informal that they've lost sight of making dinner special for themselves."*
>
> *Jefferson Sa, clinician*

SPAGHETTI WITH BREADCRUMBS AND HERBS

This dish goes together in minutes. All you need is fresh breadcrumbs and a handful of herbs, preferably a mixture of more than one. Mint or dill combined with parsley works well, as does a combination of coriander, mint, and parsley. The breadcrumbs adhere to the spaghetti, giving texture.

(Serves 1)

1–2 teaspoons butter	Salt
2 tablespoons fresh breadcrumbs	3 ounces spaghetti or bows
	3 tablespoons mixed fresh herbs

Melt the butter in a heavy frying pan, add the breadcrumbs, and cook over medium heat, stirring constantly, for about 3 minutes or until the breadcrumbs are browned. Set the mixture aside.

Boil a pot of water, add salt to taste, and the pasta. Gently boil until the pasta is cooked through. Fresh pasta will cook in less than 5 minutes; dried pasta will take 10–12 minutes. Drain the spaghetti thoroughly. Toss first with the breadcrumbs and then with the herbs.

SPAGHETTI WITH AN UNCOOKED TOMATO SAUCE

The heat of the spaghetti slightly cooks the tomatoes, onion, and garlic. Any leftover spaghetti makes a delicious base for recycling cooked vegetables.

(Makes 1 generous serving)

1^1/3 cups peeled, seeded, and diced raw tomatoes
2–3 tablespoons finely chopped fresh onion or scallions
1 teaspoon minced garlic
1 tablespoon chopped basil (optional)

1 teaspoon olive oil
Salt and freshly ground black pepper
4–6 ounces thin spaghetti
Freshly grated Parmesan or Romano cheese (optional)

In a large bowl, mix together the tomatoes, onion, garlic, optional basil, olive oil, salt, and a generous amount of freshly ground black pepper. Let sit while you cook the spaghetti.

Bring a pot of water to a boil; add salt and the spaghetti. Cook, stirring occasionally, until the spaghetti is cooked through, but still slightly chewy (al dente). Drain the spaghetti in a colander and immediately toss it with the tomato mixture in its bowl. Top with Parmesan cheese to taste if you wish.

Note: You can also make the the tomato sauce ahead and chill. The contrast of the cold sauce with the hot pasta is interesting.

LEFTOVERS

Spaghetti Salad. If you cook too much pasta, refrigerate any leftover pasta and sauce and bring it to room temperature before adding any leftover vegetables. Even a small amount such as 1 cup pasta with sauce will make a light dinner when mixed together with ^{1}/2–^{3}/4 cup cooked *broccoli* or ^{1}/2 cup cooked *peas* or *corn* kernels (or a mixture of both) and *oil* and *vinegar* to taste. Add 1 tablespoon fresh herbs, such as *basil* or *parsley*, to freshen the taste.

PESTO

Pesto, the Northern Italian basil and Parmesan cheese sauce, is best made in small batches. This recipe makes enough for a generous serving of pasta (3–4 ounces)—or a modest serving with enough left over to be spooned over a baked potato, added to an omelet, or put in mayonnaise for the dressing of a chicken or cooked vegetable salad. I like the addition of a sprig of sweet marjoram and half a leaf of sage—but the customary herb is fresh basil. Pine nuts are traditional, but you can use walnuts. Either a food processor or blender works well—don't overblend or you will lose the texture.

(Makes 1/2 cup pesto)

1 cup packed basil leaves
1 sprig of sweet marjoram
(optional)
1/2 teaspoon chopped fresh
sage (optional)
2–3 tablespoons olive oil
2–3 tablespoons grated
Parmesan cheese

2 tablespoons pine nuts or
chopped walnuts
2 cloves garlic, minced (about
1 teaspoon)
Salt (optional)

In a blender or food processor, blend together the basil, optional sweet marjoram and sage, olive oil, Parmesan, pine nuts, and garlic until the basil is incorporated into the sauce. Season with salt if necessary. (I usually don't add salt because the cheese is salty.) Serve over cooked pasta. Any leftover pesto should be covered with a film of olive oil and refrigerated.

LEFTOVERS

In chicken salad. Add 1 tablespoon of leftover pesto to *Chicken Salad* (page 149).

Baked Scallops with Pesto (page 120).

SUPER-QUICK PASTA WITH CANNED TOMATOES AND CAPERS

You can assemble this dish in 10 minutes with pantry shelf items on a night when the refrigerator is bare. The anchovies aren't discernible as such; they meld into the sauce, deepening the flavor. You'll use only the canned tomatoes, not their juices, which you can freeze for soups, or purée with some celery leaves and lemon juice and serve over ice for a pick-me-up.

(Serves 1)

1 tablespoon olive oil	4 anchovies
2/3 cup chopped onion (preferably a red Bermuda, for color)	1/2–1 teaspoon whole capers
	Salt and freshly ground black pepper
A 14 1/2-ounce can whole tomatoes	2–3 ounces angel hair pasta

Bring a large pot of water to a boil. Heat the olive oil in a heavy pan. Stir in the onion, lower the heat to medium, and cook, stirring frequently, for 2 minutes. Lift out the tomatoes from the can, add them to the onion, and press down with a wooden spoon or a potato masher to break them up slightly. (Or you could chop them on a chopping block—but it's a messier procedure.) Cook over high heat for 2 minutes, stirring frequently, then cover the pan, lower the heat, and cook 3 minutes longer. Finely chop the anchovies and add them to the pan, along with the capers. The tomatoes should be cooked down to a purée. If they seem to be dried out, moisten them with 2–3 tablespoons of juice remaining in the can. Taste and season with salt and pepper.

Cook the pasta: Add salt to the boiling water along with 2–3 ounces angel hair pasta. Boil rapidly for 4–5 minutes or until done. Drain and add to the tomato-sauce pan. Swirl around so that all the sauce is incorporated. Serve immediately.

VARIATION

With tuna and shells. This is a heartier sauce for a more substantial

Super-Quick Pasta with Canned Tomatoes and Capers (continued)
pasta. Omit the anchovies. After the tomato mixture is cooked, stir in a drained 3¼-ounce can *tuna fish* packed in water. Cover the pan and cook slowly for 5 minutes. Season generously with black pepper. Serve with *shells* or *rigatoni.*

Note: Use some of the remaining anchovies in a *Caesar Salad* (page 30) or in *Pasta with Broccoli Florets* (page 208).

MOCK FETTUCINE ALFREDO

Try this recipe on a night when you're so tired that even buying take-out is too much effort. You need only cook the pasta and mix it with the cheeses. The heat of the cooked pasta softens the cheeses so they form a sauce. Be sure to use a high-quality Parmesan, because that's all you taste.

(Makes 1 medium-sized serving)

2–3 ounces fettucine or
  spaghetti
1 ounce cream cheese, either
  fresh or frozen
3 tablespoons grated Parmesan
  cheese

1 tablespoon cream or sour
  cream (optional)
Freshly grated black pepper

Cook the pasta in a large pot of boiling salted water until it is cooked through but still has some texture (al dente)—about 5 minutes with fresh pasta, 10 minutes with dried. Drain the pasta and place it back in the pot. Do not rinse. Toss the cream cheese with the pasta until it softens and coats the strands. Then add the Parmesan cheese. Taste and add cream if you wish. Sprinkle with black pepper to taste.

VARIATIONS

Fettucine with Herbs. Add 2 tablespoons chopped herbs, such as *basil,* chopped *chives,* or a mixture of *basil, parsley,* and *sweet marjoram.*

Fettucine with Crabmeat. Omit the Parmesan or cut it down to 1 tablespoon. Add 2 ounces (about ¾ cup) of fresh *crabmeat* after the cream cheese. Sprinkle with a pinch of *nutmeg* if you wish.

FETTUCINE WITH AN ONION SAUCE

On days when your refrigerator is empty, if you have onions, dried pasta, and olive oil you can put together this peasant dish from Italy. It's customarily made with more oil, but by sautéing then braising the onions (about a 30-minute procedure), you not only use less oil but also end up with a more pronounced onion flavor in the sauce. If you set aside 3 tablespoons of the onion sauce, you'll have a head start on either a soup or a sautéed vegetable later on in the week (see Leftovers). *(Serves 1)*

1 large sweet white or red onion, or 2 medium yellow onions	Salt
	3–4 ounces fettucine or bows
	Freshly ground black pepper
1 teaspoon olive oil	1–2 tablespoons grated
1/4–1/2 teaspoon sugar	Parmesan cheese (optional)
1 teaspoon butter or olive oil	

Peel and slice the onion. You should end up with about 3 cups (although the amount isn't critical). Heat the olive oil in a heavy pan and stir in the onion. Toss continuously, over medium-high heat, until the slices are coated with oil and have wilted slightly. Turn down the heat, cover the pan, and cook, stirring frequently, for about 20 minutes. Watch carefully after about 15 minutes because as the water in the onion evaporates, it can suddenly burn. (One reason they're usually stewed in oil.)

Stir in 1/4 teaspoon sugar (or 1/2 teaspoon sugar if you're using yellow onions) and butter. Cover the pan and cook, stirring occasionally, for another 15 minutes. The onion will have wilted down to about 2/3 cup and will have a thick purée-like consistency. Set aside, reserving 3 tablespoons for *Sautéed Cabbage with Onions* or *Cabbage and Soba Soup* (see Leftovers).

About 10–15 minutes before the onion is cooked through, boil a pot of water, add salt to taste, and the pasta. Cook the pasta over medium heat until it is cooked through but still retains some texture (al dente). (The cooking time will depend upon the type of pasta.) Drain it thoroughly and toss with 1/2 cup of the onion mixture—or use all of the sauce if you prefer. Season with salt and a generous amount of freshly grated black pepper and, if you like, toss with cheese.

the mixture to a boil, lower the heat, and gently boil for 5 minutes. The cabbage should be barely cooked through. Add the noodles and carrot and additional water (or stock) if necessary. Cook another 5–7 minutes or until the noodles are barely cooked through. Season with soy sauce, chopped garlic, and ginger to taste. Cover the pan and let the flavors meld for a few minutes before serving.

Note: This soup stays in good condition for 3–4 days if refrigerated in a glass bowl and covered tightly.

SHRIMP CARBONARA

This is a takeoff on the delicious Italian spaghetti with a bacon-egg sauce, traditionally made with pancetta, a mild Italian bacon (see first variation). This shrimp version, which is equally good, goes together in about 10 minutes—and even faster if you use angel hair pasta. The egg is cooked by the hot spaghetti.

(Serves 1)

3–4 ounces dried angel hair
    pasta or spaghetti
Salt
1–2 teaspoons olive oil
3 tablespoons finely chopped
    sweet onion
6 peeled raw shrimp, coarsely
    chopped (about 3 ounces)

1 medium egg
2 tablespoons grated Parmesan
    cheese
Freshly ground black pepper
1 tablespoon minced fresh basil
    or parsley
Balsamic vinegar

Bring a large pot of water to a boil, and add the pasta and salt. Continue cooking the pasta in boiling water until it is cooked through but still retains some texture—about 5–6 minutes for angel hair pasta, 10–12 minutes for spaghetti.

Meanwhile heat the olive oil in a frying pan, add the onion, and cook over medium heat, stirring frequently, for 3 minutes. Stir in the shrimp and cook, stirring constantly, until they are cooked through, about 1–2 minutes. Remove from the heat and set aside. In a large mixing bowl beat the egg, and add the Parmesan cheese, a generous amount of black pep-

Shrimp Carbonara (continued)

per, the basil, and a dash of balsamic vinegar. Drain the pasta thoroughly and toss with the cheese mixture. Add the reserved shrimp and onion and toss again. Serve immediately.

VARIATIONS

With ham or bacon. Substitute 3 tablespoons coarsely chopped cooked *ham* (preferably ham sold in chunks), *bacon, or pancetta* for the shrimp, and *parsley* for the basil.

With zucchini. Omit the shrimp. Substitute 4 tablespoons chopped raw *zucchini.* Increase the cooking time to 4 minutes for the zucchini. Substitute *sweet marjoram* for the basil. You can also add 1/4 teaspoon chopped *rosemary or sage.*

With leftover asparagus and garlic. Substitute 2 stalks sliced cooked *asparagus* for the shrimp. Add 1 teaspoon minced *garlic* along with the onions. Substitute 1 teaspoon minced *tarragon* for the basil.

Note: You can buy pancetta at most Italian grocery stores and many supermarket deli counters.

PASTA WITH BROCCOLI FLORETS

The anchovies, which are barely discernible, round out the flavor of the dish. Broccoli is usually sold by the bunch; you want to end up with about 1 cup florets (about 1/3 pound broccoli).

(Serves 1)

1–1 1/3 cups raw broccoli florets
2 ounces spaghetti
2–3 teaspoons olive oil
1 teaspoon minced garlic
1 tablespoon minced scallions
2 anchovies, finely chopped
    (optional)

1/8 teaspoon hot pepper flakes
    or 1/2 teaspoon minced
    jalapeño pepper
Salt and freshly ground black
    pepper

Bring a pot of water to a boil, add the broccoli, and gently boil for 3–5 minutes, or until the broccoli is cooked through. Lift out with a slotted spoon and set aside (covered with a kitchen towel to keep warm). In the same pot of water, cook the pasta until it is cooked through but still has some texture (al dente), anywhere from 8 to 10 minutes, depending upon the type of pasta. Drain.

About 5 minutes after the pasta starts cooking, heat the olive oil in a frying pan large enough to hold the pasta. Add the garlic, scallions, optional anchovies, and hot pepper flakes. Cook over medium heat, stirring constantly, for 2 minutes or until softened. Add the reserved broccoli and cook 1 minute longer. Gently stir in the pasta. Taste and season with salt and pepper. Serve immediately.

VARIATION

With cheese. Sprinkle with 1 tablespoon grated *Parmesan* or *Romano* before serving.

SPAGHETTI WITH GARLIC AND CLAMS

This is a great pantry shelf item for nights when the refrigerator is empty and you don't want to go shopping. Frozen parsley works well in this recipe—but you need fresh garlic. You can freeze the leftover canned clams in their liquid (they become a little rubbery but are still edible).

(Serves 1)

Salt

3–4 ounces spaghetti

2–3 teaspoons olive oil

2 teaspoons minced garlic
  (about 2 cloves)

Freshly ground black pepper

1–2 tablespoons chopped
  parsley or a mixture of
  parsley and chives

A 7-ounce can minced clams

Bring a pot of water to a boil, add salt to taste, and pasta. Cook until done. Most dried spaghetti is cooked through in 10–12 minutes.

Meanwhile, heat the olive oil in a small frying pan. Add the garlic and stir for 1 minute. Add a generous amount of black pepper, the parsley, and about 1/2 the can of clams. (The amount of clams depends upon your appetite.) Cook just long enough for the clams to be heated through, 1–2 minutes. Set aside until the spaghetti is done.

Drain the spaghetti and toss with the clam sauce.

SPAGHETTI IN A LEMON-CREAM SAUCE

This sauce, which I first tasted in Northern Italy, takes less than 5 minutes to put together. Add a few diced shrimp—or sliced leftover artichoke hearts—and you have a festive main course. It's an excellent way to use up any leftover heavy cream.

(Serves 1)

1/3 cup heavy cream
1/4 teaspoon minced garlic
1/4–1/2 teaspoon minced fresh lemon zest
1 portion spaghetti (about 2 ounces)

Salt
1 teaspoon butter (optional)
2 teaspoons minced parsley or chervil
Grated Parmesan cheese (optional)

Pour the cream into a small saucepan and add the garlic. Bring the cream to a boil, and gently boil it until it is reduced by about 1/3. You want the cream just to thicken slightly. Add the lemon zest and set the pan aside.

Bring a large pot of water to a boil, add the spaghetti, and salt to taste. Boil the spaghetti over high heat until it is cooked through, yet still has some texture (al dente). Drain thoroughly, add the butter, if using, then toss with the sauce. Sprinkle with the parsley or chervil. Serve with grated Parmesan cheese, if you wish.

VARIATIONS

With shrimp or crabmeat. Add 5 cooked, diced *shrimp* or 1/4 cup cooked *crabmeat* along with the lemon zest.

With sorrel. Add 1–2 tablespoons thinly sliced raw *sorrel* along with the lemon zest.

With mushrooms. Add 1/4 cup cooked *mushrooms* along with the lemon zest.

With fresh peas and scallion. Add 1/3 cup barely cooked fresh *peas* (or thawed frozen baby peas) and 1 tablespoon chopped *scallion* along with the lemon zest.

With leftover asparagus or artichokes. Add 1/3 cup sliced cooked *asparagus* or *artichoke hearts* at room temperature along with the lemon zest.

STIR-FRIED SPAGHETTI WITH VEGETABLES

It's worth cooking a little extra spaghetti to have on hand for this quickly prepared main dish that uses up a small portion of leftover poultry or meat. (It's also good as a vegetarian main dish.) If you add the soy sauce at the very end, it retains a less salty flavor.

(Serves 1)

2 teaspoons vegetable oil
1 teaspoon minced garlic
1/2 cup sliced scallions (green and white parts) or onions
1/3 cup thinly sliced seeded red pepper
1 cup thinly sliced cabbage
3/4 cup thinly sliced poultry, pork, beef, or lamb (optional)

1 1/2–2 cups leftover spaghetti
1 tablespoon cider or rice wine vinegar
1 teaspoon sugar
1 1/2–2 tablespoons soy sauce
1 tablespoon chopped coriander
Salt and freshly ground black pepper (optional)

Heat the oil in a large frying pan and add the garlic. Stir it rapidly for 30 seconds, then stir in the scallions, red pepper, and cabbage. Add the leftover poultry or meat, if using. Continue stirring, over medium heat, for about 3 minutes, or until the vegetables are wilted slightly. Stir in the spaghetti. Cook about 2 minutes longer, or until the spaghetti is heated through. Add the vinegar, sugar, soy sauce, and coriander, and cook 30 seconds longer, stirring constantly. Taste and season with salt and pepper if you wish.

VARIATIONS

With sesame oil. Add 1/2 teaspoon *Oriental sesame oil*, 1/4 teaspoon *red pepper flakes*, and 1/8 teaspoon *dry mustard*.

With celery and broccoli. Omit the poultry or meat. Add 1/2 cup diagonally sliced *celery* and 3/4 cup *broccoli* sliced about 1/2 inch thick along with the red pepper. Add 2–3 tablespoons water along with the soy sauce.

LO MEIN NOODLES WITH BROCCOLI

This is one of the most useful recipes you can have in your repertoire as a single cook because it stretches small amounts of vegetables. Some nights you might prefer to start from scratch—other nights, you can recycle leftovers. The crisp texture of fresh broccoli contrasts nicely with the soft Chinese-style noodles—but other vegetables, such as asparagus, carrots, peas, sliced spinach or kale (or a combination of vegetables) work equally well. The amount of noodles depends upon your appetite—if you cook too much, the leftovers are tasty either hot or cold.

(Makes 1 generous serving)

2 cups chicken, beef, vegetable, or fish stock
1 1/2 cups trimmed broccoli florets and/or stems cut into 1/2-inch pieces
2–4 ounces lo mein noodles
Freshly ground black pepper
3 tablespoons sliced scallions

2 tablespoons sliced celery (optional)
1 teaspoon minced garlic
1/2 teaspoon fresh or frozen grated gingerroot or lemon rind (optional)
Salt (optional)

Place the stock in a saucepan, bring it to a boil, and add the broccoli pieces. Cook them for 2–3 minutes, or until barely cooked through. Remove them from the pan with a slotted spoon and set aside. (The broccoli will continue to cook as it sits.) Add the noodles to the broth and sprinkle with black pepper. Lower the heat and simmer the noodles until just cooked through, about 5 minutes. Remove the pan from the heat and stir in the scallions, optional celery, and garlic. Cover the pan and let sit for 2 minutes. Add the broccoli and ginger. Taste and season with salt, if you wish.

VARIATIONS

With scallops or shrimp. Add 2 ounces thinly sliced *scallops* or 5 whole *shrimp* after the noodles have cooked for 4 minutes. Remember that both scallops and shrimp become tough if they are overcooked.

With tomatoes and/or mushrooms. Add 1 small peeled, seeded, and chopped *tomato* and 1/4 cup thinly sliced *mushrooms* along with the scallions. Omit the broccoli if you wish.

With Italian pasta. Substitute either dried or fresh Italian pasta, such as *shells* or *fettucine,* for the lo mein noodles. The dried pasta will take longer to cook than the dried Chinese noodles, so you'll need to put the broccoli back in the pan and reheat it for a minute before serving.

PENNE WITH GREENS AND TOMATOES

Think of this as a vehicle for leftovers. Although I suggest raw greens, this recipe is also quite good with leftover sautéed greens or broccoli—or even thinly shredded raw romaine lettuce. I use cream cheese and sour cream as a binder, but you could replace them with heavy cream. As only the penne is precooked, it's quick to assemble. Any leftovers freeze well and reheat well in a microwave.

(Makes 2 servings)

2 tablespoons cream cheese
2 tablespoons sour or heavy
   cream
3 tablespoons grated Parmesan
   or Romano cheese
1/3–1/2 cup grated Monterey
   Jack or fontina cheese
1 teaspoon chopped fresh
   rosemary or basil
1/4–1/2 teaspoon chopped fresh
   thyme
1 cup coarsely chopped drained
   canned tomatoes (or

3 peeled, seeded, and
   chopped ripe tomatoes)
1 cup uncooked penne (or
   2 cups cooked)
3 cups washed, stemmed, and
   chopped fresh greens (such as
   kale, spinach, escarole,
   chicory, or bok choy) in any
   combination
2 tablespoons chopped red
   pepper (optional)
Olive oil

In a large mixing bowl, beat together the cream cheese, sour cream, cheeses, herbs, and tomatoes. Set aside. Bring a pot of water to the boil, add the raw penne, and cook for about 7 minutes, or until the penne is barely cooked through. (It will finish cooking in the oven.) Drain the penne and combine with the cheese-tomato mixture. Stir in the greens and red pepper, if using.

Penne with Greens and Tomatoes (continued)

Place the pasta mixture in a greased baking dish, such as an 8 × 8-inch square pan. Drizzle the top with olive oil to taste (no more than 2 teaspoons).

Bake in a preheated 450°F oven for about 15 minutes or until cooked through.

VARIATIONS

With olives. Add 2 tablespoons chopped *black olives* along with the greens.

With leftover meats. Add coarsely chopped leftover *meatballs, sausage, ham, or poultry* along with the penne. Cooked chopped *shrimp or tuna* is also quite good.

STIR-FRIED PENNE WITH KALE AND ZUCCHINI

This is a satisfying vegetarian meal-in-one. You can cook the penne and chop the vegetables in the morning, store them in the refrigerator, and be eating in minutes once you walk in the door from work.

(Makes 1 generous helping)

$1/2$ cup uncooked penne
Salt
2 tablespoons olive oil
1 teaspoon minced garlic
3 cups coarsely chopped kale,
    leaves only

1 small zucchini, diced
1 stem bok choy, thinly sliced,
    or $1/4$ cup sliced Chinese
    cabbage (optional)

Bring a pot of water to a boil, add the penne and salt to taste, and cook for about 7 minutes, or until cooked through but retaining some texture (al dente). Drain and set aside.

In a large frying pan, heat the olive oil, add the garlic, and stir for 1 minute. Add the kale, zucchini, and optional bok choy, and stir constantly 3–4 minutes or until the vegetables are barely cooked through. Stir in the penne (if it has been refrigerated, cook for 1–2 minutes until reheated). Serve immediately.

LEFTOVERS

Add chicken or beef *broth, shell beans,* and chopped fresh *tomatoes* to taste. Simmer for 5 minutes. Serve with *Cornbread* (page 269).

SHELLS WITH SAUSAGES, TOMATOES, AND PEPPERS

This filling pasta dish is loaded with fresh vegetables rather than sauce. If you'd prefer a more traditional treatment, add 1/4 cup *Fresh Tomato Sauce* (page 98) or two peeled and chopped tomatoes. For a low-fat version, skip the cheese.

(Makes 1 generous serving)

1–11/2 cups dry pasta, such as shells or bows
1 tablespoon olive oil
1/2 cup cubed frying peppers
1/3 cup sliced onion
3 ounces Cajun-style or hot Italian sausage, cut into 1/4-inch-thick pieces
2/3 cup seeded and chopped tomatoes (do not peel)

1 cup sliced yellow summer squash or zucchini
1 tablespoon chopped basil or coriander or 2 tablespoons chopped parsley
1/2 cup grated aged provolone or Parmesan cheese (optional)

Bring a pot of water to the boil, add the pasta, and gently boil until it is cooked through but retains some texture (al dente), about 8–10 minutes depending on type of pasta. Drain in a colander.

Meanwhile, heat the olive oil in a large frying pan. Add the frying peppers and onion, and stir to coat with the oil. Add the sausage, and continue cooking slowly, until the sausage is cooked through (the amount of time depends upon whether the sausage is precooked). Pour off all but a thin film of the fat, and stir in the tomatoes and squash. Cook, stirring frequently, for 3–5 minutes, or until the squash is barely cooked through. Toss with the pasta, add the basil or coriander, and toss again. Sprinkle with the optional cheese. Serve immediately.

Shells with Sausages, Tomatoes, and Peppers (continued)

VARIATION

With vegetables. Omit the sausage. Increase the amount of oil to 2 tablespoons. Add 1 teaspoon minced *garlic* and 1/2 cup *broccoli* florets along with the onion. Proceed as above.

BOWS WITH ASPARAGUS AND SCALLIONS

The pasta is the filler in this vegetable-dominated main course with a Chinese undercurrent. It's a good way to use up the stalk ends of asparagus spears (or leftover asparagus). I prefer it without soy sauce—but if you like a slight coating on your pasta, add it. You could use lo mein noodles, but the bows taste equally good and they're easier to find.

(Serves 1)

1¼–1½ cups dry pasta, such
  as bows
Salt
1 tablespoon olive or peanut oil
1 cup diced asparagus pieces
  (about 1/2-inch pieces)
3/4 cup diced scallion-bulb ends
  (1/2-inch pieces)
2 tablespoons peeled, seeded,
  and chopped red pepper
1 tablespoon peeled, seeded,
  and minced jalapeño pepper

1 tablespoon peeled and minced
  fresh gingerroot
1 tablespoon minced fresh
  coriander
Pinch of sugar
1 tablespoon soy sauce or
  2 tablespoons chicken or
  vegetable stock
Salt (optional)

Bring a pot of water to a boil, add the pasta and salt to taste, and cook over moderate heat, stirring occasionally, until the pasta is cooked through but still retains some texture (al dente). Pasta varies in its cooking time so follow the directions on the package.

Meanwhile, heat the oil in a heavy, nonreactive frying pan. Add the asparagus, scallions, and peppers. Cook over medium-high heat for 3–5 minutes, stirring occasionally, so that they brown rather than burn. The asparagus should be barely cooked through. Add the ginger and coriander and cook 1 minute longer, stirring constantly. Stir in a pinch of sugar and the soy sauce or stock.

Drain the pasta thoroughly. Toss with the vegetable mixture. Taste and correct the seasonings. Add salt if you wish.

Note: When you're using jalapeño peppers, if you seed them and remove the skin with a vegetable peeler, you end up with a more subtle "bite."

VARIATIONS

With leftover cooked asparagus. Add diced room-temperature asparagus along with the ginger.

With crabmeat. Add 1/2 cup cooked shredded *crabmeat* along with the pasta.

SPAGHETTI WITH MEATBALLS

These meatballs are light, flavorful, and just the ticket for a cool fall or winter meal with a crusty loaf of French bread and a tossed green salad. If you prefer, use ground beef (or ground turkey) rather than the pork/beef mixture. Letting the meat mixture sit before you form the meatballs makes them lighter. You'll end up with 8–10 meatballs, enough for a hearty dinner with leftovers for a meatball sub—or you could halve any remaining meatballs, cover them with sauce, and freeze for another meal.

(Makes 2 meals)

1/3 cup minced Italian flat leaf parsley or basil
1/3 cup fine breadcrumbs (from 2–3 slices stale bread)
1 teaspoon minced garlic
1–2 tablespoons Parmesan cheese
Milk
1 egg, beaten

Salt and freshly ground black pepper
Cayenne pepper
4 ounces lean ground beef
4 ounces ground pork
1/4 cup flour
Olive oil
4–6 cups *Tomato Sauce* (page 98)
Spaghetti

Mix together the parsley, breadcrumbs, garlic, and cheese. (If you have

Spaghetti with Meatballs (continued)

a food processor, first whirl the parsley, then pulse with the breadcrumbs, garlic, and cheese). Place the mixture in a bowl and add milk to cover (about 1/4 cup). Let sit for 15 minutes. Stir in the egg, salt, pepper, a pinch of cayenne pepper, and the meat. Let the meat mixture sit for about 30 minutes, covered.

Place 1/4 cup flour in a wide bowl. Form meatballs the size you wish, roll them in flour, shake to remove any excess, and place on a dish. (This is a rather gloppy procedure.) You will end up with about ten 2-inch meatballs. The meatballs will be soft, but will firm up while cooking.

Heat 3 tablespoons of olive oil in a large frying pan and brown the meatballs, a few at a time, turning frequently. Do not crowd the pan or they will steam, not brown. Remove them with a slotted spoon to an enameled or stainless-steel pot and cover with the tomato sauce.

Gently simmer the meatballs in the sauce for 20 minutes. Meanwhile, cook one portion of spaghetti according to the package directions. Serve with additional grated Parmesan cheese if you wish.

LEFTOVERS

Meatball Submarine Sandwich. Reheat the meatballs in the tomato sauce. Cut lengthwise almost through a small loaf of *Italian bread*. Heat a frying pan and place the bread in the pan, cut side down, to lightly toast it. If you like, drizzle the bread with olive oil first. Remove the meatballs with a slotted spoon, halve them, and place in the bread. Spoon over some tomato sauce. Serve as is or add grated *Provolone* cheese and roasted *red peppers*. Serve immediately before the bread gets soggy.

Eggplant Slices Stuffed with Meatballs

Once you have the meatballs and tomato sauce on hand, most of the work is done. You need only to prepare the eggplant slices, stuff them, and bake for a few minutes. Any leftovers make a wonderful submarine sandwich, or chop them for an omelet filling.

(Serves 1)

1/2 pound eggplant	2 tablespoons olive oil
Salt	Leftover tomato sauce (1 cup)
1 egg	Leftover meatballs (about 4)
Flour	2 tablespoons mozzarella cheese

Cut 4–5 slices 1/4 inch wide from an unpeeled eggplant. (For larger slices cut slightly on the diagonal.) Sprinkle lightly with salt and let stand for at least 30 minutes. Pat the slices dry. Beat the egg with 1 teaspoon water. Put about 1/4 cup flour into a dish. Dip the eggplant slices into the beaten egg, then into the flour. Shake off any excess flour.

Heat the oil in a large frying pan and lightly brown the eggplant slices on both sides. Drain them on a paper bag. Put 3 tablespoons tomato sauce in the bottom of a small ovenproof dish just large enough to hold the eggplant slices once they are folded over. Arrange the slices on the counter. For each slice, split a meatball and place on one half. Top with a teaspoon of tomato sauce and fold over the other half, forming an eggplant sandwich. Continue until all the slices are stuffed. Arrange the slices in a baking dish. Top with the remaining tomato sauce and sprinkle with the mozzarella cheese. Bake in a preheated 375°F oven for about 20 minutes, or until heated through.

MACARONI AND CHEESE

Homemade macaroni and cheese bears little resemblance to the commercial versions. It's an economical main dish with the bonus of using up any scraps of cheese. The wine and spices aren't necessary, but they add a dimension of flavor. Any leftovers reheat especially well in a microwave.

(Serves 1)

1 cup raw macaroni or penne	Cayenne pepper (optional)
Salt	Dry mustard (optional)
2/3 cup milk	Freshly ground black pepper
2 teaspoons butter or olive oil	(see Note)
1 tablespoon flour	1/2 cup grated cheddar cheese
1/3 cup chopped onion or	(or a combination of grated
scallions	cheeses)
1 tablespoon white wine	2 tablespoons fresh
(optional)	breadcrumbs

Bring a pot of water to a boil, and add the pasta and salt to taste. Cook until the pasta is barely cooked through (it will continue cooking in the oven). Depending upon the type of pasta, this will take about 10

Macaroni and Cheese (continued)

minutes. Heat the milk either on top of the stove or in a microwave.

Meanwhile, heat the butter in a small nonreactive saucepan. Off the heat, stir in the flour. Return to the heat and cook for 1 minute, stirring constantly. Add the milk and continue stirring until the sauce is cooked through and slightly thickened, about 3 minutes. Stir in the onion, the optional white wine, a pinch of both cayenne and dry mustard, if using, and a generous amount of freshly ground black pepper. Stir in all but 1 tablespoon of the cheese and continue cooking until the cheese has melted, about 1 minute. Remove from the heat and let sit until the macaroni is cooked through. Drain the macaroni and mix with the white sauce. Place in a buttered small casserole just large enough to hold it. Sprinkle with the breadcrumbs and the 1 tablespoon reserved cheese. Bake in a preheated 350°F oven for about 15 minutes, or until bubbling. Let cool slightly before serving.

Note: The macaroni and cheese develops an entirely different flavor if you crush fresh peppercorns with a hammer or side of a bottle so that the peppercorns are in larger pieces than would be possible when ground in a pepper mill.

FOOLPROOF RICE

You can cook rice just like you cook pasta. If you cook extra, you'll have the makings for *Dirty Rice* or *Fried Rice* (page 221), or *Rice Pudding* (page 282) later on in the week. Rice doubles in volume once it's cooked, so decide how hungry you are and measure accordingly.

(Serves 1)

Water   1/3–1/2 cup raw rice
Salt

Bring a large pot of water to a boil, and add salt and the rice. (Water boils faster if you wait to add the salt until after it comes to a boil.) Lower the heat slightly and gently boil until the rice is cooked through but firm, stirring occasionally, anywhere from 12 to 15 minutes (after 12 minutes, taste; it may need another minute or two). Drain.

VARIATIONS

Brown Rice. You can cook *brown rice* exactly the same way, but at least double the cooking time. Brown rice usually takes 35–40 minutes to cook.

With herbs. Stir in 1 teaspoon chopped *dill, tarragon, basil,* or *coriander,* or 2 teaspoons *parsley.*

With peas. Just before serving, mix in 1/2 cup cooked *peas.*

Note: Rice reheats well in a microwave. You can also reheat rice by boiling a pot of water, adding the leftover rice, and boiling it gently for 30 seconds–1 minute. Drain immediately or it will be mush.

DIRTY RICE

Southern cooks use up leftover rice and cooked giblets (the gizzards and heart that you find packed inside whole chickens) in this tasty dish. I often make dirty rice on the same day I'm putting up stock—that way the giblets, which have been simmered in the liquid, don't go to waste. The amount doesn't matter—2 giblets would be about right.

(Serves 1)

2 teaspoons olive or canola oil
1–2 tablespoons chopped onion
    or scallions
2 tablespoons chopped celery
2 tablespoons chopped green
    pepper

3/4 cup cooked rice
Chopped cooked chicken giblets
    (1–2 tablespoons)
Salt and freshly ground black
    pepper

Heat the olive oil in a heavy frying pan. Stir in the onion, celery, and green pepper. Cook over medium heat, stirring frequently, for 3 minutes, or until the vegetables are slightly wilted. Stir in the rice and giblets and cook, stirring frequently, another 2–3 minutes, or until the rice is heated through. Taste and season with salt and pepper.

VARIATION

Fried Rice. Omit the giblets. After the rice has cooked for 2 minutes, stir

Dirty Rice (continued)
in 1 beaten *egg* that's been mixed with a dash of *hot pepper sauce* and/or *Oriental sesame oil*. Continue stirring until the egg is cooked through, about 2 minutes. Sprinkle with chopped *scallions* and/or chopped dry-roasted *peanuts* just before serving.

PILAF

This easy treatment for long-grain rice makes a flavorful change from boiled rice. The amount of liquid absorbed depends on the variety of rice.

(Serves 1)

2 teaspoons olive oil or butter
1 teaspoon minced garlic
1/3 cup raw long-grain rice
2/3–1 cup chicken, beef, or
    vegetable stock

Salt and freshly ground
    black pepper

Heat the olive oil or butter in a heavy stove-top pan. Add the garlic and cook over medium heat, stirring constantly, for 2 minutes. Add the rice, and continue stirring until the grains are coated with oil and the rice has become slightly opaque, about 3 minutes. Stir in 2/3 cup stock. Lower the heat, and continue cooking until the stock is absorbed, about 10–15 minutes. Stir occasionally and add additional stock if needed. Season with salt and pepper.

VARIATIONS

With cheese. Just before serving, stir in 1–2 tablespoons grated *Parmesan or Romano* cheese.

With leftover peas. When the rice is at the al dente stage (slightly chewy) add 1/3 cup cooked *peas*. Cook only long enough to reheat the peas.

With leftover asparagus. Cut the *asparagus* into diagonal pieces (enough to make 1/3 cup); stir into the rice along with 1 tablespoon grated *Parmesan* cheese.

With herbs. Just before serving, add 2 teaspoons chopped fresh herbs, such as *tarragon or parsley*.

RISOTTO

Traditionally, this Italian rice specialty is prepared with Arborio rice, a firm-textured short-grain rice grown in Northern Italy (stocked in the imported foods sections of many supermarkets). It's an expensive rice, but when you're cooking for one a little goes a long way. Risotto is one dish that's best kept simple. An onion and a little Parmesan cheese deepen the flavor—and vegetables are a wonderful addition—but the only essential ingredients are a good rich stock and Arborio rice. With those on hand, you can walk in the door and have risotto ready to eat in less than half an hour.

(Serves 1)

1 teaspoon butter
1 teaspoon olive oil
2 tablespoons finely chopped
  onion
1/3 cup raw Arborio rice

1 cup chicken stock
2 tablespoons grated Parmesan
  cheese
Salt and freshly ground black
  pepper

Heat the butter and olive oil in a heavy saucepan, add the onion, and cook over medium heat, stirring frequently, for about 3 minutes, or until lightly browned. Stir in the rice, and continue cooking, stirring constantly, for 1 minute. Meanwhile, heat the chicken stock.

Stir 1/3 cup of the heated stock into the rice, and continue cooking, stirring constantly with a wooden spoon, until the stock is absorbed. In 2 installments, add the remaining stock, waiting until the stock is absorbed before adding any more, and continuing to stir constantly. The whole process should take 20–25 minutes. The risotto is done when the broth is absorbed and the rice is cooked through but still firm. Stir in the Parmesan cheese and taste and season with salt and pepper.

VARIATIONS

With asparagus. About 5 minutes after you add the last installment of stock, stir in 1/2 cup *asparagus* that's been trimmed and cut into 1/2-inch pieces.

With peas and tomato. Just before the rice is cooked through, stir in 1/3

Risotto (continued)

cup fresh (or still frozen) *peas* and 1 chopped peeled and seeded *tomato*.

With zucchini or summer squash. About 5 minutes after you add the last installment of stock, stir in 1/2 cup chopped *zucchini*.

With shrimp and/or celery or fennel. Add 5 *shrimp* and/or 1/4 cup chopped *celery* (*or fennel*) about 5 minutes before the risotto is cooked through.

With spinach and basil. Just before the rice is cooked through, stir in 1/2 cup thinly sliced trimmed fresh *spinach* and 1 tablespoon chopped *basil*. If the spinach is fresh, it will cook through in less than 2 minutes.

With okra and tomato. Add 1/2 cup trimmed and thinly sliced *okra* and 1 peeled, seeded, and chopped *tomato* just before the rice is done. Cooked this way, the okra retains texture.

Note: Often in Italy an additional amount of butter, such as 1 or 2 teaspoons, is stirred in just before serving.

GRATIN OF SPINACH AND RICE

This basic technique of baking cooked greens and rice with a topping of breadcrumbs and cheese is one that can be reused over and over, depending upon the kinds of greens and vegetables you have on hand. Sometimes I make this with spinach—other times with escarole, chicory, or kale. If I have zucchini or summer squash in the refrigerator, I'll use that—but something as different-tasting as asparagus works equally well. Remember this is essentially a peasant dish and the ingredients (and proportions) are up to you. It's a great way to use up cooked leftover vegetables.

(Serves 1)

1 tablespoon olive oil
1 1/2 cups stemmed and chopped
    raw spinach (or 3/4 cup
    chopped, cooked spinach)
1 tablespoon minced garlic
1 tablespoon chopped scallion

2 tablespoons chopped red
    pepper
1/2 cup chopped raw summer
    squash or zucchini
1/3 cup peeled, seeded, and
    diced tomato

3/4 cup cooked brown or white
   rice
1 1/2 tablespoons grated Romano
   or Parmesan cheese
1 teaspoon chopped rosemary

or 1 tablespoon chopped
   basil
3 tablespoons fine dry breadcrumbs

Heat 2 teaspoons of the olive oil in a heavy frying pan. Add the spinach, garlic, scallion, and red pepper. Cook, stirring frequently, over moderate heat for 3 minutes, or until the spinach is wilted. Add the summer squash and cook 1 minute longer. Turn off the heat and add the tomato, rice, 1 tablespoon of the cheese, and the rosemary. Pat the mixture into a small, oiled casserole about 6 inches in diameter. Sprinkle with the breadcrumbs and the remaining 1/2 tablespoon cheese. Drizzle with the remaining 1 teaspoon olive oil. Bake in a preheated 400°F oven for 25–30 minutes, or until the mixture is cooked through and the breadcrumbs are browned. Serve either hot or at room temperature.

Note: I prefer the contrast in textures between the barely cooked squash and the spinach and rice. If you'd like a more uniform texture, cook the squash in boiling water for 2 minutes, drain it, and add to the rice mixture before baking.

VARIATION

With egg custard. Omit the breadcrumbs. Beat 1 medium *egg* with 1/2 cup *milk* and stir into the cooked vegetable mixture along with the remaining 1 teaspoon olive oil. Sprinkle with the 1/2 tablespoon Romano cheese. Bake in a preheated 350°F oven for 25–30 minutes, or until a knife inserted in the center comes out clean. Serve at room temperature.

SHRIMP AND RICE WITH PEAS

You can barely taste the curry powder, which deepens the flavor of this dish that utilizes leftover peas. Use a good-quality curry powder, such as Madras Curry Powder imported from India, or the Spice Islands version. The nutty-flavored basmati rice (available at many specialty stores and

Shrimp and Rice with Peas (continued)

supermarkets) is especially delicious cooked in this manner. (Many super-markets carry popcorn rice, which is basmati rice given a jazzier name. If you can't find it in your area, the McKnight Milling Company in Wynne, Arkansas, produces the Cache River brand of basmati rice. Nudge your supermarket staff to order it through their specialty foods catalog.)

(Makes 1 generous serving)

2–3 teaspoons butter
3/4–1 teaspoon curry powder
1/2 cup chopped onion
1/2 cup chopped celery
1 tablespoon chopped fresh tomato
1/2 cup long-grain rice
1 cup fish or shrimp stock or water

5 cooked or raw shrimp, halved lengthwise
1 cup peas, cooked (or frozen)
2 tablespoons chopped parsley
Salt and freshly ground black pepper

Heat the butter in a heavy stove-top casserole. Stir in the curry powder and onion, and cook, covered, over medium heat for 5 minutes, stirring occasionally. Uncover, and add the celery, tomato, and rice. Stir so that the rice is coated with the butter and curry powder and add the stock. Bring the mixture to a boil, cover it, lower the heat, and cook for 15 minutes, stirring occasionally. Add additional liquid if necessary. The rice should be cooked through but still retain texture (al dente). Stir in the shrimp and peas, cover the pan, and cook another 2 minutes. Stir in the parsley, taste, and season with salt and pepper. Serve in a big bowl with country bread or *Cornbread* (page 269) on the side.

VARIATIONS

With zucchini or broccoli. Omit the peas. Add 1 cup sliced *zucchini* along with the celery, *or* stir in 1/2 cup blanched *broccoli* florets along with the shrimp. Proceed as above.

With leftover chicken or turkey. Omit the shrimp. After the rice has cooked for 15 minutes, add 1/2–3/4 cup thinly sliced cooked *chicken or turkey* that has been marinated in 1 tablespoon *lime juice* for 30 minutes. (You can omit the lime juice, but it makes the poultry taste fresher.) Proceed as above.

With lima beans and corn. Omit the peas. Stir in 1/2 cup cooked *lima beans* and 3/4 cup cooked *corn* kernels along with the shrimp.

With red or black beans. Omit the peas. Add 1/2 cup leftover cooked *red or black beans* after the rice has cooked for 15 minutes.

LEFTOVERS

Rice Soup. Any leftovers are delicious added to chicken or vegetable stock for a light soup. Simmer just long enough to reheat the ingredients. Stir in 2 teaspoons chopped *sweet marjoram, chives,* or 1 tablespoon chopped *scallion* greens just before serving.

Mock Risotto. Reheat the leftover rice and vegetables. For every 2/3 cup leftovers, stir in 1 tablespoon *cream* and 2 tablespoons grated *Parmesan or Romano* cheese. Cover the pan and let the mixture sit for 1 minute before serving.

GARLIC AND CHEESE GRITS

Grits are no longer the exclusive purview of the South: It's now possible to buy them throughout much of the country. Southerners start eating grits at breakfast and continue throughout the day. In my part of the world, cheese grits are made with processed American cheese; I think the flavor (and texture) is better with grated provolone, fontina, or cheddar. Try them with smoked meats, such as turkey, pork, or ham—or with freshly grilled vegetables on top.

(Serves 1)

1 teaspoon butter	1–2 tablespoons grated
1–2 teaspoons chopped garlic	provolone, fontina, or ched-
1 cup water	dar cheese
3 1/2 tablespoons regular grits	Salt

Heat the butter in a heavy stove-top casserole with a lid. Add the garlic, lower the heat, cover the pan, and cook for 2 minutes. Do not let the garlic brown. Add 1 cup water, bring it to a boil, and stir in the grits. Lower the heat and simmer, stirring often, for 8–10 minutes, or until the grits are the consistency you like. Stir in the cheese. Taste and add salt. Serve immediately.

Garlic and Cheese Grits (continued)

VARIATIONS

With scallions. Add 2 tablespoons finely sliced *scallions* (both white bulb and green leaves) along with the cheese.

With hot pepper. Add 1 tablespoon peeled, seeded, and minced *hot pepper* along with the cheese.

OMELET

An omelet is the harried cook's standby, for it takes less than 5 minutes to put together, usually with ingredients on hand. It's also an excellent vehicle for small amounts of leftovers. You'll need, however, a heavy pan 7 to 8 inches in diameter, with sloping sides. Many appliance shops sell omelet pans, but before you buy one, lift it first. Frequently, these pans look serviceable but are much too lightweight for you to make a decent omelet. (The cooking surface of the pan should be thick enough so that it distributes the heat evenly, cooking rather than burning the eggs.) Omelet pans are traditionally used just for omelets, and merely wiped out after each use. If you wish an all-purpose pan, buy one with a nonstick finish.

It takes practice to make a good omelet. Remember that the more filling you use, the more difficult it is to roll the omelet. (Most restaurants serve humongous omelets, where the omelet itself is only a container for the filling. If that's what you're in the mood for, that's fine, but in a traditional 2-egg omelet, the filling is usually no more than 1 1/2–2 tablespoons.) Unless it's cheese, the filling must be hot, so prepare it before you start the omelet.

(Serves 1)

2 medium eggs	2 teaspoons butter
2 teaspoons water	
Salt and freshly ground black pepper	

Using a fork, beat the eggs with the water, a pinch of salt, and black pepper to taste. Heat the butter in the omelet pan until it bubbles. Pour the eggs all at once into the pan. They will begin to set immediately at the edges. Simultaneously, slide the pan back and forth. You want to keep the omelet moving so that the eggs don't stick to the bottom of the pan. Either stir the eggs gently with the fork or slide a spatula under them and lift slightly so that the egg in the center cooks. Keep the heat high, but even, so that the omelet cooks but doesn't brown. When the surface looks slightly opaque but still creamy, it is ready to be folded. Add any filling at this point. Tip the pan and, with a fork, lift the edge nearest the handle. Assuming everything is going well, the omelet will start to roll on itself, and you can shake the pan and the omelet will slide out onto the plate.

VARIATION

Three-Egg Omelet. Add 1 egg. Increase the amount of water to 1 tablespoon and the amount of butter to 1 tablespoon. Proceed as above. Use 3 tablespoons filling.

Fillings

Here are a few ideas to get you thinking. Leftover chopped broccoli, spinach, or other greens are good sautéed first in butter and spread with a grating of nutmeg. Small quantities of cooked fish, chicken, and meat, reheated in butter and combined with parsley or other fresh herbs, also work well.

Grated Cheese. Add 2 tablespoons grated cheese, such as *cheddar* or *Swiss,* just before the eggs are set so that the cheese starts to melt before folding.

Fresh Herbs. Just before folding, sprinkle with fresh herbs to taste, such as 2 teaspoons chopped fresh *tarragon, basil, dill, parsley,* or *chives.*

Tomato, Onion, and Pepper. Heat 1 teaspoon butter in a heavy frying pan. Stir in 2 teaspoons chopped *pepper* and 1 tablespoon chopped *onion* or scallions. Cook for 1 minute, stirring constantly, then stir in 2 tablespoons peeled, seeded, and chopped *tomato.* Cook over medium heat for about 4 minutes, stirring occasionally, or until the tomato has cooked down. Season with salt. Add 1 teaspoon chopped *basil.*

Avocado and Jalapeño Pepper. Dice 1 1/2 tablespoons room-temperature

Fillings (continued)

avocado. Combine with 1/2–1 teaspoon minced *jalapeño* pepper, and 1 tablespoon grated *Monterey Jack* cheese. Or substitute 2 teaspoons peeled, seeded, and diced *tomato* for the pepper.

Crabmeat. Mix 2 tablespoons crabmeat with mayonnaise to moisten.

Smoked Salmon and Cream Cheese. (If you live in a city, many bagel shops sell a cream cheese–smoked salmon spread. Use 1 tablespoon along with 2 teaspoons chopped scallions.) Or chop 1 tablespoon *smoked salmon* and combine with 2 teaspoons chopped *chives* or *scallions,* and 1–2 teaspoons *cream cheese.*

Sausage and Onion. Crumble 2–3 tablespoons *sausage,* such as Italian or home-style. Film the surface of a frying pan with oil and fry the sausage over medium heat until it is thoroughly cooked through. Remove with a slotted spoon and spread on the surface of the omelet. Sprinkle with 1/2 teaspoon *scallion* greens or *chives.*

Asparagus and Cheese. Diagonally cut enough cooked *asparagus* to make 2 tablespoons. Sauté in 1 teaspoon butter until heated through. Spread on omelet and sprinkle with 1 tablespoon grated *Parmesan* cheese.

Mushroom. Heat 1 teaspoon butter in a frying pan. Add 1/4 cup chopped *mushrooms,* 1/2 teaspoon chopped *garlic,* and 2 teaspoons chopped *onion.* Cook over medium heat until mushrooms are cooked through, about 3–5 minutes. Do not let the onion brown. Pour off any excess butter, and add 1 tablespoon *heavy cream.* Stir to coat, and immediately fill omelet.

RED PEPPER FRITTATA

A frittata is a flat Italian omelet that's an excellent way to use up small amounts of fresh vegetables and leftovers. Served cold, it is a good sandwich filling on a roll with a little olive oil, or with lettuce, tomato, and onion. Although it's a peasant dish, I first tasted frittata at an elegant two-star Michelin restaurant in Turin, where it graced the appetizer list at an exorbitant price. You can make it for pennies.

(Serves 1)

1–2 teaspoons olive oil
3 tablespoons coarsely chopped
    red pepper
3 tablespoons chopped onion or
    scallions
1 tablespoon chopped celery
2 eggs
Dry mustard (optional) or hot
    pepper sauce

2 teaspoons water
1 teaspoon flour
Salt
2 teaspoons chopped basil, pars-
    ley, or a combination of basil
    and a sprig of mint

Heat the olive oil in a 6–7 inch well-seasoned frying pan. Add the pepper, onion, and celery. Cook the mixture over medium-low heat, stirring frequently, for 5 minutes. Meanwhile, beat together the eggs with a pinch of dry mustard or a dash of hot pepper sauce, the water, the flour, and salt to taste.

Pour the eggs over the vegetables. Cook over low heat, without stirring, until the eggs have set and the bottom of the frittata is lightly browned. Sprinkle with the herbs, press down on them with the back of a spatula so that they adhere to the surface, and turn the frittata. Cook about 1 minute longer or until set. Serve, herb side up, cut into quarters.

VARIATIONS

Asparagus Frittata. Substitute 1/3 cup peeled *asparagus,* cut into 11/2-inch lengths, for the celery. Omit the red pepper if you wish.

Spinach and Mushroom Frittata. Substitute 1/2 cup cooked *spinach* and 1/4 cup chopped *mushrooms* for the red pepper and celery. Beat 1 tablespoon of grated *Parmesan* cheese into the eggs.

Potato and Ham Frittata. Reduce the amount of red pepper to 1 tablespoon. Omit the celery. Add 1/2 cup coarsely chopped *potatoes* and 1/4 cup *ham* along with the red pepper.

Zucchini Frittata. Omit the red pepper. Substitute 1/2 cup cooked thinly sliced *zucchini.* Reduce the sautéing time to 3 minutes. Add 1 tablespoon *Parmesan or Romano* cheese.

Note: I make frittata successfully using only 1 teaspoon oil, but add the additional teaspoon before pouring in the eggs, if you prefer. Be sure the heat is low, otherwise the eggs will scorch.

STRATA

Stratas are an excellent convenience food: These custard-based dishes not only need to sit for a while before being cooked (even overnight), but also are a thrifty way to use up stale bread and dribs of cheese, meats, and vegetables. This is but one version; use your imagination (and the contents of your refrigerator) to work out countless variations.

(Makes 1–2 servings)

2 eggs
1 cup milk
1/4 teaspoon dry mustard
2 1/2–3 cups coarsely torn stale
   bread
1/2 cup chopped onion
1/2 cup finely chopped cooked

ham or leftover cooked
   poultry
1/4 cup seeded and minced
   jalapeño peppers
2/3–1 cup shredded cheddar
   or Monterey Jack cheese
   (or a combination of both)

Beat together the eggs, milk, and dry mustard. In a greased 6-cup casserole put half the bread. Sprinkle with the onion, ham, peppers, and half of the cheese. Pour over half of the milk mixture. Add the remaining bread and milk. Press down with the palms of your hands so that the bread is submerged in the milk (at least momentarily). Cover and put in the refrigerator for at least 2 hours or overnight. Uncover, and bake in a preheated 350°F oven for 20 minutes. Sprinkle on the remaining cheese and bake 15–20 minutes longer, or until the custard is set and the cheese is lightly browned. The strata will puff up slightly and then collapse. Serve with a *Fruit Salad* (page 40) or a tossed green salad.

LEFTOVERS

Stratas reheat well in the microwave or in a slow oven (325°F). The time varies depending upon the portion size.

SWEET ONION TART

While it may seem a bit much to make this for one, especially after a long hard day, occasionally it's nice to treat yourself. This works best in a 2-cup shallow gratin pan or a recycled pot pie pan from a 9-ounce frozen pie. This tart is particularly good made with sweet onions, such as the Vidalia onions from Georgia. Do cook the onions the length of time I mention, so that they develop almost a caramelized flavor. The tart pastry is easy to make—just pat it into a pie pan. Any leftovers are good for brown-bagging it, packed for lunch and eaten at room temperature.

(Makes one generous serving)

No-Fuss Pastry

2/3 cup flour
1/4 teaspoon sugar
Salt

3 tablespoons butter, chilled
1 medium egg, beaten

Filling

1 teaspoon butter
2 cups thinly sliced sweet
    onions (about 2)
1 medium egg
3/4 cup milk

Nutmeg
Salt and freshly ground black
    pepper
1/4 teaspoon dry mustard
1/4 teaspoon Dijon mustard

To make the crust: This is a snap to do in a food processor, but it works equally well with a mixer. Combine the flour, sugar, and salt to taste. Pulse in the butter until it is the size of lentils, then add the egg. Combine until the mixture forms a ball. (You may need to add another tablespoon flour, but the dough should be soft.) Pat it into a pan. Set aside.

To make the filling: Heat the butter in a heavy frying pan and stir in the onions. Cook over low heat, stirring frequently, for about 20 minutes, or until the onions are wilted and are almost sticking to the pan.

Beat the egg with the milk, then add a pinch of nutmeg, a touch of salt, a generous sprinkling of black pepper, and the mustards.

Arrange the onions in the baked pie shell, then pour over the egg mix-

Sweet Onion Tart (continued)

ture, lightly pressing down on the onions so that they are virtually covered by the mixture.

Bake in a preheated 400°F oven for 35–40 minutes, or until the crust is golden and the custard is firm. Let stand for 10 minutes before serving.

VARIATIONS

Onion and Ham Tart. Add 1/4 cup finely diced *ham* to the onions about halfway through the sautéing time.

Onion and Bacon Tart. Omit the butter. Fry 2 strips *bacon* until crisp. Crumble and set aside. Measure out 1 tablespoon of fat and use it to cook the onions. Proceed as above, sprinkling the bacon bits over the pie shell before adding the onions.

Onion and Herb Tart. Add 2 tablespoons minced *parsley,* or 1 tablespoon chopped *basil* and 1 tablespoon chopped *parsley* to the egg mixture. Proceed as above.

Onion and Tomato Tart. Reduce the amount of onions to 1 cup. Cook as above. Peel and seed 1 large *tomato* and cut into 1/2-inch slices. Arrange the onions in the pan and top with the tomato slices. Add 2 tablespoons grated *Parmesan* cheese to the egg mixture and pour over the onions and tomato. Proceed as above.

Onion and Mushroom Tart. Reduce the quantity of onions to 1 1/2 cups and add 1 cup sliced *mushrooms* to the sautéed onions halfway through the cooking time. Proceed as above.

LUNCHES

When you're busy, it's tempting to regard lunch merely as a fueling stop: The last thing on your mind is a balanced meal or good-tasting food. You munch a bag of chips and an apple at your desk, grab a hamburger and some french fries—or head for one of the salad bars (and load your plate with salad dressing and croutons) rather than take the time to bring a lunch from home.

This kind of snacking-out may be the new American way of life, but it's particularly unhealthy for single people, who, as a rule, eat more poorly than couples or families. Many of us fill up on junk foods at breakfast and lunch, lose energy come mid-afternoon and grab a candy bar, and then stick a frozen dinner into the microwave or buy take-out again at night because we're too tired to cook. Or we're ravenous come evening, plunk down in front of the TV with a trencherman's plate of food, and then go to bed sated, yet exhausted. We know we're eating poorly (and spending far too much money along the way), but it seems too much trouble to brown-bag lunch when just getting out of the house on time in the morning is a major accomplishment.

I'm not suggesting that you should fix lunch every day of the week: One advantage of being single is that you can eat your main meal at lunch with friends, and then enjoy a light supper, such as soup and a sandwich, a fruit salad, or some grilled vegetables without considering the dinner wishes of a partner or family. Eating lunch out is a treat I manage at least once a week.

The rest of the time, however, I follow what might be called "the leftover theory of lunch management." The actual time involved works out to about an hour a week (less time than standing in lines at take-out counters), most of which is spent planning dinner menus that incorporate additional vegetables, legumes, and grains to recycle in lunches. By using leftovers in midday meals, I not only eat better but also save a surprising amount of money.

To get you thinking about the possibilities, let me suggest some of the lunches I would prepare during a typical week. Because I want to limit the amount of fat and preservatives I eat, I prefer to roast poultry and meat and use the leftovers for sandwiches rather than buying commercial lunch meat—although there are a number of low-fat choices on the market. (But read the package labels: One low-fat bologna I checked out had corn syrup as an additive.)

The most compelling reason to utilize leftover meat is that it tastes better. For example, usually on a Sunday, I roast a good-sized chicken (see page 143). I might stuff it with lemon wedges, crushed garlic, an onion, a carrot, and fresh herbs, such as sage, parsley, and thyme. The chicken is the basis for Sunday supper. After dinner, I strip the meat from the bones, store it in the refrigerator for sandwiches, and simmer the bones, skin, and pan vegetables in water for soup. I'll usually end up with 8 cups of broth, enough to make four soup meals. Sometimes I'll prepare *Onion Soup* (page 248), or I might opt for a fresh *Carrot Soup* (see page 151). If I am serving mashed potatoes with the chicken, I add the potato broth to the stock and any leftover potatoes to soup. So far, I have the makings for at least three lunches: one chicken sandwich and two soups with some chicken left over for another meal.

The next day for my dinner meal I might cook extra rice or beans. If I have made brown rice, I will prepare a brown rice salad for the following day with lots of roasted red peppers, onions, sliced raw zucchini, minced basil, and scallions, lightly moistened with lemon juice and olive oil. I'll eat this with a slice of bread and a piece of fruit. If I'm cooking green beans, I'll make sure that I'm steaming extra potatoes, and I'll toss the leftover blanched beans and potatoes in a mustard-flavored oil and vinegar dressing and accompany it with some rye bread for a flavorful light lunch.

When I don't feel like cooking ahead of time, in just a few minutes I can put together some French-style hors d'oeuvre. I'll grate carrots and toss them with black pepper and lemon juice; marinate sliced tomatoes and onions in oil and vinegar; dice cooked potatoes, along with celery and onions, with barely enough mayonnaise to bind them, and bring along some raw fennel to munch on. (Fennel also aids in digestion.) I'll pack them in separate plastic containers and eat with a piece of fruit and country-style French bread.

No matter which lunch I prepare, I always include a slice of good-quality bread, preferably one made with whole grains. It's worth searching out the best bread you can find and freezing it. Almost every city has a health-food bakery that specializes in flavorful sourdough, whole wheat, or multigrain breads. If you're buying packaged bread at the supermarket, remember that ingredients are listed in order of quantity, so select one where whole wheat is first on the list. And if, like me, you live in a community where spongy white bread is the only store-bought option, learn to bake your own using one of the bread recipes in this book.

Most of us realize that we should be increasing the amount of complex carbohydrates, vegetables, and fruits in our diets and decreasing the quantity of fat, sugar, and protein we consume. When I prepare sandwiches, I keep this in mind. I focus on adding vegetables to the sandwich (both for flavor and bulk) rather than loading up on meats or cheese and oils (including those in mayonnaise). You can buy Dijon or whole-grain mustard in most supermarkets and train yourself to prefer its taste to that of gobs of mayonnaise. You can also cut mayonnaise with plain yogurt—

it's hard to tell the difference. Most cheeses have a high fat content and should be used in moderation. If you buy well-aged sharp cheese, which has a more assertive flavor, you'll be satisfied with less. A meat or cheese sandwich made with hearty bread, spread with mustard, then a layer of vegetables such as tomatoes (cut parallel with the stem so they bleed less), cucumbers, shredded raw cabbage, or lettuce is more satisfying than one composed strictly from meats and cheeses. Herbs are also a delicious sandwich addition. During tomato season, my favorite sandwich is a small amount of aged Vermont cheddar cheese and several slices of vine-ripe tomatoes, piled on sourdough bread and topped with basil and a light drizzle of olive oil. Tuna fish sandwiches made with a reduced quantity of mayonnaise (or the new mayonnaise substitutes) and sliced raw cucumbers on whole wheat bread are both filling and satisfying. Sliced avocado, chicken, and tomato sandwiches are wonderful, but if you're watching fat, mash an avocado slice and use it as a spread rather than as a main ingredient.

It's also important to pack a beverage (so you don't go down to the cola machine and get tempted by all the snack foods). If you like fruit juices, that's fine, but if you're watching your weight remember that they're usually high in calories. Also be sure that you're buying fruit juices, not fruit drinks—most of which have quantities of corn syrup sweeteners. I've found an excellent thirst quencher to be chilled bottled water with a dash of bitters and a piece of lime. During the winter I like a thermos filled with mulled cider; on hot summer days mixing iced herbal tea with a small amount of fruit juice (such as apple-raspberry) is delicious. If you're watching your diet, V-8 juice is low in calories. The new coolers developed for chilling baby bottles and children's lunches cost about $6 in most hardware stores. A slender reusable ice pack fits easily into a bag for lunch if you want a less bulky option.

Regardless of what lunch you pack, be sure to add a snack, such as a piece of fruit or a sandwich portion for the 4 p.m. blues—or to eat just before you head home from work. This keeps your energy level high in the early evening as you're facing the crowds on the bus or highways or getting ready to fix dinner.

SOUPS AND BREADS

SOUPS

Many single persons eat soup at least once a day: It just doesn't happen to be homemade. Yet making a soup is one of the simplest, most gratifying ways you can cook for yourself—and it's a great way to use up leftovers. Admittedly, putting a soup together isn't quite as easy as opening a can, but it runs a close second. Most warm soups are no more difficult to make than simmering ingredients in water or broth until they are the consistency you wish. You can change the consistency to fit your mood: Sometimes you'll wish to purée the liquid with the ingredients in a blender or food processor; other times you can leave them whole for texture. Once you learn which ingredients marry well, you can clean out your refrigerator into the stockpot and savor the satisfaction of eating tasty food that otherwise would have gone to waste.

People who have trouble making soup usually are scrimping on the ingredients. Only in a fairy tale can you make soup out of a stone—although you can certainly use less-than-perfect vegetables to make a broth. Be sure to remove any rotten spots before adding them to the stockpot.

In this chapter I've given you directions for making some flavorful easy-to-prepare soups. If you end up with more than you expected, just freeze the remainder in portion-sized amounts. Except for cream-based soups, most soups freeze well. If you'd prefer to store the soups in the refrigerator, be sure to boil them up every second day to keep them from spoiling. If you follow this precaution, most soups will keep in good condition for four or five days. Before reheating, to freshen the flavor add a teaspoon or two of minced herbs, or a dash of cider vinegar. And when you get down to a smidgen, freeze it and use in casseroles, particularly those made with rice, where a quarter cup of a puréed carrot or onion soup, for example, can work wonders.

VEGETABLE BEAN SOUP

Virtually every supermarket sells a soup mix of beans, dried peas, and lentils, a thrifty choice for solo cooks because a 1-pound package (the standard size) is large enough for at least 3 separate meals of soup. Just before serving, you can add leftover vegetables (see first variation).

(Makes 2¹/₂–3 cups)

1 cup dried bean soup mix
Water, vegetable, or ham stock
¹/₄ cup peeled and diced carrot
²/₃ cup peeled and chopped
   onion
1 teaspoon minced garlic (about
   1 clove)

¹/₃ cup sliced celery
1 cup canned crushed tomatoes
   or 1¹/₂ cups peeled, seeded,
   and chopped fresh tomatoes
Sprig of thyme (optional)
Salt and freshly ground black
   pepper

Rinse and examine the beans. Put them in a medium-sized saucepan, add 4 cups water, and bring to a boil. Boil the mixture for 2 minutes, then let sit for 30 minutes. Drain and rinse the beans, cover with 4 cups of water or stock, and cook uncovered for 1 hour. Add the carrot, ¹/₃ cup of the onion, the garlic, and the celery. Simmer, covered, for 1 hour. The beans should be almost cooked through. Add the remaining onion, the tomatoes, and the thyme, if using. Cook, covered, for 20–30 minutes, or until the soup is the consistency you prefer. You may need to add additional water or stock. Taste and add salt and pepper.

VARIATIONS

With leftover vegetables. Just before serving add ¹/₂–1 cup chopped or sliced leftover vegetables, such as *fresh beans, broccoli, zucchini, winter squash, turnips,* or *corn.* Cover the pan and let the vegetables sit in the mixture until they are heated through, or cook, stirring, for 1 minute.

With greens. Add 2 cups sliced greens, such as *spinach, kale, or swiss chard* leaves about 20–30 minutes before the soup is done.

With herbs and/or pasta or rice. Add 1 tablespoon chopped *parsley, coriander, or basil* just before serving along with ¹/₂–1 cup *leftover macaroni, other pasta,* or *rice.*

Vegetable Bean Soup (continued)

With ham or sausage. If you're using *ham* pieces add them along with the water after the mixture has soaked for 30 minutes. Add cooked sliced *sausage* just before serving.

LEFTOVERS

Any leftover soup freezes beautifully. To reheat uniformly in the microwave, freeze it in ice-cube trays and reheat as many cubes as you wish. One cube equals about 2 tablespoons.

Note: One of the best—and most reasonably priced—soup mixes, the A-1 Mix, is produced in Maine by the Kennebec Bean Company. The legume mix, which includes 16 old-time favorites, such as Soldier and Jacob's Cattle, is selected to cook through at the same rate—not always the case with bean soup mixes. You can mail-order this mix, as well as 23 varieties of dried beans, directly from the company (Kennebec Bean Co., P.O. Box 219, North Vassalboro, Maine 04962).

CHICKEN NOODLE SOUP

This basic soup lends itself to add-ons, such as leftover cooked vegetables (see Variation). It's particularly attractive prepared with matchstick-sized pieces of chicken and a garnish of scallions.

(Makes about 2 1/2 cups)

1 1/2 cups chicken stock	Thinly sliced leftover chicken
1/3 cup peeled and finely	(optional)
chopped carrot	Freshly ground black pepper
1/3 cup chopped celery	1 tablespoon sliced scallion
3/4–1 cup dried noodles	(optional)

Pour the chicken stock into a saucepan and bring it to a boil. Add the carrot and celery, lower the heat, and simmer the vegetables for 10 minutes. Stir in the noodles and cook, stirring occasionally, until the noodles are cooked through but retain some texture, about 5–8 minutes, depending upon the noodle. Stir in thinly sliced cooked chicken to taste, if you like. Add a generous amount of black pepper and the optional scallions. Cover the pan and steep for 2 minutes off the heat before serving.

VARIATIONS

With leftover vegetables. Add 1/3 cup of one or more of the following: *peas, lima beans, corn,* sliced *broccoli, beans*—or 1–2 tablespoons diced *rutabaga* or white *turnip.*

With herbs. Add 1 tablespoon of chopped *sweet marjoram* or *parsley* along with the black pepper.

CARROT AND HERB SOUP

This carrot soup is a flavorful supper or lunch standby that's ready in about 15 minutes from start to finish. Either coriander or sweet marjoram tastes great—but you can always use chopped parsley or chives. The balsamic vinegar variation has a full, rich flavor.

(Makes 2¹/2–3 cups)

2 cups chicken or vegetable stock
2/3 cup peeled coarsely chopped carrot (about 2 medium)
1/4 cup chopped celery
1/3–1/2 cup peeled, coarsely chopped potato
1/2–2/3 cup peeled and chopped onion
Salt and freshly ground black pepper
2 teaspoons chopped fresh coriander, sweet marjoram, or parsley

Place the stock, carrot, celery, potato, and onion in a heavy stove-top pot. Bring the mixture to a boil, reduce the heat, and simmer for about 10 minutes, or until the vegetables are cooked through. Purée the vegetables and liquid in a blender, or place the cooked vegetables in a food processor, pulse until they are puréed, and combine with the liquid. Taste and season with salt and pepper. Stir in the herbs and serve.

VARIATION

With balsamic vinegar. Omit the herbs. Add a dash or two of *balsamic vinegar* and a generous amount of black pepper.

Note: Any leftover soup freezes well. Purée once again before reheating.

GREEK-STYLE LEMON SOUP

You can put together avgolemono, the tart Greek chicken stock, lemon, and egg soup, in under 10 minutes if you have chicken stock and rice (either fresh or frozen) on hand. Cook the soup gently once you have added the egg—otherwise it will curdle.

(Makes 1¹/2–2 cups)

1¹/2–2 cups chicken stock
¹/3 cup cooked rice
1 medium egg
1–1¹/2 tablespoons freshly squeezed lemon juice

2 teaspoons minced fresh mint or parsley
Salt and freshly ground black pepper (optional)

Heat the chicken stock in a stainless-steel or enamel pan. Add the rice. Meanwhile, beat the egg until it is foamy and add the lemon juice. Stir in about ¹/2 cup of the chicken stock into the egg mixture, then, off the heat, add the egg mixture to the soup, whisking constantly. Simmer the soup until it thickens slightly. *Do not let boil.* Stir in the herbs and season with salt and pepper if you wish. Serve immediately.

VARIATION

With dill, corn, and greens. For a heartier, nontraditional version, just before serving substitute *dill* for the mint, and add ¹/2 cup fresh or frozen *corn* kernels and 2–3 tablespoons very thinly sliced fresh young greens, such as *collards* or *spinach.* The corn and greens should be barely cooked through.

WATERCRESS AND PORK SOUP

This easy soup, a favorite of my friend Peter Richards, can be made with a good-quality canned chicken broth.

(Makes about 3 cups)

2 cups chicken stock (low-sodium if canned)

1 boneless pork cutlet, cut into ¹/8-inch-thick slices

1–1¹/₂ cups chopped
watercress (about ¹/₂ bunch)
1 tablespoon sliced scallions

2 teaspoons chopped coriander
Salt and freshly ground black
pepper

Pour the chicken stock into a saucepan, bring it just to a boil, and add the pork. Lower the heat to a simmer, and simmer the pork for 5 minutes, stirring occasionally. The pork should be cooked through. Stir in the watercress, and cook 1 minute longer. The watercress should retain some crunch. Add the scallions and coriander. Taste and season with salt and pepper. Serve immediately.

VARIATION

With an egg. Beat an *egg.* Just before you take the soup off the heat, pour the egg very slowly into the soup in a thin stream, stirring constantly.

GAZPACHO

The Spaniards, who certainly know what hot weather is like, invented this icy tomato-based soup. It's an ideal light meal for muggy, summer weather because you can prepare it in the morning and come home to a dinner that's ready. Gazpacho takes about 15 minutes to make—and that includes chopping the vegetable garnish.   *(Makes about 2¹/₂ cups)*

1 tablespoon lemon juice or
white wine vinegar
¹/₃ cup fresh breadcrumbs
1 teaspoon minced garlic

2 teaspoons olive oil
2¹/₂ cups peeled, seeded, and
chopped ripe tomatoes
Salt

Condiments

About 1 tablespoon peeled and
chopped cucumber
About 1 tablespoon chopped
scallion

About 2 teaspoons chopped
green pepper

Place the lemon juice in a glass bowl, add the breadcrumbs, garlic, and olive oil. Let the mixture sit so the breadcrumbs absorb the liquid. Purée

Gazpacho (continued)

with 2 cups of the tomatoes in a blender. Add $^1/_3$–$^1/_2$ cup water if you prefer a thin soup. Refrigerate until very cold. Before serving, stir in the remaining tomatoes, and the amounts of the cucumber, scallion, and pepper you prefer.

Note: Traditionally, the gazpacho condiments are served in little bowls so that you can add them in the proportion you prefer.

COLD AVOCADO SOUP

This light soup is just right on a steamy summer night. Adjust the amount of lemon juice to suit your palate.

(Makes 1$^3/_4$ cups)

1$^1/_4$ cups chicken or vegetable
    stock
$^1/_4$ cup nonfat yogurt
1 cup peeled and diced avocado

1–2 teaspoons freshly squeezed
    lemon juice
Salt

Place the stock and yogurt in a blender. Blend on low speed until combined. Add the avocado and 1 teaspoon of the lemon juice and purée at high speed. Taste and add salt and remaining lemon juice if you wish.

VARIATION

With lemongrass and cream. **Simmer** the stock for 20 minutes with 1 teaspoon chopped *lemongrass*. Strain the stock and purée with $^1/_4$ cup all-purpose *cream* and the avocado. Season with salt and a dash of *cayenne pepper*. Serve hot with toasted pita bread or restaurant-style tortilla chips.

CHILLED SALMON AND CUCUMBER SOUP

This refreshing summer soup is an excellent way to use up a leftover piece of salmon. The amount of salmon isn't critical.

(Makes about 2^1/2–3 cups)

^{1}/2 cup diced onion
1^1/2 cups fish or bottled clam stock
1 cucumber, peeled, seeded, and diced
2 teaspoons chopped fresh dill

^{3}/4 cup plain yogurt
Leftover cooked salmon fillet or 4 ounces steamed salmon
Salt and freshly ground black pepper
Sprig of dill, for garnish

Mix the onion with the fish stock and all but 1 tablespoon of the cucumber. Place the mixture in a saucepan and cook over low heat until the cucumber is tender but not mushy. Pulse in a food processor or blender with the fresh dill and yogurt until combined. Chill.

Just before serving, flake the salmon into pieces and add to the soup. Season to taste with salt and freshly ground black pepper. Garnish with the reserved tablespoon of cucumber and a sprig of fresh dill.

MARIE O'DAY'S CABBAGE, CARROT, AND BARLEY SOUP

I grew up with this soup, which holds for several days in the refrigerator or freezes well. It's an ideal way to utilize both leftover barley and the carcass and leftover meat from a roast chicken or turkey. Be sure to finely dice the vegetables.

(Makes about 5–6 cups)

4–5 cups rich-flavored chicken stock
2 cups finely diced carrots
2 cups finely diced cabbage
1 cup cooked barley

^{3}/4–1 cup diced cooked chicken
Freshly ground black pepper
2 teaspoons minced sweet marjoram (optional)

Place the chicken stock in a pot, add the carrots and cabbage, and

Marie O'Day's Cabbage, Carrot, and Barley Soup (continued)
bring the broth to a boil. Lower the heat, and simmer for 15 minutes. Add the barley and simmer for 5 minutes longer. Add the chicken meat and simmer just long enough for the chicken to be reheated. Taste. If the chicken stock is too watery, strain out the chicken and vegetables and boil the broth until it has the desired flavor. Then add the chicken and vegetables, reheat, season with pepper to taste and the sweet marjoram, if using. Add salt at the table.

VARIATION

Scotch Broth. Substitute 2 cups *cooked lamb* or *beef* for the chicken. You could add 1/2 cup cooked *parsnip*. Proceed as above.

MUSHROOM AND CELERY SOUP

You can enjoy this recipe either as a soup or recycled as a sauce with roast chicken or pork chops. It's even good baked over meatballs. For best flavor use a densely flavored stock, such as the one produced in *Braised Chicken with Vegetables* (page 150). Serve with a crusty loaf of bread or *Double Cornbread* (page 270).

(Makes about 2 cups)

1 tablespoon butter	1/3 cup chopped celery
1/3 cup chopped onion (1 medium)	1 tablespoon chopped herbs, such as dill, parsley, or a
1 cup finely chopped mushrooms	combination of basil and sweet marjoram
1 tablespoon flour	Salt and freshly ground black
2–21/4 cups heated chicken or vegetable stock	pepper

Heat the butter in a heavy saucepan. Add the onion and cook over moderate heat for about 2 minutes, stirring occasionally. Add the mushrooms and cook for about 3 minutes, stirring, until they are slightly wilted. Off the heat, stir in the flour, then add the stock, stirring constantly. Add the celery. Bring the mixture to a boil, lower the heat, and simmer for about 10 minutes. Add the herbs and immediately remove from the heat. Let the soup sit for a few minutes to meld the flavors. Season with salt and pepper to taste before serving.

VARIATIONS

Cream of Mushroom Soup. Omit the celery and herbs. Add 1/2 cup all-purpose *cream* after the soup has simmered for 10 minutes. Do not let the mixture boil.

Hungarian-Style Mushroom Soup. Use chopped *dill* as the herb. Add 1 tablespoon *sour cream* to each soup bowl just before serving.

WINTER SQUASH, POTATO, AND ONION SOUP

I cook extra winter squash and mashed potatoes for this hearty soup that gets its beautiful golden color from the winter squash. The proportions of vegetables are arbitrary, but you need a goodly amount of squash for maximum flavor. If you have leftover green salad, add it to the mixture.

(Makes 2 1/2–3 cups)

2 teaspoons butter
1 1/2 cups thinly sliced onions
1 1/2 cups chicken or beef stock
   or vegetable water
3/4 cup cooked, mashed winter
   squash
3/4 cup cooked mashed potatoes
1 fresh tomato, peeled, seeded,
   and chopped (about 3/4 cup)

1 tablespoon chopped fresh
   coriander
1 teaspoon chopped fresh chives
Pinch of nutmeg
Salt and freshly ground black
   pepper to taste

Heat the butter in a heavy casserole, add the onions, stir to coat with butter, and cover the pan. Stew over low heat, stirring frequently, for about 20 minutes. Stir in the stock, winter squash, mashed potatoes, and tomato. Cover and cook another 10 minutes, or until the mixture is warm. Purée in a blender or food processor. Just before serving stir in the coriander and chives. Season to taste with a pinch of nutmeg and salt and pepper.

Winter Squash, Potato, and Onion Soup (continued)

Note: If you have leftover soup, freeze it in 1/4-cup amounts. Added to soups or casseroles it adds a deep, full flavor.

VARIATIONS

Pumpkin Soup. Substitute 1/2 cup cooked *pumpkin* for the winter squash.

With rutabaga. Add 1/4 cup mashed *rutabaga or turnip* along with the winter squash.

ONION SOUP

This a wonderful standby, both for the freezer and as an ingredient in other recipes, such as braised beef dishes. I like it best prepared with chicken broth (rather than beef broth), which results in a lighter, more subtle-tasting soup. It's essential to cook the onions the length of time indicated. They reduce almost to a purée.

(Makes 8 cups)

1 tablespoon butter	6–8 cups chicken, vegetable, or
7–8 cups thinly sliced onions	beef broth, heated
2 tablespoons flour	Salt and freshly ground pepper

Melt the butter in a large saucepan. Stir in the onions and toss in the butter until lightly coated. Cover the pan and slowly simmer the onions for 20 minutes. Uncover and cook 30 minutes longer, stirring occasionally. With the pan off the heat, stir in the flour, then cook over low heat, stirring, for 3 minutes. Add the broth and simmer slowly for 20 minutes. Taste and season with salt and pepper before serving.

Note: For a lighter soup, omit the flour.

LEFTOVERS

Microwave Vegetarian Rice Casserole. In a microwave casserole place 1/2 cup long-grain *rice*, 2/3 cup onion soup, 1 tablespoon chopped *red or green pepper*, 2 teaspoons chopped *lemongrass or coriander*, and 1/4 cup sliced *mushrooms.* Cover and microwave over high heat for 5 minutes. Uncover, turn the heat to medium, and cook 10 minutes longer. Stir in 1 small *zucchini,* thinly sliced (about 3/4 cup), cover, and cook 5 minutes longer. Stir and season with salt and freshly ground black pepper before serving.

Creamy Onion Gravy. This gives a down-home flavor to sautéed or fried chicken. Into about 1 tablespoon of the pan drippings, off the heat stir in 1 tablespoon flour. Cook, stirring, for 3 minutes and pour in 1/2–2/3 cup heated onion soup. Stir until the gravy thickens and add 2 tablespoons *light cream.* Season with salt and lots of freshly ground black pepper.

BEEF GOULASH SOUP

This soup is halfway between a soup and a stew. The sweet rose paprika is stocked in the gourmet section of most supermarkets. This paprika, traditionally used in Eastern European cooking, tastes particularly good with beans, peppers, and cabbage. Be sure to cook it in fat for best flavor. This makes enough for 2 generous meals. Freeze any leftovers for another day.

(Makes about 6 cups)

1 tablespoon canola oil, lard, or rendered chicken fat	1 cup thinly sliced carrots
2 cups chopped onions	1–11/2 pounds stew beef, cut into 11/2-inch cubes
2 teaspoons finely chopped garlic	2–3 cups beef stock
2 tablespoons rose paprika	1 tablespoon chopped sweet marjoram
2 medium green peppers, cut into 1/4-inch-thick rings	Salt and freshly ground black pepper

Heat the oil in a large ovenproof pot and add the onions and garlic. Cook over medium heat, stirring frequently, for about 5 minutes, or until lightly browned. Stir in the paprika and continue cooking for 2 minutes longer to remove the raw taste of the spice. Stir in the peppers, carrots, and stew beef until they are coated with the paprika. Add beef stock to cover meat and vegetables, adding water if necessary.

Cover the pan and bake in a preheated 350°F oven for about 1 hour. Skim off the fat, and set half the soup aside for another meal (see Note).

Beef Goulash Soup (continued)
Season the remaining soup with the sweet marjoram and salt and pepper to taste. Serve in a large soup bowl, accompanied by a dense country bread.

VARIATIONS

Goulash Soup with Sour Cream. Dice enough *rutabaga or kohlrabi* into 1/2-inch pieces to make 1 cup and steam until tender, about 10–15 minutes. Heat the leftover soup, add 1/2 cup chopped *celery,* and cook for about 5 minutes, or until the celery is cooked through but still retains texture. Stir in the rutabaga or kohlrabi along with 2 tablespoons *sour cream.* Taste and season with salt and pepper. Add 2–3 teaspoons *catsup* or 1/4 cup chopped *tomatoes* if you wish.

With potatoes and tomatoes. Add 1 cup diced cooked *potatoes* and 1/4 cup fresh chopped *tomato* to the leftover goulash. Season with 2 teaspoons chopped *dill* and salt and pepper to taste.

Note: This soup freezes well.

VEGETABLE STOCK

You can use this as the basis for soups or casseroles. I usually freeze it in 1/2-cup amounts. If you leave the skin on the onions, it adds color to the stock. There's no need to peel the vegetables, just rinse them first.

(Makes about 8 cups)

3 medium carrots, chopped	1 bay leaf (optional)
2 medium onions or 1 large cleaned leek, chopped	Parsley sprigs
1 cup chopped yellow turnip	1 thyme sprig
3 stalks celery, chopped	10 peppercorns
4 cloves whole garlic (optional)	1 large tomato, seeded and chopped

Place the carrots, onions, turnip, celery, garlic, bay leaf, about 6 sprigs parsley, thyme, and the peppercorns in a large pot. Cover with 8 cups of water. Simmer over low heat for 1 1/2 hours, adding extra water as needed. Add the tomato and simmer 20 minutes longer. Strain, cool, and freeze.

CHICKEN STOCK

Making chicken stock is easy; if you can simmer water, you can make stock. No need to add vegetables—for a delicate stock, just simmer chicken pieces (or a cooked chicken carcass) in water. The vegetables add a more complex flavor. If you buy whole chickens, stash away the necks, wing tips, and gizzards in a heavy plastic bag in the freezer until you want to make stock. Leaving skin on the onion adds color to the stock.

(Makes about 8 cups)

3–4 pounds chicken pieces, such as a cooked chicken carcass or uncooked necks, backs, wings, or gizzards (do not use livers)

3 stalks celery
3 carrots
1 large onion, halved
1/2 teaspoon peppercorns (optional)

Place the chicken, celery, carrots, onion, and peppercorns in a large, heavy pot, and cover with about 2 quarts of cold water. Slowly bring the water to a simmer, and simmer for 2–2 1/2 hours, occasionally skimming the scum and fat from the surface and adding more water as needed.

Pour the stock through a colander into a large bowl, let cool slightly, then refrigerate to finish cooling, uncovered (if it is covered as it cools, it might sour). Refrigerate the stock until the fat congeals on the surface. Remove the fat and taste the stock. If it seems too watery, boil it down to concentrate the flavor. Refrigerate the stock for up to 4 days, or freeze it in 1/2-cup amounts. The stock will keep in good condition in the freezer for up to 6 months.

VARIATIONS

Rich Chicken Stock. Substitute a 5-pound *fowl* for the chicken pieces. Add 2 cloves *garlic*, 2 cleaned *leeks*, 1 sprig of *thyme*, and 1/2 a *bay leaf.* Proceed as above.

Oven Chicken Stock. Preheat the oven to 450°F. Place the chicken, celery, carrots, and onion in a roasting pan and roast, uncovered, for 20–30 minutes, or until lightly browned. Pour off the fat, cover the chicken and vegetables with water, and lower the heat to 350°F. Cook, stirring occasionally and adding water as needed, for 2 hours. Pour the stock through a colander and proceed as above.

ADDITIONAL SOUP RECIPES IN THIS BOOK

BREADS

Nothing tastes quite like homemade bread. Whether it's a slice of warm yeast bread, a flaky biscuit, or a stack of tender pancakes—fresh bread adds a special fillip to a meal. I probably make more bread now that I'm single than I ever did when I was married. Thanks to the new rapid-rise yeasts and the high-gluten flours developed for bread machines, making yeast breads is far more foolproof than it was many years ago.

In this section you'll find bread recipes that are particularly useful for solo cooking. Even if you're just beginning to bake yeast breads, you can succeed with French bread kneaded in a food processor or mixer. This bread is wonderful with main courses or sandwiches. Nothing goes to waste because once the bread has cooled, you can slice it into serving portions and freeze them immediately in a heavy plastic bag. When you're preparing a meal all you need do is open the bag and take out the slices, which will defrost in 10–15 minutes at room temperature. (And if you're taking a sandwich to work, make it with frozen bread, which defrosts during the morning and ends up tasting fresher than bread that has been refrigerated.)

There are so many biscuit and cornbread mixes on the market that it might not seem worth making quick breads from scratch. However, many of the commercial mixes have a surfeit of preservatives that leave a slightly metallic aftertaste, so it's worth taking a minute or two longer and starting from scratch. It's up to you. However, unless you're baking up a storm, it's best to store the flours in the refrigerator (or freezer), where they'll stay in good condition longer. And if you decide to bake your own quick breads, buy the smallest size container of baking powder and replace it every six months (more often if you live in a humid climate) so that it retains its potency.

Making pizza is a useful way to use up leftover vegetables, small amounts of cheese, or meat. You'll find recipes for pizza crust and several toppings. If you have the time, it's handy to mix together a batch (or two) of dough, form it into a pizza round, precook it for 10 minutes, and freeze the cooled round. Then, when you're in a hurry, all you need do is top the frozen round with whichever combination you prefer, stick it in the oven, and sit down to dinner in 10–15 minutes.

FRENCH BREAD

This recipe is based on one developed by food chemist Shirley Corriher. The dough is sticky, but don't be tempted to add much more flour or the texture will suffer. (I oil my hands while forming the dough, which works well.) Shirley's addition of cider vinegar helps approximate the flavor and aroma of bread you find in France.

Cuisinart manufactures small French-bread pans with curved sides that work well with this recipe. If you don't have these pans, use a soufflé dish. Freeze any extra loaves for another meal.

(Makes 3 thin loaves)

1 package dry yeast	1 teaspoon salt
1 teaspoon sugar	1 teaspoon cider vinegar
1 cup warm water (110°F)	1 tablespoon vegetable oil
2 cups bread flour, approximately	

Stir the yeast and sugar into the water and let sit for 5 minutes, until the surface bubbles. Place the flour and salt in the bowl of a food processor, and pulse on and off for a moment. Add the yeast mixture. Pulse the machine on and off about 8 times, then add the cider vinegar.

When the dough starts to form a ball, process it for 15–20 seconds to knead. Add additional flour, a tablespoon at a time, if the dough is soupy and does not form a ball. It will be sticky. (Alternatively, you can mix the dough by hand or by using a heavy-duty electric mixer. Beat for 2 minutes. The dough will be sticky; do not try to knead on the counter.)

Oil a mixing bowl with the vegetable oil, place the dough in the bowl, and turn to coat with oil. Let rise in a warm place until the bread is doubled in bulk (about 40 minutes). Make a fist with your hand, and punch down the dough. Cover the dough, and let the dough sit for 15 minutes before forming into loaves.

Either shape into 3 long, skinny French loaves to fit the Cuisinart loaf pans, or form into a ball and place in a greased soufflé dish. Cover and let rise until doubled in bulk. Bake the bread in a preheated 425°F oven for 20 minutes for the French loaves, or 30–35 minutes for the country-style loaf. Remove the bread from the pans or dish and cool on a rack.

VARIATION

Basil-Cheese French Bread. Add 3 tablespoons minced *fresh basil* and 2 tablespoons *Parmesan cheese* to the flour and salt mixture. Proceed as above.

WHOLE WHEAT POTATO BREAD

This is a versatile choice for the solo cook because the potatoes keep the bread moist and fresh-tasting for several days. Potato bread is delicious made with white flour (particularly good toasted), but it's also tasty made with a mixture of whole wheat and white flours with wheat germ mixed in—or with leftover oatmeal or mixed grain cereals or minced herbs. I prefer the flavor of bread that has a lower yeast content and a slow rise, but if you're in a hurry, add the additional package of yeast. When you drain the cooked potatoes, save the water for the bread recipe—it adds a pleasant flavor.

(Makes 2 loaves)

1–2 packages dry yeast
2 cups lukewarm potato water
   or water
1–2 tablespoons sugar
1 cup cooled mashed potatoes
1/3 cup butter, softened, or
   canola oil

31/2 cups white bread flour
1 teaspoon salt
3 cups whole wheat flour
   (preferably stone-ground),
   approximately
2/3 cup fresh wheat germ

In a large bowl, dissolve the yeast in 1/2 cup of the water. Stir in 1 teaspoon of the sugar and let it sit until the yeast starts to bubble, about 5 minutes. Add the remaining water and sugar. Beat in the potatoes, softened butter, and white flour. Add the salt. Then slowly add the whole wheat flour and wheat germ. The amount of flour will vary depending upon the humidity in the air. You will have a stiff dough.

Knead the dough until smooth (about 10 minutes). Place it in a greased bowl, turn it over, and cover with a clean dishtowel. Let it rise until doubled in bulk, about 11/2 hours. Punch down the dough, let sit for 15 minutes to relax the gluten in the flour (which makes it easier to form), then shape into 2 loaves. Place in 2 greased 9 × 5-inch bread pans.

Whole Wheat Potato Bread (continued)
Let rise until doubled in bulk. Bake the bread in a preheated 400°F oven for 30–40 minutes. Remove from the pans and cool on a rack before slicing with a bread knife.

VARIATIONS

White Potato Bread. Use only white flour.

Herb-Nut Potato Bread. After you add all the flour, add 3 tablespoons minced fresh herbs, such as a mixture of *sweet marjoram, parsley,* and *basil,* along with 3 tablespoons chopped *nuts.* Knead and proceed as above.

Oats and Bran Bread. Substitute 1 cup *rolled oats* and 1/2 cup *bran* for 1 1/2 cups of the whole wheat flour and the wheat germ.

LEFTOVERS

Italian Tomato and Bread Salad. See page 32.

Croutons. Slice bread into 1/2-inch pieces. Trim the crusts (use for breadcrumbs) and cut into 1/2-inch cubes. Place on a cookie sheet and bake in a preheated 325°F oven for about 20 minutes, turning occasionally, or until lightly toasted. Store in a tin. Croutons will usually stay in good condition for at least 1 week.

SAVORY BREAD ROLL

This stuffed bread loaf, loosely based on the meat and vegetable mixtures found in Italy, is tasty either hot or cold. For a heartier bread version, substitute half a recipe of *Whole Wheat Potato Bread* (preceding recipe).

(Makes 1–2 servings)

1 recipe *Pizza Dough* (page 259)
2 tablespoons olive oil
1 tablespoon chopped garlic
1/2 cup chopped onion
2 cups stemmed and chopped
  fresh spinach or kale
1/2 cup chopped celery
1/3 cup diced ham or Genoa
  salami (optional)

1 tablespoon chopped red or
  green pepper
1/2 cup diced mushrooms
1/2 cup diced pitted black olives
4 ounces grated mozzarella
  cheese
2 tablespoons grated Parmesan
  or provolone cheese

Make the pizza dough and place it in a covered bowl to rise. Meanwhile, heat 11/2 tablespoons of the olive oil in a large frying pan. Add the garlic and onion and cook, stirring frequently, for 2 minutes. Stir in the spinach, celery, ham, if using, and pepper. Continue cooking for 5 minutes, stirring frequently, or until the spinach is wilted. Add the mushrooms, cook 2 minutes longer, stirring constantly, and the olives. Scrape the mixture into a glass bowl and let it cool.

Punch down the pizza dough and let sit for 15 minutes so that the gluten relaxes and the dough is easier to work. Roll it out to a 10 x 12-inch rectangle. The dough should be about 1/2 inch thick. Oil the surface with the remaining 1/2 tablespoon olive oil. Cover the dough to within an inch of the edges with the filling and the grated cheeses. With the longest edge parallel to you, roll up the dough like a jelly roll, tuck the ends under, and place it diagonally, seam side down, on an oiled cookie sheet. Cut two deep slashes in the top to allow steam to escape.

Immediately bake in a preheated 400°F oven for 40–50 minutes, or until the bread is cooked through and the top is golden brown. Cool before cutting into slices.

MEDITERRANEAN PICNIC LOAF

Slightly stale French bread tastes brand-new in this robust sandwich that you can make the night before for lunch the next day. The loaf doesn't get soggy because you coat the stale bread with oil before adding the filling. Adjust the size of the sandwich and the amount of anchovies, olives, and tomatoes to suit your taste.

(Serves 1)

Fresh garlic
Good-quality olive oil
Day-old, firm-textured French or
    Italian bread

Greek or Italian olives
Anchovies
Tomatoes
Freshly ground black pepper

Smash the garlic and marinate it in $1/4$ cup olive oil for a few hours. Halve the bread, then brush with the garlic-scented oil. (Use the leftover oil for cooking.) Finely chop olives and anchovies and spread on the bread. Slice tomatoes parallel to their cores (so they don't ooze) and arrange on the bread. Season with pepper and wrap tightly in aluminum foil, pressing down slightly in the process. Let sit overnight or up to 24 hours. Cut into 2-inch slices, if you wish.

> *"Cooking after working all day is a great way to unwind because it allows you to be creative, develop new skills and talents that maybe you didn't think you had—and there's no pressure. You can take your time and be a perfectionist if you wish. I cook with a lot of herbs—I have my own little herb garden around the house that contains rosemary, thyme, sage, basil, oregano, and the usual chives. Usually I bake or stir-fry food; in the summer I particularly like to grill outside. Pizzas are a great meal if you live alone. You can make your own dough and go for it."*
> *Diane Fulkerson, businesswoman*

PIZZA

I opt for pizza at least twice a month because it's a handy way to clean out the refrigerator. Often the best pizzas are invented with leftovers, or small amounts of vegetables. Making your own pizza takes little more than an hour from start to finish with the new rapid-rise yeast. Or you can buy frozen bread dough, defrost it, and measure into 1 cup portions, taking the measurement before it rises. Leftover pizza is great for breakfast—or lunch at work.

(Makes an 8–9-inch pizza)

Pizza Dough

This dough is ready to bake in about 1 hour. I use bread flour, which has more protein than all-purpose flour, giving a better texture to any kind of yeast bread. (The protein content is listed on the bread package. Aim for one with a percentage of 12 or higher. Commercial bread flour has a percentage of 16.) Vary the pizza dough by adding half whole wheat flour and a tablespoon of rye flour. The cornmeal in the dough adds texture. The amount of flour varies depending upon the humidity in the air. (On a humid day, you'll need more flour.) This makes a pizza with a thin, almost crisp crust.

3 tablespoons warm water
3 tablespoons milk
1 1/4 teaspoons dry yeast (about
   1/2 package)
1/4 teaspoon sugar or 1/2 teaspoon honey

3/4 cup bread flour
1/2 teaspoon salt
1 tablespoon olive oil
2 1/2 tablespoons cornmeal

Mix together the water, milk, yeast, and sugar and let sit for about 5 minutes. Then add 1/3 cup of the bread flour and beat until well combined. Stir in the salt, olive oil, 2 tablespoons of the cornmeal, and the remaining flour. You may need to add more flour or water, depending upon the humidity in the air. You want the dough to be moist. Place on a floured countertop and knead for 5 minutes (or knead in a food processor, or a mixer with a dough hook attachment, for 2 minutes). The dough

Pizza (continued)

will look smooth with a satinlike surface. Place the dough in an oiled bowl, turn, and cover it with a clean dishtowel. Let the dough double in bulk, about 30 minutes. Punch the dough down, and let it rest for 10–15 minutes so the gluten relaxes and the dough is easy to form.

To assemble the pizza: Sprinkle an ungreased baking sheet or pizza stone with 1/2 tablespoon cornmeal. Roll out the dough on a floured board—or just put the dough on the cookie sheet or stone and roll it out there. Flatten it slightly with your fingertips. I think it's easier to make a rectangle than a circle—but it's up to you. You want to end up with a 6 × 8-inch rectangle (or a 9-inch circle) that's 1/4–1/3 inch thick, depending upon the thickness of the crust you prefer. Let the dough rise for about 15 minutes. Place a topping (recipes follow) on the pizza, drizzle over a little olive oil, and bake in a preheated 425°F oven for about 15–20 minutes, or until the dough is cooked through. Let cool slightly before cutting into pieces and serving.

Note: Some of the new-style yeasts formulated for bread machines are meant to be mixed with the dry ingredients rather than the liquids. Read the package instructions and assemble the dough accordingly.

LEFTOVERS

Leftover pizza is great for breakfast or lunch. It also freezes well: Wrap individual slices in plastic wrap or freezer paper and store them in the freezer. Reheat individual slices, or have a smorgasbord pizza dinner by reheating as many pieces (and kinds) as you like in the oven. Place frozen slices on a cookie sheet and bake in a preheated 400°F oven for 12–15 minutes or until warmed through.

Fresh Tomato Sauce with Mozzarella Topping

This delicate sauce is the one to choose when fresh tomatoes are in season.

(For 1 small pizza)

2 tablespoons olive oil
1 1/2 cups peeled, seeded, and
  chopped fresh tomatoes
Salt and freshly ground black
  pepper

1 recipe Pizza Dough (see page
  259)
1 tablespoon grated Romano or
  Parmesan cheese (optional)
4 ounces grated mozzarella cheese

Heat 1¹/₂ tablespoons of the olive oil in a nonreactive frying pan. Stir in the tomatoes. Cook, stirring frequently, for 7–10 minutes. Taste and add salt and pepper. Cool slightly. Spread the tomato mixture on the pizza dough. Sprinkle with the optional Romano or Parmesan and drizzle with the remaining ¹/₂ tablespoon oil. Bake in a preheated 425°F oven for 10 minutes, sprinkle with the mozzarella cheese, and continue baking until done, about another 10 minutes.

Variation

With anchovies. Proceed as above, only after you spread out the tomato mixture, sprinkle with 2 teaspoons chopped *anchovies*.

Note: The high butterfat content of the mozzarella causes it to burn easily. Always add it halfway through the baking process.

Asparagus, Mushroom, and Scallion Topping

Asparagus and mushrooms take center stage in this vegetarian pizza with less cheese than most versions. This is a good way to use up cooked leftover asparagus.

(For 1 small pizza)

9 fresh or leftover asparagus
   spears
1 teaspoon olive oil
¹/₂ cup chopped scallions, both
   green and white parts
1 teaspoon garlic

4 ounces sliced mushrooms
1 recipe Pizza Dough (see page
   259)
3 tablespoons grated Romano or
   Parmesan cheese
¹/₄ cup grated mozzarella cheese

Look over the asparagus spears. You are going to arrange them in a pinwheel design on the pizza, tips pointing to the center, so trim the spears to fit. If they are raw, blanch them in a pot of boiling water for 2 minutes, immediately run them under cold water, and drain on a clean dishtowel. Pat them dry.

Meanwhile, heat the olive oil in a nonreactive frying pan, add the scallions and garlic, and cook over moderate heat, stirring frequently, for 2 minutes. Stir in the mushrooms, raise the heat, and cook 2 minutes longer, stirring constantly. Remove from the heat.

Pizza (continued)

Arrange the asparagus on top of the dough, fanning out the spears. Fill in between the spears with the scallions and mushrooms. Sprinkle with the Romano cheese. Bake in a preheated 425°F oven for 10 minutes. Sprinkle with the mozzarella cheese, and bake for 5 minutes longer, or until the cheese is melted and the crust is browned.

Variation

With shrimp. Arrange 8 raw, oiled *shrimp* between the asparagus spears along the edge of the pizza—echoing the curve of the dough. Proceed as above.

Sweet Onion and Red Pepper Topping

Just one large white onion combined with a peeled red pepper makes a colorful and smooth-tasting late-summer pizza. Try the variation with anchovies: their salty taste plays against the sweetness of the pepper and onion. If possible, use top-quality Parmesan cheese: pregrated and bottled cheese masks the fresh vegetable flavors.

(For 1 small pizza)

1 1/2 tablespoons olive oil
3 cups thinly sliced sweet white
   onions
2/3 cup peeled, seeded, and
   sliced red peppers
1 recipe Pizza Dough (see page
   259)

2 tablespoons good-quality
   Parmesan cheese
1/3 cup grated provolone or
   fontina cheese

In a heavy stove-top pan with a lid, heat the olive oil. Add the onions, stir so that the slices are covered with oil, and cook for 1 minute, stirring. Cover the pan and let simmer over low heat for 10 minutes, stirring occasionally. Stir in the red peppers, cover the pan again, and cook another 10 minutes. Stir frequently so that the onions don't stick and burn. Drain the onions and peppers in a colander.

Roll out the dough and cover with the onions and peppers. Sprinkle with the Parmesan cheese. Bake in a preheated 425°F oven for 10 minutes. Sprinkle with the provolone cheese and bake another 5–8 minutes, or until the cheese is melted. Let cool slightly before serving.

Variation

With anchovies and garlic. Add 1 teaspoon chopped *garlic* along with the onions. Proceed as above, garnishing the top of the vegetables with *anchovies* to taste before adding the cheeses.

Sausage, Vegetable, and Mushroom Topping

(For 1 small pizza)

A 2–3-inch piece pepperoni or kielbasa sausage
1–1¹/2 tablespoons olive oil
1 pepper, seeded and sliced
1 onion, peeled and sliced
¹/3 cup sliced mushrooms
¹/4 cup tomato sauce (canned is fine)

1 recipe Pizza Dough (see page 259)
1 tablespoon chopped fresh basil
3 tablespoons grated Parmesan cheese
¹/3 cup grated fontina, mozzarella, or cheddar cheese

Thinly slice the sausage and cook for 2 minutes in the olive oil over medium heat along with the pepper, onion, and mushrooms. Stir constantly. Transfer to a strainer in the sink and let drain. Spread the tomato sauce on the dough, then sprinkle with the basil. Top with the vegetables, and sprinkle with the Parmesan cheese. Drizzle a touch of olive oil over the top (about 1 teaspoon or to taste). Bake in a preheated 425°F oven for 10 minutes, sprinkle with the fontina cheese, and bake 5 minutes longer, or until the cheese is melted and the crust is browned.

Shrimp and Basil Topping

(For 1 small pizza)

8 medium shrimp
1 teaspoon olive oil
1 recipe Pizza Dough (see page 259)
4 tablespoons tomato sauce
1 tablespoon chopped fresh basil

3–4 tablespoons grated Parmesan or Romano cheese
¹/3 cup grated mozzarella, fontina, or cheddar cheese

Mix together the shrimp and olive oil. Spread the dough with the

Pizza (continued)

tomato sauce. Top with the shrimp, basil, and Parmesan cheese. Bake in a preheated 425°F oven for 10 minutes. Sprinkle with the mozzarella cheese and bake 5 minutes longer, or until the cheese is melted and the crust is browned.

Mushroom and Crabmeat Topping

This is another example where a small amount of an expensive ingredient (crabmeat) is affordable for one, while it would be extravagant for a family.

(For 1 small pizza)

1 tablespoon olive oil
1/3 cup chopped scallions
11/2 tablespoons seeded, peeled, and chopped red pepper
11/2 cups sliced mushrooms
1 tablespoon chopped parsley
3/4 cup cooked crabmeat (about 2 ounces)

1 recipe Pizza Dough (see page 259)
1/2 cup peeled, seeded, squeezed, and chopped fresh tomato
2 tablespoons grated Parmesan cheese
3/4 cup grated fontina or provolone cheese

Heat 1/2 tablespoon of the olive oil in a heavy frying pan. Add the scallions, red pepper, and mushrooms. Cook over high heat, stirring constantly, for 3 minutes. Scrape into a bowl and add parsley and crabmeat.

Brush the dough with the remaining 1/2 tablespoon olive oil. Arrange the tomato in a circle in the center of the dough. Scatter the crabmeat mixture around it, completely covering the surface. Sprinkle the pizza with the Parmesan cheese and bake in a preheated 425°F oven for 10 minutes. Sprinkle with the fontina cheese and place back in the oven just long enough for the cheese to melt, about 3 minutes.

BISCUITS

These add a festive touch to a dinner of leftovers. The amount of fat depends upon how "short" you'd like the biscuits to taste. Adding leftover winter squash turns the biscuits an attractive golden hue. You can freeze any leftover biscuits and microwave them while still frozen for about 20 seconds. Let them sit for a minute and they'll taste almost brand-new.

(Makes about five 2½-inch biscuits)

1 cup flour	2–3 tablespoons shortening
1½ teaspoons baking powder	⅓ cup milk
1 teaspoon sugar	

Mix together the flour, baking powder, and sugar. Cut in the shortening with a pastry blender until the fat is the size of large peas. Pour the milk over the flour mixture. Toss with a fork. Turn out on a floured board and knead about 4 times, then pat out into a large circle. Cut into rounds with a floured glass or biscuit cutter. Bake in a preheated 425°F oven for about 12 minutes.

VARIATIONS

Winter Squash, Pumpkin, or Sweet Potato Biscuits. Reduce the milk to ¼ cup. Combine 2 tablespoons leftover *squash, pumpkin,* or *sweet potato* along with the milk and egg. Proceed as above.

Cream Biscuits. Substitute *heavy cream* for the milk and reduce the shortening by 1 tablespoon.

Shortcakes. Increase the sugar to 1 tablespoon and use ¼ cup *butter.* Cut the biscuits into 3-inch rounds (size of a large glass). Makes three 3-inch biscuits.

Cobblers. Use the fruit mixture amounts in *Peach Crisp* and its variations (page 274). Halve the biscuit recipe, but use 3 tablespoons milk. Drop the soft dough over the fruit, partially covering it, sprinkle with 1 teaspoon of sugar, and bake in a preheated 425°F oven for about 25 minutes.

PEACH BREAKFAST PINWHEELS

If you have some super-ripe peaches, try these breakfast pinwheels flavored with the fresh peach juice and honey. The biscuit dough is soft. Don't let that deter you when you're cutting the pinwheels—it will all even out in the baking. A light honey, such as a wildflower blend, gives the best flavor.

(Makes five 2¹/2-inch pinwheels)

¹/2–³/4 cup peeled and diced
  peaches
¹/4 cup (4 tablespoons) honey
¹/4 teaspoon cinnamon
Milk, as needed

1 recipe *Biscuits* (page 265),
  replacing the milk with the
  peach juices (see below)
¹/2 cup chopped pecans
2 teaspoons butter

Mix the peaches, 3 tablespoons of the honey, and the cinnamon together and set aside for at least 15 minutes. Drain the peaches, pouring any peach juices (and honey) into a liquid measuring cup. If the peaches are juicy, you should have ¹/3 cup liquid. Otherwise, add enough milk to reach that level. Make biscuits, substituting the peach liquid for the milk. Turn the dough out onto a floured board and pat it into a ¹/2-inch-thick rectangle.

Spread the remaining 1 tablespoon honey over the dough and top with the reserved peaches. Sprinkle with the nuts and dot with the butter. Roll up like a jelly roll, sliding a spatula under the dough to lift it. Slice the dough into 1¹/2-inch pieces and place them, cut-side down, in a buttered 6-inch round baking pan or ovenproof frying pan. If the peaches have exuded any more liquid, drizzle it over the dough. Bake the pinwheels in a preheated 425°F oven for 20–25 minutes or until completely cooked through and lightly browned.

LEFTOVERS

These biscuits will keep in good condition for 1 day thanks to the honey. I suspect they'll be gone by then, but for longer storage freeze them and reheat (frozen) in a 400°F oven for 15 minutes.

CREAM SCONES

If you live in a community where there's no bakery (as I do), your only option for fresh morning-baked goods is to make your own. Be fore-warned—scones are addictive, particularly spread with honey or raspberry preserves. The amount of butter and sugar depends upon your taste buds. Freeze any leftover scones.

(Makes 2 large or 4 small scones)

1 cup all-purpose flour	1/3 cup heavy cream
1 teaspoon baking powder	1–2 tablespoons butter, melted
1–2 teaspoons sugar	1 medium egg

In a large bowl, mix together the flour, baking powder, and sugar. Measure out the cream in a glass measuring cup, add the butter and egg, and beat with a fork until blended. Pour into the dry ingredients and stir only until combined. The mixture will be soft. Place on a floured surface, knead for a few moments, then pat into a 4-inch circle. Cut into halves or quarters. Place the scones slightly apart on a greased cookie sheet and bake in a preheated 425°F oven for 12–15 minutes. Serve immediately.

Note: For a glossy surface, reserve about 1 teaspoon of the egg, cream, and butter mixture and brush it on the tops of the scones just before baking.

FLOUR TORTILLAS

Frozen tortillas are so easy to buy at the supermarket that you might think it's not worth the effort of making them. But I find that more often than not store-bought tortillas have been frozen and refrozen, leaving them with a brittle texture and a cardboard taste. This recipe, which takes only a few minutes to prepare, gives you fresh tortillas with a flavor that's superior to even the best frozen brand. Traditionally, tortillas are made with lard or vegetable shortening—I prefer olive oil, which is better for your health.

Flour Tortillas (continued)

(Makes three 8-inch tortillas)

3/4 cup all-purpose flour   1/4 cup warm water
1/4 teaspoon salt   Cornmeal or flour
2–3 teaspoons olive oil

Place the flour and salt in a mixing bowl. Beat together, then add the oil and water. Beat with the mixer until the dough forms a ball. If you have a mixer with a dough hook, knead the dough with a hook for about 2 minutes. Otherwise knead by hand on a floured surface for 3–5 minutes, or until the dough is shiny and elastic. Place the dough back in the bowl, cover it with a towel, and let it sit for at least 15 minutes to relax the gluten in the flour, making the tortillas easy to roll out.

Divide the dough into 3 balls. Lightly dust a flat surface with cornmeal or flour. Using a rolling pin, roll each piece of dough into an 8-inch circle. Heat a heavy ungreased frying pan. One at a time, place each tortilla in the pan. Cook the first side 30–45 seconds. Turn the tortilla over and cook an additional 15–30 seconds, or until it is cooked through but still slightly soft. If you aren't filling the tortillas immediately, cover them with a clean dishtowel so that they don't dry out.

VARIATION

Whole Wheat Flat Bread. There's nothing traditional about these, but they're tasty with Indian food. Substitute 3/4 cup *whole wheat flour* for the all-purpose flour, increase the water to 1/3 cup, and add 1/2 teaspoon *brown sugar.* Proceed as above.

LEFTOVERS

To freeze: Layer between 2 pieces of waxed paper, wrap in foil, and freeze for another meal.

In chicken soup. Slice leftover tortillas into paper-thin slices and drop into *clear chicken soup* just before serving.

Tortilla Chips. Cut into bite-sized pieces and deep-fry in *canola oil* until lightly browned. Use to scoop up salsa.

PANCAKES

It's tempting to reach for a mix when you make pancakes, but this recipe takes only a couple of minutes to put together. If you prepare the batter and let it sit while you make your coffee, the flour particles swell, giving the pancakes a slightly more tender texture. Check the batter before cooking, and if it's too thick add another tablespoon or two of milk. You're aiming for a consistency a little thicker than buttermilk.

(Makes 3–4 pancakes)

1 tablespoon melted butter or
    canola oil
1 medium egg
$1/4$ cup milk

$1/2$ cup flour
$3/4$ teaspoon baking powder
1 tablespoon sugar

Beat together the butter, egg, and milk in a mixing bowl. (One with a pouring spout is handy.) Combine the flour, baking powder, and sugar and add them to the milk mixture, stirring just enough to moisten the ingredients.

Lightly grease a frying pan and heat it until a drop of batter dropped on the surface starts to cook immediately. For each pancake, pour about 3 tablespoons of batter into the pan. Turn the pancake over with a spatula when small bubbles appear on its surface. Continue cooking until all the batter is used up. Serve with maple syrup or sugar.

VARIATION

Whole Wheat Orange Pancakes. Use $1/4$ cup *whole wheat flour* and $1/4$ cup white flour. Use 5 tablespoons milk and 3 tablespoons *orange juice*. If you wish, add $1/2$ teaspoon *grated orange rind*.

CORNBREAD

Cornbread is the most versatile of the quick breads, for you can eat it plain as an accompaniment, add vegetables for a more hearty version, or recycle it as a stuffing or pudding. This version is a cross between the

Cornbread (continued)

dense cornbread favored in the South and the fluffier, sweeter bread of the North. The olive oil and sour cream are by no means traditional—but they add flavor and moisture. Note that you bake the cornbread in a small-sized pan such as a 6-inch ovenproof frying pan.

(Makes a 6-inch cornbread)

1/2 cup sour cream
1/2 teaspoon baking soda
1/2 cup all-purpose flour
1 cup cornmeal (preferably stone-ground)
2 teaspoons baking powder

1/4 teaspoon salt
1 teaspoon sugar
1/2 cup milk
1 1/2 tablespoons olive oil or melted butter
1 medium egg

Combine the sour cream and baking soda and let sit for 10 minutes (the mixture will start to bubble and increase in volume). Mix together the flour, cornmeal, baking powder, salt, and sugar. Beat together the sour cream, milk, olive oil, and egg. Stir into the dry ingredients. Spoon into a greased 6-inch round baking pan. Bake in a preheated 425°F oven for 20–25 minutes, or until cooked through. Serve immediately.

VARIATIONS

Double Cornbread: **After combining the sour cream and flour mixtures,** stir in 1/2 cup cooked *corn* kernels and 1 tablespoon chopped *jalapeño peppers* (optional). Proceed as above.

With vegetables. **Increase the amount of olive oil to 2 tablespoons. Heat** it in a frying pan and add 1/3 cup chopped *red or green pepper,* 2 tablespoons shredded *fresh basil,* and 1/2 cup chopped *green onion or scallion tops* (or 1/3 cup chopped *onions*). Cook, stirring constantly, over high heat for about 2 minutes, or until the vegetables are slightly wilted and cooked through. Cool slightly and add to the cornbread batter along with 1/2 cup cooked *corn kernels*—either scraped from leftover corn on the cob or canned. Proceed as above.

Note: Any leftover cornbread can be used to stuff chicken or pork chops (see *Stuffed Pork Chop,* page 188).

DESSERTS

Many desserts, such as cakes or traditional pies, are impractical to make for one. This doesn't mean that if you have a sweet tooth, however, you have to feel deprived. Desserts such as cookies, custards, or crisps all cook up beautifully and can be prepared in quantities that are feasible when you live alone.

I've given you several cookie recipes that not only are made in smaller quantities than most traditional recipes, but also keep very well. The Scottish shortbread, for example, actually needs to age before it tastes right. Stored correctly, it will stay in good condition for several weeks. Gingersnaps usually taste better after a day or two.

A bowl of ripe fruit is the ideal way to end a meal. It's hard to improve upon sliced fresh peaches mixed with blackberries or blueberries, some juicy strawberries dipped in sour cream and brown sugar, or soft raspberries or ripe figs.

And should you end up with extra fruit that will spoil if you don't use it up immediately, you can convert it into a baked treat, such as baked bananas, a sour cream banana cake, or a berry crisp.

BAKED BANANA WITH ORANGE SAUCE

This is a delicious way to recycle a banana that's almost too ripe to eat. During baking, the ingredients mingle to create a caramelized sauce. Baste frequently so the sauce doesn't separate. If you wish, serve it with heavy cream or a top-quality vanilla or butter pecan ice cream.

(Makes 1 serving)

1 ripe banana	2 tablespoons brown sugar
2 tablespoons freshly squeezed orange juice	1 tablespoon butter
	Cinnamon

Peel the banana and split lengthwise. Place it in a small, shallow buttered ovenproof dish. Add the orange juice and sugar. Dot with the butter and sprinkle with cinnamon to taste. Bake in a preheated 350°F oven for 20–25 minutes or until tender, basting with the pan juices frequently. Serve immediately.

VARIATION

With rum or bourbon. **Just** before serving, heat 3 tablespoons of *rum* or *bourbon,* pour it over the bananas, and ignite with a match. Shake the pan until the flames die down.

SOUR CREAM BANANA CAKE

This cake tastes best made with on-the-verge bananas—the riper, the better. Thanks also to the sour cream, it stays fresh-tasting for at least 3 days if wrapped tightly in foil. There's no need for frosting. Either serve the cake plain or dust it with powdered sugar.

(Makes an 8-inch tube or 9-inch square cake)

1/2 cup (8 tablespoons) butter, softened
11/3 cups sugar
2/3 cup mashed bananas (about 2)
2 small eggs

1 teaspoon pure vanilla extract
2 cups all-purpose flour
1 teaspoon baking soda
1/4 teaspoon cinnamon
Salt
1/2 cup sour cream

Cream the butter in a mixer for 1–2 minutes, then gradually add the sugar. Continue beating until the butter and sugar are well combined, about 3 minutes. Add the bananas, eggs, and vanilla, and beat for 30 seconds. Combine the flour, baking soda, cinnamon, and a pinch of salt, and stir into the banana mixture. Add the sour cream and mix only until combined.

Spoon into a well-greased 6-cup tube pan (or a 9-inch square pan). Bake in a preheated 350°F oven for 50–55 minutes. The cake is done when a thin knife inserted into the center comes out clean. Cool in the pan for 10 minutes before turning out onto a rack.

VARIATIONS

Banana Orange Nut Cake. Add 1 tablespoon finely minced *orange zest* and 1/2 cup chopped *pecans or walnuts* along with the sour cream. Proceed as above.

Banana Rum Cake. Add 2 tablespoons *dark rum* along with the bananas, and increase the flour by 1 tablespoon. Proceed as above.

PEACH CRISP

I consider crisps the ultimate dessert comfort food, but they really taste best fresh because the topping gets soggy as it sits. This recipe makes just enough for a generous serving (with maybe an extra bite or two).

(Serves 1)

1¹/3 cups peeled and sliced
    peaches
2 teaspoons lime or lemon juice
2 tablespoons brown sugar
Cinnamon
2 tablespoons flour

1 tablespoon sugar
1 tablespoon butter
2 tablespoons chopped nuts
Heavy cream or vanilla ice
    cream (optional)

Toss together the peaches, citrus juice, brown sugar, and a pinch of cinnamon. Put in a small, buttered 2-cup baking dish. Combine the flour and sugar, then cut in the butter with a pastry blender, two knives, or your fingers. The butter should be in pea-sized pieces. Sprinkle over the peaches, then sprinkle with the nuts. Bake in a preheated 350°F oven for 35–45 minutes, or until the peaches are cooked through, the juices are bubbling, and the topping is slightly browned. Serve plain, or topped with cream or ice cream to taste.

VARIATIONS

Apple Crisp. Substitute 2 cups peeled and sliced *apples* for the peaches, and 1 tablespoon *orange juice* for the lime or lemon juice. Proceed as above.

Pear Crisp. Substitute 2 cups peeled and sliced *pears* for the peaches. Use lime juice and a pinch of *nutmeg* rather than cinnamon. Proceed as above.

Baked Mixed Fruit Crisp. Use a mixture of 1¹/3 cups *blueberries,* diced peaches or *plums,* and *strawberries.* Proceed as above.

FRUIT SHORTCAKES

Most of us OD on strawberry shortcake, but that's only one choice among the soft fruits for shortcake. Equally good are peach, nectarine, raspberry, blackberry—or combination shortcakes, such as peach and blueberry. This recipe makes enough for one dessert maven—or two moderate eaters. Adding the fruit juices to the heavy cream means less sugar and a more complex flavor. Do not use a commercial cream topping—all the fresh-fruit taste will be masked.

(Makes 1 or 2 servings)

1 cup peeled and thinly sliced
   (if necessary) fruit
1–2 tablespoons sugar
2 teaspoons orange juice
   (optional)

1/4 cup heavy cream
1 recipe *Shortcakes*
   (page 265)

Mix the fruit with the sugar and optional orange juice. If you have a stone fruit, such as peaches or nectarines, gently squeeze the fruit to exude some juices. (Omit this step with super-ripe fruit.) Let the fruit sit for at least 15 minutes.

Whip the cream in a very small bowl. Spoon out a tablespoon of the fruit juices and add them to the cream. Split each shortcake and arrange it on a plate. Spoon over any fruit juices, then top with the fruit and whipped cream. Serve immediately.

BREAD PUDDING

Concurrent with the bread machine, Americans have rediscovered bread pudding. Many of the young regional chefs offer some unusual variations, with exotic fruits and liquors—but I still enjoy a good basic pudding, made with scraps of stale bread, milk, eggs, and butter. Unlike many desserts, it can be cut way back in quantity without losing its essence. Any leftovers are delicious for breakfast.

Bread Pudding (continued)

(Serves 1)

2 tablespoons butter	2–3 tablespoons sugar
1 1/2 cups coarsely torn pieces of leftover bread	1/4 teaspoon pure vanilla extract
1 cup milk	1 tablespoon dark rum or bourbon (optional)
1 egg	

Heat the butter in a frying pan and slowly cook the bread in it, tossing frequently. Place the bread in a buttered 6-cup baking dish. Beat the milk, egg, and sugar together. Stir in the vanilla and rum, if using. Pour over the bread, and toss lightly. Let the mixture sit for 5 minutes. Bake in a preheated 350°F oven for 25–35 minutes. Remove from the oven when a knife inserted in the center comes out clean. The top will puff up and fall slightly as it cools. Let the pudding sit for at least 15 minutes before serving with heavy cream or ice cream (such as butter pecan), if you wish.

VARIATIONS

With fruits. Heat the butter and sauté 1/4–1/3 cup peeled and sliced *pears, peaches,* or *apples* for 3 minutes. Add 1 tablespoon of the sugar, and cook, stirring, until the sugar melts and coats the fruit. Soak the bread in the milk, and mix with the remaining ingredients, including the fruit-butter mixture. Proceed as above.

Banana Bread Pudding with Butterscotch Sauce. This is an excellent way to use up a frozen *banana.* Just peel and slice it while still frozen. Heat 2 tablespoons butter in a frying pan, add 3 tablespoons *brown sugar,* and cook together, stirring until the sugar melts. Add the sliced banana, and cook just long enough to let the banana slices defrost. Meanwhile, beat together the egg, milk, vanilla, and 1 teaspoon bourbon or rum. Pour over the bread, then add the banana sugar mixture. Stir together. Proceed as above. Serve topped with *Quick Butterscotch Sauce.*

Quick Butterscotch Sauce

This makes enough for one serving. Double the proportions if you have a guest.

(Makes 1/4 cup)

2 tablespoons water	1/4 cup sour cream
2 tablespoons brown sugar	1/4 teaspoon pure vanilla extract

Heat together the water and brown sugar. Stir constantly until the sugar starts to brown and caramelize. Remove from the heat and immediately stir in the sour cream. Keep stirring until the sauce forms (about 1 minute). If necessary, add a teaspoon of warm water. Add the vanilla extract. Pour sauce over the bread pudding before the sauce hardens.

BROWNIES

One could argue that there's no such thing as too many brownies, since there is always a line of eager volunteers to eat up any extras. This recipe makes about 6 pie-shaped brownies—enough for you and a friend or two. It's easy to make and freezes well. I think a pinch of cinnamon adds a more complex flavor, but if you're a purist, omit it.

(Makes 2–3 servings)

3 ounces semisweet chocolate	3/4 teaspoon pure vanilla extract
6 tablespoons butter	2/3 cup flour
Cinnamon (optional)	1/2 cup chopped nuts, such as pecans or walnuts
3/4 cup sugar	
2 medium eggs	

Melt together the chocolate and butter either on top of the stove or in a microwave oven. Place the mixture in a mixing bowl and beat for 1 minute. Add, one at a time (in this order), the cinnamon (if using), sugar, eggs, vanilla, and flour. Beat only enough to incorporate the ingredients. Add the nuts. Pour into a buttered 6-inch round cake pan. Bake in a preheated 350°F oven for 25–30 minutes. Cool slightly before cutting into wedges.

LEMON SUGAR COOKIES

These cookies not only keep for three to four days in a covered tin, but also you can freeze half the dough raw, and then slice and bake cookies without defrosting the dough. The lemon flavor intensifies as the cookies sit. If you have a food processor, whirl the sugar and lemon peel together.

(Makes 2 dozen 3-inch cookies)

1 lemon
1/2 cup (8 tablespoons) butter, softened
3/4 cup sugar, plus sugar for coating

1 egg
11/2 cups flour
1 teaspoon baking powder
Pinch of salt

Thinly peel the lemon (avoiding the white pith, which is bitter). Finely chop the lemon peel. Squeeze the lemon and reserve the juice.

Cream the butter in a mixing bowl. Gradually add the sugar and continue beating until smooth. Beat in the egg and the reserved lemon peel and 2 teaspoons fresh juice. Beat in the flour, baking powder, and a generous pinch of salt.

Pour some sugar into a dish. Pinch off a walnut-sized piece of dough and roll the dough between your palms to form a ball. Roll the doughball in the sugar, place on a greased cookie sheet, and slightly flatten with the palm of your hand. Continue forming the cookies until the sheet is filled.

Bake in a preheated 350°F oven for about 12 minutes, or until the edges of the cookies are lightly colored. Remove from the sheets and cool on racks. Repeat the process with the remaining dough.

Note: To freeze the dough, sprinkle sugar on a flat surface. Form the dough into a 11/2-inch-thick tube and roll it in the sugar. Gently lift the dough, wrap in foil or plastic wrap, and freeze. To bake cookies, slice the frozen dough into 1/4-inch rounds and bake as above for 12–15 minutes.

GINGERSNAPS

The honey variation gives these cookies a cakelike texture and keeps them moist for days. Crumble one to give an elusive flavor to a pot-roast gravy.

(Makes 18 cookies)

1/3 cup butter
3 tablespoons sugar, plus sugar
  for rolling
1/4 cup molasses
1 egg
1/2 teaspoon pure vanilla extract
11/4 cups flour (half whole

wheat and half white flour
  is good)
2 teaspoons ground ginger
1/2 teaspoon cinnamon
1/8 teaspoon ground cloves
1 teaspoon baking soda

Cream the butter, add the sugar and molasses, and continue beating until they are combined. Beat in the egg and vanilla. Stir together the flour, ginger, cinnamon, cloves, and baking soda and add to the butter mixture. The dough will be slightly sticky. (It can be refrigerated for several hours or overnight, or baked immediately.) Form walnut-sized pieces, roll them in sugar, and place on a greased baking sheet. Bake in a preheated 350°F oven for 12–15 minutes, or until cooked through. Cool on a rack. If stored in a covered tin, the cookies will keep in good condition for almost 2 weeks.

VARIATION

Honey Gingersnaps. Replace the 3 tablespoons sugar with 1/4 cup *honey*. Increase the flour to 11/3 cups. Proceed as above.

SNICKERDOODLES

This old-fashioned cookie has been one of my favorites for more than 25 years because it's a snap to make, keeps well, and provides a generous mouthful. (It's also delicious.)

(Makes about 22 cookies)

3/4 cup sugar
1 teaspoon cinnamon
1/4 cup (4 tablespoons) butter,
    softened
1/4 cup shortening

1 medium egg
3/4 teaspoon cream of tartar
1/2 teaspoon baking soda
11/3 cups flour

Measure out 2 tablespoons of the sugar, and mix with the cinnamon in a small bowl. Set it aside. Cream together the remaining sugar, butter, and shortening for about 2 minutes. Add the egg. Then stir in the cream of tartar, soda, and flour. Scoop out about a 11/4-inch ball of dough. Roll it between your palms to round it and roll the ball in the cinnamon-sugar mixture. Place it on an ungreased cookie sheet. Repeat with the remaining dough, spacing the cookies about 2 inches apart.

Bake the cookies in a preheated 400°F oven about 10 minutes or until cooked through. Cool on a cookie rack.

BAKED CUSTARD

Custard is a simple, yet satisfying, dessert that is easily reduced in volume to serve one. In a pinch you can bake the custard in a small ovenproof dish (or an ovenproof glass measuring cup) but custard cups, which are sold at well-stocked discount and cookware supply stores, are not only attractive but also just the right depth. It's important to cook the custard slowly, surrounded by water that does not boil. This keeps the texture smooth and free from "weeping" when it is served. Any leftover custard is good for breakfast.

(Makes 1 generous serving)

2 medium eggs
2–3 tablespoons sugar
3/4 cup hot milk

1/4 teaspoon pure vanilla extract
Nutmeg

Beat the eggs and sugar together until well combined, about 1 minute. Pour the hot milk over in a slow stream, mixing constantly. Add the vanilla.

If you have a sieve, pour the custard through it into 2 custard cups (1/2–3/4-cup capacity). (This gives a smoother texture; you can just pour the egg mixture into the cups directly.) Sprinkle the surfaces with grated or ground nutmeg. Place the cups in a deep baking dish large enough to hold them comfortably and pour boiling water halfway up their sides. Place the dish in a preheated 350°F oven and bake for 25–30 minutes, or until a knife inserted in the center of a custard comes out clean. Cool, then refrigerate before serving.

VARIATIONS

With rum. Add 1 teaspoon *dark rum* along with the vanilla.
With cream. For a richer version, substitute *cream* for the milk.

RICE PUDDING

There are dozens of versions of rice pudding. This simple rendition makes enough for a generous serving.

(Serves 1)

1 medium egg	$1/2$ teaspoon pure vanilla extract
2–3 tablespoons sugar or	$1/2$ cup cooked rice
$1^1/2$ tablespoons honey	$1/8$ teaspoon cinnamon or
$3/4$ cup milk	nutmeg (optional)

Beat the egg and sugar together for 1 minute. Add the milk and vanilla and beat 30 seconds longer. Stir in the rice and the optional cinnamon. Pour into a 2-cup glass baking dish. Bake in a preheated 350°F oven for 35–40 minutes, or until cooked through. Serve either warm or cold.

SCOTTISH SHORTBREADS

Shortbreads are ideal cookies for a single person because they keep nicely for two or three weeks in a tightly covered tin. In fact, their flavor improves with age. I've tasted more than my share of shortbread in Scotland, and favor this recipe with rice flour—which adds a crunchy texture—given to my sister Dawn by a Scottish friend. Most health-food or Oriental grocery stores carry rice flour. Try with tea, or serve with sliced fresh raspberries, strawberries, or peaches.

(Makes 24 cookies)

1 cup ($1/2$ pound) butter,	$1^3/4$ cups all-purpose flour
softened	$1/2$ cup plus 2 tablespoons rice
$1/2$ cup plus 1 tablespoon sugar,	flour
plus sugar for dusting	

Beat together the butter, sugar, and flours until well combined. Form the dough into a ball, and halve it. Place one half on a cookie sheet. Then either roll or pat it into a 1/2-inch-thick circle about 7 inches in diameter. Repeat with the remaining dough.

Score each circle into 12 wedges; then, using the tines of a fork, prick the surfaces and crimp the edges. Bake the shortbreads in a preheated 300°F oven for about 50 minutes, until they are cooked through but not browned. Remove from the oven, and cut along the score lines. Cool, and store in a tin for at least 1 week before serving

BERRY PIE FOR ONE

A standard-sized fruit pie is impractical to make for one, unless you have loads of friends who will eat up the leftovers. However, it's possible to make a much smaller-sized pie that gives you one generous serving and a tad more for a snack. I've found that smaller-sized pies taste better made with only a top crust (otherwise there's too much crust and too little filling). As it's almost impossible to buy a small-sized pie plate, I use an ovenproof 6-inch frying pan or a 2-cup shallow au gratin or ovenproof casserole dish. Either size works out well. The amount of flour depends upon how thick you prefer the juices to be.

(Makes 1 generous serving)

1 1/2 cups fresh or frozen berries, such as blackberries or blueberries
1/4 cup sugar

2–3 teaspoons flour
1/2 teaspoon grated lemon rind
1/2 teaspoon butter
1/2 recipe *Piecrust* (page 294)

In a shallow 2-cup ovenproof dish, mix together the berries, sugar, flour, and lemon rind. Dot with the butter.

Roll out the piecrust to approximate the shape of the pan. Either place over the berries and tuck down the sides of the crust alongside the dish edge, or crimp the edges of the dough with a fork. Cut a large X in the center of the dough and prick the surface with the tines of a fork. Bake in

Berry Pie for One (continued)

a preheated 425°F oven for 25–30 minutes, or until the crust is lightly browned and the berries are bubbling.

VARIATION

Pear or Apple Pie. Use 1^1/$_2$–2 cups peeled and sliced fruit. Add a dash of *nutmeg* or *cloves* and ^{1}/$_4$ teaspoon *cinnamon.* Omit the lemon rind, if you wish. Proceed as above.

ODDS AND ENDS

You'll find some of my favorite recipes in the following pages: beverages, syrups—even a cheese made from yogurt. These recipes have nothing in common save for the fact that they taste good. I find them handy additions to my solo cooking; I trust that you'll find them useful as well.

LIME-GRENADINE COOLER

The ingredients that make a rum punch taste so good work equally well in this tart nonalcoholic drink that's refreshing served over ice. Most liquor stores (and many supermarkets) sell bitters and grenadine syrup. Grenadine, because it's made from pomegranates, turns the drink an attractive peach-blush red.

(Serves 1)

1/4 cup freshly squeezed lime
   juice
1/4 cup freshly squeezed
   orange juice
2–3 teaspoons grenadine syrup

1 teaspoon sugar
1/8 teaspoon bitters
1/2 cup water or club soda
Mint leaves, optional garnish

Mix together the lime juice, orange juice, grenadine syrup, sugar, bitters, and water. Pour over ice and garnish with mint leaves if you have any.

VARIATION

Planter's Punch. Add 1 1/2 ounces *dark rum,* such as Appleton or Myers's.

STRAWBERRY-GRAPEFRUIT COOLER

This festive-looking, refreshing drink is low in calories and high in vitamin C. It's a great pick-me-up for the early-evening blahs. The bitters, which are available at any liquor store, are an ingredient in many cocktails. The best-flavored variety is Peychaud's, a New Orleans favorite that has a slight licorice aftertaste.

(Makes about 1 cup)

1/2 cup freshly squeezed grapefruit juice, or a combination of grapefruit and orange juice
1/4 cup water

1/2–2/3 cup ripe strawberries, hulled
2–3 ice cubes
Bitters (I like at least 1/2 teaspoon)

In a blender, frappé the juice, water, strawberries, and ice. Shake in bitters to taste. Blend again and serve in a clear glass.

VARIATIONS

With rum. Add *dark rum* to taste.
With banana. Add 1/2 *banana* along with the strawberries.
With mango and banana. Add 2/3 cup ripe *mango* and 1/2 banana. Omit the strawberries.

> "I love to cook. Life is so hectic that to cook is comforting: The properties of food don't change—all you have to do is know them and they react the same every time. As I live alone, I never have a set mealtime. Dinner can be anywhere between three hours ago and now. I make a game out of shopping. A friend and I go 'French housewifing' and shop store to store. I know where to find the best fruit and produce, which store has the best French bread, or the best aged meat. I don't always have the time to do this, but it's a priority for me. Cooking is a delightful experience."
>
> Debby Freedman, teacher

PEAR JUICE

If you buy a whole batch of pears that
ripen all at once, rather than waiting
until they spoil and have to be thrown
out, either freeze them whole and
use while still frozen in blended drinks,
or make pear nectar using this technique. Steaming gives the best flavor,
but if you don't have a steamer, gently boil them. You'll need at least 5
ripe pears to end up with 1 cup juice. (I like pear juice so much that during the fall I buy baskets of ripe pear drops, or seconds, at farm stands. I
trim out the bruises and make this juice. However, if you're canning pear
juice, do not use drops.) Once it's refrigerated, the juice stays in good
condition for at least four days.

Full-flavored ripe pears, such as   Water
    Bartletts   Fresh limes (optional)

Wash the pears, stem them, and chop into eighths. Put the pears into
a large nonreactive pot and add water to at least 2 inches above the top of
the pears. If you like, add 2 tablespoons strained lime juice. Simmer over
low heat until the pears are soft, about 45 minutes to 1 1/4 hours. (The
time varies depending upon the type of pear.) Mash the pears and let sit
for 15 minutes. If you're steaming the pears, steam them in a steamer-
juicer until they are soft. Then mash them and continue cooking until
they have released their juices.

Put the cooked pears and liquid through a food mill. The juice will be
thick. Taste the juice and if it is watery, put the juice back in the pan and
gently boil until it has the depth of flavor you wish. Watch carefully because the pear solids can burn. Cool the nectar, pour it into a glass bottle,
and refrigerate. Shake before serving. If you wish, add freshly squeezed
lime juice to taste.

STRAWBERRY ICE CREAM SODA

At least once a summer, it's fun to have an old-fashioned ice cream soda made with farm-ripened berries. Any soft berry, such as raspberries, blackberries, or dewberries, works equally well.

(Serves 1)

1/4 cup crushed strawberries,
   plus 1 whole, for garnish
Sugar
1/4 cup light cream

Chilled club soda
Vanilla ice cream
Mint or lemon verbena,
   optional garnish

Sweeten the crushed berries to taste with the sugar. Place the purée in a tall glass, stir in the cream, and fill with club soda, leaving room for a scoop of vanilla ice cream. Garnish with a fresh berry cut into slices accordion-style and, if you like, a sprig of fresh mint or lemon verbena.

CHOCOLATE SAUCE

There's no need to have a jar of chocolate sauce cluttering up your refrigerator when it's so easy to make exactly the amount you wish. Once, while visiting Kentucky, I sampled some chocolates laced with whiskey, an addictive treat that can't be shipped out of state because of Federal regulations. Ever since then I've added bourbon to chocolate sauce; if you prefer, substitute cream or water.

(Makes 1/3 cup sauce)

1/3 cup milk chocolate chips,
   such as Hershey's, or semisweet chips

2 tablespoons heavy cream
1 teaspoon bourbon or water

Place the chocolate chips and cream in a heavy stove-top pan. Over low heat, stirring constantly, cook the mixture until it thickens slightly, about 2 minutes. Add the bourbon and continue cooking until the harsh alcohol taste disappears, about 1 minute. Serve warm over ice cream, cake, brownies, brownies with ice cream . . . or even over fresh pineapple or bananas. You can also use the sauce as a dip for fruit such as whole strawberries or peach slices.

VARIATIONS

Sour Cream Chocolate Sauce. This version has a tart aftertaste and a thicker, more satiny texture. Substitute 2 tablespoons *sour cream* for the heavy cream.

Frozen Banana with Chocolate Coating. I like my banana best partially frozen; however, at that stage the chocolate frosting is a little sticky. Place the banana on a rack over waxed paper. Pour the hot sauce over the banana, turn, and coat the other side. Freeze until firm.

LEFTOVERS

Reheat any leftovers in a microwave, or put in a tall jar and let sit in a bowl of boiling water, stirring occasionally, until liquid. Use in chocolate ice cream sodas.

Chocolate-Stuffed Pecans. Even if you only have about 1 tablespoon of sauce, that's enough to give you several nut candies to store in the refrigerator. Put any leftover sauce in the refrigerator or freezer until it becomes firm enough to hold its shape in a spoon. Take a pecan, spread with about 1/4 teaspoon sauce, and top with an equal-sized pecan. Continue until all the sauce is gone. Store the pecan candies in plastic wrap in the refrigerator.

Note: This is particularly delicious made with semisweet chocolate bits.

COFFEE SYRUP

Recycle your leftover coffee in this syrup to pour over ice cream or brownies. You can make any amount you wish—the basic proportions are equal amounts of brown sugar and coffee. Increase the butter in 1/2-teaspoon increments.

(Serves 1)

1/3 cup leftover coffee (do not use instant)
1/3 cup firmly packed brown sugar

1/8 teaspoon pure vanilla extract
1/2 teaspoon butter

Combine the coffee and sugar in a small pan. Boil it gently, uncovered, until the mixture thickens slightly (about 10 minutes). Stir in the vanilla and butter. Use while still warm.

VARIATIONS

With whiskey. Add 1–2 teaspoons *bourbon* or *coffee liqueur.*

With sour cream. Stir in *sour cream* (or heavy cream) along with the vanilla and butter.

LEFTOVERS

Use as flavoring for a coffee milkshake.

PEAR SAUCE

This is the equivalent of an applesauce made with pears—but with a more complex flavor. This version, which contains mustard, keeps at least one week in the refrigerator. Omit the sugar if the pears are sweet.

(Makes about 2 cups)

2 cups diced peeled ripe pears (about 1 1/4 pounds)
1/2 cup water

1 tablespoon sugar (optional)
2 tablespoons white vinegar
2–3 tablespoons Dijon mustard

Place the pears and water in a medium-sized pot and cook until soft, stirring frequently to prevent burning. (The time varies depending upon the type of pears: Bartlett pears cook down in 10–15 minutes.) Drain, saving the juices for cooking, and cool slightly. Add the sugar, vinegar, and mustard. Whirl in a food processor until smooth or purée in a food mill. Serve with pork chops, ham, or baked chicken.

LEFTOVERS

Add to meat casseroles for a subtle fruit aftertaste.

MORNING GRUEL

This hearty "gruel," inspired by the grains-yogurt breakfast combinations served in Switzerland and Germany, will give you ample energy for the morning's chores. Bananas and strawberries add potassium and vitamin C. Vary the amount of oatmeal and yogurt to suit your taste.

(Serves 1)

2–3 tablespoons plain low-fat
    yogurt
1/2–1 teaspoon honey
1/3–1/2 cup old-fashioned oats
1/2 sliced banana or 1/2 cup
    sliced strawberries

2 teaspoons chopped nuts,
    such as hazelnuts or walnuts
    (optional)

In a cereal bowl, mix together the yogurt and honey. Stir in the oats and fruit. Let sit for 2–3 minutes to let the oatmeal soften and the flavors meld slightly. Sprinkle with nuts, if you like.

VARIATIONS

With brown rice. Add *leftover brown rice* to taste.

With peaches, nectarines, apples, mangoes, papayas, or pears. Substitute 1/2 cup sliced fruit for the banana or strawberries.

YOGURT CHEESE

For years I bought yogurt cheese until a Lebanese friend pointed out how easy it is to make (and fresh-tasting to eat). All you need to do is drain plain yogurt until it becomes firm. My friend drains his yogurt through cheesecloth, but I find coffee filters work beautifully.

(Makes about 1¹/₃ cups)

2 pounds plain yogurt

Spoon the yogurt into a colander lined with a single layer of dampened coffee filters. Place over a deep bowl to drain. Let sit for at least 12 hours. The longer the yogurt drains, the denser it becomes. If you want a cheese to spread on pita bread or crackers, let it drain for 24 hours. Yogurt cheese will keep for up to 2 weeks in the refrigerator if kept covered.

VARIATION

Garlic Cheese. Form the cheese into walnut-sized balls, and place in a clean glass jar. Add several peeled cloves of garlic. Cover with olive oil, seal, and store in the refrigerator, where the cheese will last for months. Or form balls and roll in freshly ground black pepper. Some of the ground pepper will float around in the oil, but that doesn't affect the taste.

CHEESE SPREAD

This bottomless crock of cheese is an excellent way to use up scraps of cheese that otherwise would harden in the refrigerator. Once you have made the first batch of spread, you can add to it every once in a while, blending in shredded cheese or butter and cream cheese as needed. I like a base of cheddar—and sometimes Parmesan for flavor.

(Makes about 2 cups)

4 cups shredded cheddar cheese
4 ounces cream cheese
¹/4 cup (4 tablespoons) butter

1 tablespoon plus 1 teaspoon prepared horseradish
1 tablespoon olive oil

1/8 teaspoon hot pepper sauce   1 tablespoon soy sauce (optional)

Let the shredded cheese stay at room temperature until it is soft. Combine with the cream cheese, butter, horseradish, oil, hot pepper sauce, and soy sauce if used. Mix together until smooth. (This is easiest done in a food processor.) Pack into a crock or glass bowl, cover with plastic wrap, and let it age in the refrigerator for at least 2 days before serving. If you replenish the cheese and flavorings, the crock will last indefinitely. It will keep for up to 3 months without replenishing.

VARIATION

Sherry Cheese Spread. Omit the soy sauce and add 1–2 tablespoons *dry sherry. Or* use 1 tablespoon *bourbon.* Proceed as above.

SESAME SAUCE

Serve this sauce with baked fish or with raw vegetables in a pita bread sandwich.

(Serves 1)

1/2 teaspoon minced garlic   2 tablespoons cold water
1/3 cup tahini (sesame seed paste)   Salt
2–3 tablespoons freshly squeezed
   lemon juice

Mash the garlic into a paste with the back of a knife blade. Place in a mixing bowl or food processor and add the tahini. Process until the garlic is thoroughly incorporated. Add the lemon juice first, then the cold water. The sauce should end up the consistency of a thick mayonnaise. Wait until serving to add salt.

VARIATION

Hummus. Mix with 1/3–1/2 cup puréed cooked *chickpeas.*

LEFTOVERS

Any leftover sauce will keep in good condition for at least 1 week in the refrigerator.

PIECRUST

Piecrust is a snap to make once you understand certain principles. The flour should be all-purpose (not bread or pastry) for a flaky crust. Before you roll out the dough, let it rest in the refrigerator for about 20 minutes. This allows time for the flour to more fully absorb the water, resulting in a dough that's easier to handle. Chill the fat for a half hour in the freezer for best results, and use ice water as the liquid. The amount of water you need depends upon the humidity in the air. I prefer a pastry blender (rather than my fingertips) to cut the flour and fat together, which keeps handling to a minimum. Excess handling makes piecrusts tough.

(Makes a double crust for a 9-inch pie)

2 cups all-purpose flour	2 tablespoons butter
7 tablespoons vegetable shortening	5–6 tablespoons ice water

Place the flour in a bowl and cut the shortening and butter into it until the fat is the size of small lentils. The mixture will not appear uniform—some particles will look like cornmeal. Sprinkle with the water, a tablespoon at a time, lightly tossing with a fork. Your aim is to use only enough water so that the pastry barely holds together when pressed into a ball. At that stage, take a leftover plastic shopping bag, pour the pastry particles into it, and press them together. If the dough looks as if it needs another tablespoon of water, wait until after it comes out of the refrigerator, because often it's unnecessary to add it once the dough has rested. Place in the refrigerator for about 20 minutes.

Halve the dough, pat it into 2 slightly flattened balls, and place on a lightly floured surface. Rub a rolling pin with flour. Starting in the center of one ball, roll the dough out in all directions, lifting the dough occasionally so it doesn't stick to the surface. You're aiming for a finished circle about 10 inches in diameter. Line the pie pan, add the filling, and repeat the procedure with the other ball to make the top crust.

Most standard directions for forming the edges of a crust tell you to fold the top crust over the bottom one. I find it easier to reverse that process, folding the bottom crust over the top and adjusting the thickness as I go along. The easiest way to crimp the edges is to press the tines of a fork along the rim, but I prefer using my fingers (middle finger of one hand flanked by the thumb and index finger of the other) to indent the dough at even intervals, forming the triangular edges traditional with American pies. Cut vents in the top before cooking to allow steam to escape. The baking temperature will vary with each pie, but as a rule of thumb, bake filled pies for 15 minutes at 425°F and then lower the heat to 350°F for the remaining baking time.

Note: Do *not* make this dough in a food processor.

INDEX

A Note About the Author

Jane Doerfer is the director of Going Solo in the Kitchen, a cooking school for solo cooks in Apalachicola, Florida. She has written, collaborated on, or produced four other books: *The Pantry Gourmet, The Victory Garden Cookbook, The Legal Sea Foods Cookbook,* and *Crockett's Tool Shed.* A former food columnist for *Horticulture* magazine and food editor for *New England Living* magazine, Doerfer has taught cooking for more than twenty years.

A Note on the Type

This book was set in ITC Stone, a typeface designed by Sumner Stone for the International Typeface Corporation in 1988. Stone is really three typefaces—Serif, Sans, and Informal; each stands on its own but is also part of an integrated family planned to be compatible when mixed on a page.

Composed by North Market Street Graphics,
Lancaster, Pennsylvania
Printed and bound by R. R. Donnelley & Sons,
Harrisonburg, Virginia

Drawings by Philippe Lardy
Designed by Anthea Lingeman